Praise for
Creating Value in Nonprofit–Business Collaborations

"Austin and Seitanidi fill a gaping hole in our understanding of cross-sector partnerships by illuminating what types of value are created in them, how they are created, and who benefits. The book provides a way to talk concretely about real results, and offers strategies for boosting them. With over 100 examples from around the globe, leaders will be able to translate these ideas into action and chart paths to greater impact."
— **Jeff Bradach**, co-founder and managing partner,
The Bridgespan Group

"This is the most complete analysis on the creation of value in cross-sector partnerships."
— **Bruce W. Burtch**, called "The Father of
Cause-Related Marketing"

"Companies take note! Finally, you have a solid compass for navigating rich collaborative ventures with nonprofit organizations. The pay-offs will surprise you."
— **Thomas Donaldson**, The Mark O. Winkelman
Endowed Professor, The Wharton School,
University of Pennsylvania

"Austin and Seitanidi's book offers an in depth and highly systematic account of how value is created in business-NGO partnerships. It is also brimming with case examples that ground the analysis in real-world experience. Scholars and practitioners interested in how partnerships work will enjoy this book's thorough coverage and rich practical wisdom."
— **Barbara Gray**, professor of organizational behavior and
director of Center for Research in Conflict and
Negotiation at The Pennsylvania State University

"Multisector partnerships have been all the rage in CSR for a long time. This book finally moves the debate beyond the hype and provides a detailed analysis of how collaboration between business and civil society can create tangible value for all parties involved."
— **Dr. Dirk Matten**, professor of strategy, Hewlett-Packard Chair in Corporate
Social Responsibility, Centre of Excellence in Responsible Business,
Schulich School of Business, York University

"Collaboration always sounds like a good thing . . . but is it? Austin and Seitanidi provide a thoughtful and accessible answer: collaboration can provide value, and they indicate why and how. The book is particularly welcome as it is both well-grounded and practical."
— **Jeremy Moon**, FRSA, professor and director, International Centre for Corporate
Social Responsibility (ICCSR), Nottingham University Business School

"Cross-sector partnerships have become ubiquitous, but far too often they do not live up to their potential. Austin and Seitanidi have done a huge service to nonprofit and business leaders alike by providing practical insights into how to nurture collaboration in a way that creates less heat and much more light."
— **Mario Morino**, chairman, Morino Institute and Venture Philanthropy Partners

"Austin and Seitanidi's book on partnerships is an excellent and truly welcome input to the understanding and debate about partnerships on an international scale. Both distinguished authors have contributed remarkably to exploring and debating the role of partnerships over the last two decades—way back in a time where partnerships were perceived by many as controversial and long before the ideas of business co-constructing value with governments and NGOs entered the mainstream scene of management theory. The book provides intelligent and reflective thinking for both practitioners and scholars about stages, processes, and outcomes of partnerships but also importantly about the type of mindset for partnerships either to fail or succeed. In particular, I appreciate how important questions are raised about how shared value is constituted collectively and related to the collective's interests, keeping in mind the advancement of democratic ideals."

—**Mette Morsing**, professor, Copenhagen Business School,
CBS Sustainability Platform

"This is a timely, informative, and accessible book on business collaboration and partnership. It is relevant and valuable to those studying large firms and small."

—**Laura J. Spence**, PhD., professor of business ethics, Royal Holloway,
University of London; Section Editor, *Journal of Business Ethics*

"Austin and Seitanidi provide an innovative and important roadmap to the creation of shared value through collaboration, co-creation, and co-evolution. Indeed, in a world full of wicked problems, this book should prove invaluable to practitioners and scholars alike, as its ideas are theoretically sound yet grounded in collaborative practices of the sort demanded by our complicated future."

—**Sandra Waddock**, Galligan Chair of Strategy,
Carroll School of Management, Boston College

"Scaling the opportunity of collaboration requires that we unravel the mystery of what makes it smart and effective beyond inspiration and perspiration. The practical research and analysis in this book takes us along this pathway, opening the way to a more systematic approach to success and impact."

—**Simon Zadek**, senior fellow, Global Green Growth Institute; senior advisor,
International Institute for Sustainable Development; visiting scholar,
Tsinghua School of Economics and Management

Creating Value in Nonprofit–Business Collaborations

New Thinking and Practice

James E. Austin
M. May Seitanidi

JB JOSSEY-BASS™

A Wiley Brand

Published by Jossey-Bass
A Wiley Brand
One Montgomery Street, Suite 1200, San Francisco, CA 94104-4594—www.josseybass.com

Jossey-Bass books and products are available through most bookstores. To contact Jossey-Bass directly call our Customer Care Department within the U.S. at 800-956-7739, outside the U.S. at 317-572-3986, or fax 317-572-4002.

Wiley publishes in a variety of print and electronic formats and by print-on-demand. Some material included with standard print versions of this book may not be included in e-books or in print-on-demand. If this book refers to media such as a CD or DVD that is not included in the version you purchased, you may download this material at http://booksupport.wiley.com. For more information about Wiley products, visit www.wiley.com.

Library of Congress Cataloging-in-Publication Data

Austin, James E.
    Creating value in nonprofit–business collaborations : new thinking and practice/James E. Austin, M. May Seitanidi.—First edition.
        1 online resource.
    Includes bibliographical references and index.
    Description based on print version record and CIP data provided by publisher; resource not viewed.
    ISBN 978-1-118-82442-9 (pdf)—ISBN 978-1-118-82435-1 (epub)—ISBN 978-1-118-53113-6 (cloth)
    1. Public-private sector cooperation.   2. Value.   I. Seitanidi, Maria May.   II. Title.
HD3871
658'.046—dc23

2013047035

Printed in the United States of America
FIRST EDITION

HB Printing   10 9 8 7 6 5 4 3 2 1

Contents

Figures and Table

FIGURES

TABLE

*To the fellow researchers and nonprofit and business practitioners
whose creativity, talents, and commitment serve to create
collaborative value for individuals, organizations, and society.
May this book honor their past efforts and contribute
to their future progress.*

Foreword

Twenty-five years ago—before the era of corporate social responsibility, before the publication of the significant body of academic literature on cross-sector collaboration that this book comprehensively synthesizes and insightfully elaborates—a cold call came in to the corporate offices of the Timberland Company from City Year, the then-fledgling nonprofit.

City Year was launching a corps of fifty young people in Boston to demonstrate the power of national service to unite diverse American youth, solve pressing social problems, and bolster our nation's democracy. The nonprofit was in search of boots because it wanted to unify its members in appearance and spirit and protect them during physically demanding service projects. Timberland answered the call and donated fifty pair. This in-kind donation began what would evolve into a rich partnership, one that the two of us—as leaders of our two organizations through the most robust years of this partnership—are proud to call, in Jim Austin and May Seitanidi's language, transformational.

Over the past quarter of a century, more than eighteen thousand City Year corps members in twenty-four cities nationwide have given a year of service in their Timberland boots. At the same time, Timberland, with inspiration from City Year, has embedded a deep ethos of service into the company's culture, advocating—for its employees and for everyone else—the importance of doing well *and* doing good.

We have to admit that in the early days of our partnership, we had no rules—no effective framework to guide our collaboration. It was a little like cutting our way through a thick forest, clearing a path to partnership. But even though we had no rules, we did have regular discussions about how to invent the rules. And over time we developed processes and systems for our collaboration. They worked, and our partnership flourished.

But imagine having a road map for a transformational partnership, a map drawn from a rich field of research, a map featuring illustrative examples taken from nonprofit–business collaborations that have co-generated real value for the participating nongovernmental organizations (NGOs) and the companies alike. That road map is what this book provides. Not only does it review the large corpus of literature on the topic of cross-sector collaboration and provide an impressive list of bibliographical resources for readers who want to delve deeper, it also—and this is perhaps more important—finds and fills in or clarifies the blank spots and gray areas in current research and practice. In these ways, this book offers readers a new conceptual and analytical framework, one that, as an outgrowth of the coauthors' earlier seminal work, is highly applicable to the needs of practitioners. The presentation of this framework is accompanied by vivid examples of company–nonprofit collaborations that illustrate each of the framework's concepts, and the book includes a superb final chapter that lays out twelve smart practices, based on the framework, for maximizing collaborative value creation.

As we look back over the quarter century of our partnership, the concepts presented in this book ring true to us. To take just one example, we actually did evolve through the collaboration continuum discussed in Chapter Four, moving from the philanthropic phase to the transactional phase to the integrative phase and finally to the transformational phase.

That first gift of boots from Timberland to City Year was philanthropic, but we almost instantly made the transition to the transactional phase. On the one hand, Timberland became City Year's uniform provider, donating not only boots but all uniform parts and becoming a lead corporate sponsor. On the other hand, City Year led staff service days and diversity trainings for Timberland—City Year's goal was never just to get a check; from the beginning of the organization, City Year asked its sponsors to get involved, to come out and do service, and to start seeing service as a vehicle for bringing people together.

As our collaboration grew, we were also quick to understand that our partnership was about much more than what each of us could get from or do for the other. And so we moved from the transactional phase to the integrative phase, and somewhere along the way we entered the transformational phase. Jeffrey Swartz joined the City Year board and later assumed the position of chair and helped lead the organization through a period of expansion. Timberland made a total corporate commitment to City Year, directing the vast majority of its philanthropic dollars to the organization. At the same time, Timberland's unique culture of service began to take root through the company's very close collaboration with Michael Brown, with his City Year co-founder Alan Khazei, and with their colleagues at the nonprofit. As a result, service essentially became an element of the company's DNA. For example, Timberland's Serv-a-Palooza eventually grew into a worldwide day of service across two dozen nations, and the company launched its "path of service," through which employees are granted paid time off to serve their communities.

Jeff had a vision of building on his grandfather's breakthrough product (the boots) and his father's corporate success (the Timberland brand) by adding a unique, powerful, authentic contribution—belief. And soon the *boots, brand, belief* formula came into sharp focus. It was a powerful formula for a rapidly rising company, and it helped define what an authentic, high-quality lifestyle brand can aspire to and achieve. As for City Year, its transformational partnership with Timberland led to an organizational DNA that has generated a series of transformational corporate partnerships. These have helped to build a dynamic national organization and to inspire an innovative federal program of national service that by its very design *requires* high-quality nonprofit–private sector partnerships.

The framework presented in this book is a remarkable one. But it represents only one of the many helpful and resonant concepts captured in the pages that follow. For example, one of the most compelling concepts that the coauthors present is the idea of synergistic value, whereby two partners collaborate to produce an innovation that neither could have produced alone. And, indeed, although we are proud of everything that City Year and Timberland have done together over the many years of our partnership, there is no instance of synergistic value that we are more proud of than our having come together to champion the founding of AmeriCorps in the halls of Congress and to help make it possible for more than 775,000 young Americans to date, including City Year's corps members, to serve their country.

At City Year and Timberland, we have often recalled the inspirational words of Robert F. Kennedy: "Each time a man stands up for an ideal, or acts to improve the lot of others, or strikes out against injustice, he sends forth a tiny ripple of hope, and crossing each other from a million different centers of energy and daring, those ripples build a current which can sweep down the mightiest walls of oppression and resistance." Ripples to currents—we are excited to think about the ripples that will be generated by this important book, about the partnerships that will be formed by its future readers, and about the value creation—the currents—for individual enterprises, and for society as a whole, that companies and nonprofits can generate together.

Michael Brown
CEO and co-founder,
City Year

Jeffrey Swartz
former president and CEO,
Timberland Company

Preface

Over the past thirty years, collaboration between nonprofits and businesses has evolved, in some ways to the point of revolution. Cross-sector collaboration has moved from being a nice thing to do to being a necessary component of strategy and operations. It is difficult to find an important company or nonprofit that is not engaged in such cross-sector collaboration. In the world of nonprofits and businesses, collaboration has become essential to success.

Simultaneously, research into cross-sector collaboration has burgeoned. Its social and managerial importance as well as its conceptual and operational complexity are attracting intellectual attention from a wide range of disciplines throughout the world. Scholars have created international associations focused on this rapidly emerging field of study, and conferences on cross-sector collaboration have proliferated.

Over these last three decades, we have been deeply engaged, as researchers and as authors, in the study of cross-sector collaboration and have interacted extensively with collaborating partners in business and nonprofit groups. The seeds for this book were planted in 2000 with James E. Austin's publication of the article "Strategic Collaboration between Nonprofits and Business" in the *Nonprofit and Voluntary Sector Quarterly* (*NVSQ*)[1] and with the subsequent publication of his award-winning book *The Collaboration Challenge: How Nonprofits and Businesses Succeed through Strategic Alliances*.[2] Over the subsequent years, both of us have continued to conduct research and to publish on the increasingly complex phenomenon of cross-sector collaboration.

In 2011, the editors of *NVSQ* asked us to review the cumulative literature on collaboration between nonprofits and businesses, and to ascertain what had been learned since the turn of the twenty-first century. This request led us to conduct an exhaustive examination of the literature, an undertaking that revealed significant advances in collective knowledge of the field along with some equally significant gaps in collective understanding of how value is created in cross-sector partnering. Our immersion in that literature review led us to conceptualize a new framework for thinking about and analyzing value, and we presented our Collaborative Value Creation (CVC) Framework in two lead articles that were published in consecutive issues of *NVSQ* at the end of 2012.[3] The journal's editors offered the following comments on that work:

> Their fine effort [has] yielded much more than a review. From their in-depth and broad examination of the cross-sector collaboration and corporate social responsibility . . . literature they [have] identified various inadequacies in the way value was treated, and consequently they [have] formulated a substantive and important new framing and extension of the current literature . . . Collaborative Value Creation constitutes a central mechanism for addressing complex social issues and for generating multi-value creation leading to societal betterment. In these times of rising needs and diminishing resources, identifying insights into the way value is created, treated, and distributed requires deeper understanding and more systematic research that can lead to a paradigm change of what constitutes value. We believe that these articles will help move us in this direction by stimulating further thinking and investigation in this important emerging field.[4]

The subsequent positive feedback on those articles that we received from academic colleagues and practitioners, along with the enthusiastic encouragement of our editor at Jossey-Bass, led us to plan and write this book. That process also enabled us to elaborate, refine, extend, and test our original Collaborative Value Creation Framework and to illustrate its features with examples from practice.

We have attempted to make this book particularly relevant and accessible to practitioners while retaining many details of our base research and intellectual work. Nevertheless, the book was not written exclusively for an audience of practitioners. Although it does draw on, distill, and communicate key findings from the rich collaboration literature, it also presents a new conceptual and analytical framework for co-creating value, a framework that managers can apply. To that end, practical applications of the concepts discussed in the book are illustrated by a multitude of examples taken from actual collaborations. The book's hundreds of references to our underlying research serve as a guide to even more detailed knowledge resources on subjects of particular interest to readers.

In addition, because we recognize that many readers are likely to be collaboration scholars in search of a book to use in their own research or teaching, we have presented a wide range of examples from all over the world. We have also included a set of five questions for reflection at the end of Chapters Two through Seven, with the first three questions intended primarily for practitioners and the last two intended more for scholars and students. The questions invite readers to think about the important new concepts that the CVC Framework puts forward, and about its broader implications for organizations, individuals, and society. In Chapter Seven, the final chapter, we offer a set of twelve guidelines for practitioners in nonprofits and business who are involved in designing and managing strategic cross-sector partnerships aimed at generating ever-higher levels of planned and emergent collaborative value.

Collaboration itself can be empty. The premise of this book is that cross-sector collaborations should be designed and managed to create economic, social, and environmental value for individuals, organizations, and society. In order for those goals to be realized, it is vital that we deepen and broaden our collective understanding and practice of co-creating value.

James E. Austin
M. May Seitanidi

Acknowledgments

We are grateful to everyone who contributed to the preparation of this volume. We particularly appreciate the collaboration of Michael Brown, co-founder and CEO of City Year, and Jeffrey Swartz, former CEO of Timberland—both of them pioneers in creating value through powerful nonprofit–business partnerships—for contributing the foreword to this book. At this writing, the enduring City Year–Timberland collaboration is celebrating its twenty-fifth anniversary.

We also thank a number of our collaboration colleagues, academics as well as practitioners, who enriched our thinking with their comments on our two 2012 *NVSQ* lead articles (Austin and Seitanidi, 2012a; Austin and Seitanidi, 2012b): Bruce Burtch; Steve Waddell; Professor Andrew Crane; Professor Roberto Gutierrez; Professor Jeff Brudney, Professor Femida Handy, and Professor Lucas Meijs; the *NVSQ* editors; and a multitude of other collaboration scholars and practitioners from whom we have learned so much, and to whom we have dedicated this book.

For valuable assistance on reference documentation, we thank Urlike Weske, a graduate student at Utrecht University; and Khondker Suraiya Nasreen, a doctoral student at Hull Business School. Thanks as well to María Jesús Barroso Méndez, a doctoral student at Universidad de Extremadura, for her work on the collection of cases.

At the Harvard Business School, we are indebted to Erika McCaffrey, information research specialist, whose impressive skill enabled our exhaustive process of literature review; to Chris Jones, document specialist, for his careful assistance in preparing the manuscript; and to Paula Alexander for administrative support.

We are also grateful to Alison Hankey, senior editor at Jossey-Bass, and her team; and to Alan Venable for editorial support and guidance in the process of developing the manuscript.

Creating Value in Nonprofit–Business Collaborations

Chapter One

Collaboration: It's All about Creating Value

Businesses and nonprofits collaborate mainly to create new value for themselves or others. Collaboration between these two sectors is now widespread and growing. The strategic question no longer is whether to collaborate but rather how to co-create more value for organizations, individuals, and society. Yet we still lack understanding of where value comes from, how it is generated, what forms it takes, and who benefits. To deepen our comprehension and management of these critical issues for practitioners and academics, this book elaborates the *Collaborative Value Creation (CVC) Framework*. The framework provides a theoretically informed and practice-based approach to analyzing and creating greater collaborative value.

The Rising Importance of Collaboration

Over the past three decades, the perceived value of collaboration has vastly increased partnering between businesses and nonprofits. As of 2011, 96 percent of the world's 257 largest nonfinancial enterprises were engaged, on average, in eighteen cross-sector partnerships.[1] In 2010, 78 percent of 766 surveyed CEOs in 100 countries confirmed that collaborations "are now a critical element of their approach to sustainability issues" and that they "believe that

1

companies should engage in industry collaborations and multi-stakeholder partnerships to address development goals."[2] The perceived importance is mutual, and the partnering widespread: another 2010 survey revealed that 87 percent of nongovernmental organizations (NGOs) and 96 percent of businesses consider partnerships with each other important, and that most are engaged in eleven to fifty or more partnerships.[3] A supporting 2012 survey in California of small and midsized organizations found that 74 percent of the nonprofits and 88 percent of the companies were partnering, with over 50 percent of both having more than five partnerships.[4] In Brazil, a study of major businesses revealed that 95 percent partnered with NGOs and made social investments of about $850 million.[5] In Mexico, 61 percent of the nonprofits surveyed collaborated with businesses.[6] A survey of the top 500 firms in Holland showed that 70.1 percent have active relationships with nonprofits.[7] Academic research has amply confirmed that cross-sector partnering is considered essential to implementing strategies for corporate social responsibility (CSR) and to achieving nonprofits' social missions.[8] Furthermore, it is important to note that collaboration is not size-dependent. It occurs with organizations big and small, and the principles of value creation set forth in this book are applicable to all. In the twenty-first century, cross-sector collaboration constitutes a major leadership challenge across organizations and around the globe.

The growing complexities and magnitude of the economic, social, and environmental problems faced by societies across the planet exceed the capacities of individual organizations. A McKinsey & Company survey of 391 CEOs revealed 95 percent as reporting that, over the previous five years, society had increasingly been expecting businesses to assume greater public responsibilities, and the study's authors point to "the dawn of a new era in corporate innovation and experimentation, when new partnerships and standards will emerge, when new, more transparent measures will better reflect the full costs of doing business, and when greater private participation in the delivery of public goods and services will change companies' roles in society."[9] In addition, the number of nonprofit organizations has grown explosively, and the United Nations has estimated that one of every five people in the world has participated in some sort of civil society organization.[10]

At the same time, we are witnessing fundamental shifts in ways society and business and nonprofit managers are thinking about value. The concept of economic value creation has never been more hotly debated. From viewing value as hierarchical, with economic value at the top, we are moving toward equal priority for social and environmental value. From a single value associated with a particular sector, that is, economic value from businesses and social value from nonprofits, we are moving toward the concept of multiple value production from each sector. From the dominant logic of value coming through transactional exchanges, we are moving toward recognizing the greater value that can emanate from fused partnering relationships. The spotlight that used to shine on sole creation of value now shines on co-creation of value. The most productive pathway to progress is through strategic alliances across sectors. If your organization is collaborating only marginally, then you are being left behind. If your organization sees collaborations as strategically important, then there is still more value to be created. Throughout this century, practitioners will increasingly turn to cross-sector collaborations as powerful vehicles for organizational success and societal betterment, and so it is critically important for all of us to deepen our understanding of value co-creation.

Current Limitations in Understanding Value Creation

There is no doubt that collective knowledge about cross-sector partnering has advanced significantly over the past three decades. Nevertheless, our exhaustive examination of the literature on collaboration and corporate social responsibility[11] has revealed several important weaknesses in how value creation has been treated in this literature:

1. *Definitions.* Starting with the basic concept of what value is, we lack specific definitions.
2. *Language.* We do not have a common language and set of value reference terms.
3. *Sources.* There is no systematic categorization of sources of value.

4. *Relationships.* We do not fully distinguish among differences in the potential for value creation across different types of collaborative relationships.
5. *Dynamics.* We do not understand well enough the value-creating pathways of different collaboration processes.
6. *Location.* Only unevenly and narrowly do we specify and assess who is benefited. We have not yet uncloaked the full value of collaboration.

These weaknesses impede collective understanding and ability to realize the full potential of value creation as an outcome of collaboration.

The Collaborative Value Creation Framework

To address these limitations and enable a more specific, systematic, and comprehensive approach, we offer the CVC Framework, a new way of viewing and analyzing value and its co-creation. This is a revised, more developed, and illustrated version of a conception we proposed in 2012.[12] We will briefly introduce the framework here and then, in subsequent chapters, elaborate each of its components.

We define collaborative value as "the transitory and enduring multidimensional benefits relative to the costs that are generated due to the interaction of the collaborators and that accrue to organizations, individuals, and society."[13] With this definition in mind, we look at collaboration activities not as expenses but as investments generating returns. The CVC Framework consists of five complementary and interrelated components, each offering a distinct window through which to view, understand, and manage value creation. Each of the components is elaborated in a chapter of its own. From those chapters and the underlying literature, the final chapter distills a set of smart practices for co-creating value.

Component I: The Collaborative Value Creation Spectrum

Who creates the value? Where does the value come from? What kinds of value get created? This component provides the cornerstone of the CVC Framework by introducing the concept of a Collaborative Value Creation Spectrum that specifies four sources of value and four types of value, which provide a new set of reference terms, with each source and type of value being a unit of analysis for understanding value creation more precisely and more systematically. It serves as a mapping mechanism that enables partners to locate where their collaborative efforts fall on the value spectrum.

Component II: Collaborative Value Mindset

What is the mental framework partners should have about value creation and collaboration? How partners think about creating value collaboratively conditions, in fundamental ways, the productive potential of partnerships. This component identifies multiple dimensions of the mindset that reveal how strong the mental framework is for collaborative value creation. This element of the framework enables one, first, to identify specific attitudes and perceptions partners hold toward creating value collectively, and, second, to understand how those can be adjusted to achieve more robust co-creation of value.

Component III: Collaboration Stages

How does the type of collaborative relationship affect value creation? This component presents the *Collaboration Continuum*, to analyze how key value drivers change as partnering relationships evolve through the *philanthropic, transactional, integrative,* and *transformational* stages.

Component IV: Collaboration Processes

How do different processes in the formation and implementation of a partnership affect value creation? This component identifies how key processes in establishing and operating a partnership can generate value in its formation, selection, and implementation phases. The *Collaboration Process Value Chain* analyzes value-creation pathways to reveal how different processes can have differential value-adding effects.

Component V: Collaboration Outcome

Who benefits, and how? This component delineates beneficiary levels for outcome analysis in terms of individuals, organizations, and society as well as different kinds of value. Approaches and challenges to value measurement are presented.

Figure 1.1 graphically depicts the five interconnected components of the CVC Framework.

The CVC Framework moves beyond the growing and important recognition of multiple value creation in conceptualizations such as *triple bottom line*,[14] *blended value*,[15] and *shared value*.[16] Its distinctive perspective and approach move to a deeper and more refined examination of the co-creation of collaborative value. The framework disaggregates economic, social, and environmental value into more specific types of value, specifies key sources of that value, and identifies analytical and practice pathways for understanding the key processes that link the two.

As the preceding summary may suggest, the CVC Framework organizes collaborative value creation into constellations of key variables—collaboration value sources, types, mindsets, stages, processes, and outcomes—thereby facilitating focused and systematic analysis. It enables researchers and leaders of businesses

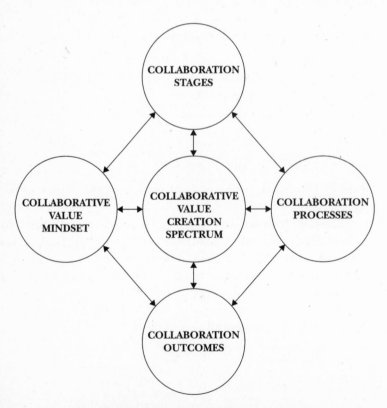

Figure 1.1.   The Collaborative Value Creation Framework

and nonprofits to examine interrelationships, dynamics, value-creation pathways, trade-offs, and outcomes at multiple levels in more precise and robust ways. The framework enables one to think more strategically about collaborative value creation for organizations, individuals, and society as well as to design collaborative value creation more carefully, manage it more productively, and measure it more accurately.

Although there are some commonalities between cross-sector collaborations (such as business with nonprofit) and same-sector collaborations (such as business with business[17]), there are many important differences. Every collaboration is shaped by distinctive contextual factors that impinge on each of the five components of the framework. Partly for this reason, this book's many partnering examples are drawn from a wide range of countries, industries, and collaboration configurations. Some value-creation collaborations also include the public sector, and you will find that much of what we say can also be applied to collaborations linking the public sector with business and non-profit partners.[18]

A Source of Research and Useful Practice

This book is built on extensive review and assessment of the relevant theoretical and applied literature in the fields of cross-sector collaboration and corporate social responsibility. Nevertheless, it is distinct from previous publications because of its dominant and different focus on the co-creation of value. Especially in that regard, the book provides new perspectives on important existing research.

The book includes a multitude of excellent case studies of business and nonprofit partnerships. These case studies are drawn from the literature, and we have added new analyses to them from our value-creation perspective. We present more than 100 examples of cross-sector collaborations from the United States, Europe, Asia, Latin America, Australia, New Zealand, and the Middle East as well as seventeen multicountry engagements. These real-world examples illustrate the managerial relevance and practical application of the framework. Specific contexts shape collaborations, but the examples reveal the broad applicability of the concepts and analytical techniques of the CVC Framework, and we use the examples to illustrate particular elements of the framework.

In some instances, we revisit the same collaboration in different chapters, to provide a cumulative and integrated application of the entire framework.

The book also serves as a distillation of and reference source for the state of knowledge on collaborative value creation. In addition to ample citations, you will find a list of nearly 500 references, which serve as a resource enabling readers to pursue identified topics in more detail. To facilitate undistracted reading of the text, a note number marks each source citation or set of source citations, as the reader will have noticed by now. The notes themselves contain a chapter-by-chapter listing of the cited sources in abbreviated form, with full source information given in the references (except for referenced interviews and sources consisting solely of URLs; information for these sources is complete in the notes). Throughout the chapters, we tap into this body of knowledge to provide intellectual and empirical support, including relevant survey and field-study data for the "why" and "how" of collaborative value creation. We believe that this aspect of the book will both provide managers with a more substantiated basis for their actions and decisions and open avenues for new conceptualizations and investigations. We try to capture the voices and insights of managers and key researchers by often quoting them directly. In addition, the book naturally draws on the authors' decades of experience in studying cross-sector collaborations and interacting with practitioners to advance the collaboration knowledge frontier.

Chapter Two moves us right into the first of the five components of the Collaborative Value Creation Framework.

The Collaborative Value Creation Spectrum

A Deeper Understanding of Value

To achieve a deeper understanding of collaborative value creation, we need new ways of conceptualizing and analyzing it. This chapter elaborates the first component of the CVC Framework: the Collaborative Value Creation Spectrum (CVCS), which provides new conceptualization, units of analysis, and definitional terms of reference. We envision value creation as a spectrum that recognizes collaboration as an activity that can produce varying amounts of value. It serves as a mapping mechanism to help partners locate and track their value-creation efforts. The goal is to understand what it takes to move across the spectrum from low value toward ever-higher levels of value creation. Many "minimalist partnerships"[1] produce just enough marginal benefits to survive, but such underachievement constitutes collaborative negligence. Being a collaboration underachiever is tantamount to throwing value away. Intelligent and responsible leadership and management aim to achieve ever-higher levels of collaborative value. To accomplish this, first *identify and understand* the *key sources* of collaborative value, which constitute focal points of analysis. Then *specify and understand* the resulting *key types* of value produced from these sources.

Figure 2.1 presents the Collaborative Value Creation Spectrum, which runs from lower collaborative value to higher collaborative value. The next section of this chapter explains and analyzes in detail how the *four sources* of value indicated in the figure—resource directionality, resource complementarity, resource nature, and linked interests—can produce ever-higher levels of value. Similarly, a subsequent section defines and shows how and why the resultant *four types* of value in the figure—associational value, transferred-asset value, interaction value, and synergistic value— are associated with movement from lower to higher levels. By the end of the chapter, we will be able to fill in the empty cells of the Collaborative Value Creation Spectrum in Figure 2.1.

In effect, the VCS component addresses two basic questions:

1. Where does value come from?
2. What types of value are created?

Within the CVC Framework, this component serves as a conceptual and analytical reference point for the other four components. Value sources and types are building blocks in the analytics of collaborative value creation. Accordingly, each of the subsequent chapters will further deepen our understanding of sources and types as we address a key question: *What enables a collaboration to generate greater value?* Those chapters examine the generation of value in terms of mindsets, evolving relationship stages,

LOW VALUE ⟶ HIGH VALUE

Sources of Value

Resource Directionality

Resource Complementarity

Resource Nature

Linked Interests

Types of Value

Associational Value

Transferred-asset Value

Interaction Value

Synergistic Value

Figure 2.1. The Collaborative Value Creation Spectrum

underlying collaboration processes, and outcomes as they affect individuals, organizations, and society in terms of economic, social, and environmental value.

Sources of Collaborative Value

To understand what gives rise to value creation as a collaboration moves across the spectrum toward greater value, one needs to identify and examine where value might come from. We have identified four interrelated yet distinctive underlying sources that can serve as focal points for analyzing and designing collaborations to generate greater value. Each value source addresses a key analytical question:

1. Who provides the resources, and how?
   (Source of value: *Resource Directionality*)
2. How good is our resource fit?
   (Source of value: *Resource Complementarity*)
3. What kinds of resources are deployed?
   (Source of value: *Resource Nature*)
4. What are our shared interests?
   (Source of value: *Linked Interests*)

We will now examine each of these sources.

Resource Directionality: Who Creates the Value?

The question of who brings value to the partnering table is fundamental to analyzing value creation. Although businesses and nonprofits can, do, and should create value on their own, cross-sector partnerships provide the opportunity to create different and multiple kinds of value. In collaborations, the degree and nature of the interaction can vary greatly, with significant implications for value creation. Within such collaborations, it is important to recognize that value creation can occur because of unilateral resource flows coming mainly from one of the partners, a situation to which we refer as *sole creation*. Or the flows can be bilateral, coming from each partner as a reciprocal exchange, and yet they can be parallel and independent: you give me something, and I'll give you something. This type of exchange is what we call *dual creation.* When the partners increase their interactions and *combine* resources, the resulting value creation from their conjoined efforts is what we label *co-creation.*

We conceive of this interaction range as moving along the VCS from sole creation to co-creation. The VCS is a mapping mechanism that enables organizations to identify where their value-creating actions fall along the spectrum. There is always some element of sole creation, but the greater the preponderance of co-creation, the greater the potential for value generation. Conjoining resources creates a new asset configuration that did not exist before. There are two key collaboration-assessment questions for partners, one descriptive and the other analytical:

1. To what degree are we co-creating value, that is, where do we fall on the spectrum?
2. What is our opportunity for increasing the degree of co-creation, that is, by moving further along the spectrum?

We can answer these questions in part by examining the flows, illustrated in the three depictions in Figure 2.2, that present the resource directionality of theVCS. If the flow is unilateral, with most of the value largely coming from one partner, then the collaboration is out of balance—a one-way street potentially leading to a dead end. Extreme one-sided creation of value is not sustainable in an alliance, because the lack of reciprocity erodes a sense of fairness in the generation and capture of benefits. In contrast, when both parties are putting commensurate resources into the alliance, albeit in separate and parallel fashion, then more value

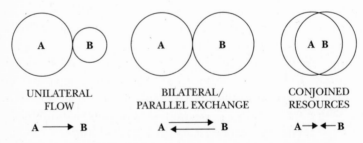

Figure 2.2.   The Value Creation Spectrum: Resource Directionality

will be created. These bilateral flows provide the basis for a reciprocal exchange and more durable relationship—each partner is putting in and getting out a fair share. Nevertheless, even greater value-creation potential lies in integrating efforts and conjoining resources so that the partners are more fully co-creating value.

Thus there are three types of resource flows: *sole creation* of value, *dual creation* of value, and *co-creation* of value. Although it is important to ask what I am giving to and getting out of the collaboration, it is even more powerful to focus on the partnership as the unit of analysis and to concentrate on making the collective pie bigger. The case examples that follow illustrate resource directionality, the first source of collaborative value, through the three types of resource flows.

Directional Flows: Case Examples

Let us turn now to two collaborations in New Zealand[2] and one in the United States.[3]

New Zealand: ANZ Bank and the Cancer Society of New Zealand

This fund-raising collaboration between the ANZ Bank and the Cancer Society of New Zealand involves the sale of daffodils. The bank advertises the program, mobilizes volunteer support, and collects and counts donations received through each branch. The type of the resource flow is predominantly unilateral, from the bank to the nonprofit. It is a longstanding relationship because the social value of the cause and the enabled work of the society provide associational value to the bank.

New Zealand: Genesis and HEET

This collaboration was between Genesis, a major New Zealand energy company, and the nonprofit Huntly Energy Efficiency Trust (HEET), and it illustrates the bilateral/

(continued)

Directional Flows: Case Examples (*continued*)

parallel exchange type of resource flow.[4] The alliance aimed to provide energy-saving curtains to low-income homes in a region where Genesis had power-generating facilities. Rather than simply providing a unilateral donation to HEET, Genesis used its marketing skills to promote the program and get other entities to donate curtains. On the other side, HEET ensured the technical appropriateness of the curtains and worked with social service agencies to identify appropriate recipients and deliver the curtains to them. Each partner was providing distinct resources and performing separate functions in a process of parallel dual value creation; both resource flows were necessary for the service delivery to function. (These were new activities for HEET, by contrast with the situation of the Cancer Society of New Zealand, discussed in the previous example; the Cancer Society of New Zealand received funds to carry on its normal activities.)

United States: Nature Conservancy and Georgia-Pacific

This example illustrates the third type of resource flow: conjoined resources. The Nature Conservancy and Georgia-Pacific, a company dealing in timber products, entered into a partnership to co-manage timbering operations in an environmentally sensitive area.[5] The organizations combined the nonprofit's knowledge of environmental science with the company's forest-management skills to increase both organizations' power to achieve economic and conservation goals in a sustainable manner.

Resource Complementarity: How Good Is the Mutual Fit?

A key source of value from collaboration is gaining access to another organization's important tangible or intangible resources that are complementary to one's own.[6] In effect, partnering changes the constellation of desirable resources available to each organization. Value resides in the resource differences. Nevertheless, organizational differences can also impede the realization of the potential value of resource complementarity.

Differences in the following areas between businesses and nonprofits (and between businesses and governments[7]) represent possible barriers to collaboration:[8]

- Mission and objectives
- Values and motives
- Strategies
- Governance
- Constituencies
- Decision-making processes
- Language
- Organizational culture
- Size and power

Sometimes the incompatibilities are too great, but partnering experiences reveal that these potential impediments are generally surmountable; sufficient organizational fit can be attained to allow the partners to tap into each other's complementary resources, many of which are in fact embedded in these differences. In effect, obstacles can become opportunities. The CVC Framework's fourth component—partnering processes, elaborated in Chapter Five—has to do with ways to facilitate fit. One is not eliminating all differences, because each organization's distinctiveness is the source of complementarity. Rather, partners aim for sufficient organizational compatibility to preserve value-enhancing differences.[9] The more ability the partners have to create a better fit and greater complementarity of their resources, the more they will advance along the VCS. The combining of each partner's distinct resources achieves completeness, as conceptualized in Figure 2.3, demonstrating resource complementarity and fit. One is not seeking complete congruence. There will likely remain spheres of activity relatively untouched by the collaboration. One strives for compatibility by focusing on the sweet spot of organizational overlap. The case examples that follow illustrate resource complementarity, the second source of value.

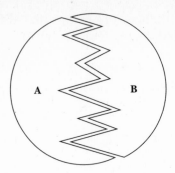

Figure 2.3.   The Collaborative Value Creation Spectrum: Resource
Complementarity

Resource Complementarity: Case Examples

The Nature Conservancy and Georgia-Pacific

This collaboration, discussed earlier, is a good example of
the combination of complementary competencies: environmental sciences from the Nature Conservancy, and forestry
management from Georgia-Pacific.

Home Depot and KaBOOM!

The long-standing partnership between the building supply
company Home Depot and the nonprofit KaBOOM! combined the company's building inputs and funds as well as
employee volunteers with the nonprofit's specialized knowledge and project-management skills for developing community playgrounds.[10]

H.E.B. and Monterrey Food Bank

When the U.S. supermarket H.E.B. expanded into Mexico, it
created an alliance with the Monterrey Food Bank.[11] H.E.B.
had food products that had been cosmetically damaged and
therefore needed to be disposed of. The Monterrey Food
Bank had the distribution system to move these surpluses to
needy consumers. The combination of these complementary

resources enabled the creation of a collaborative social-value chain.

Yad Sarah and a Pharmaceutical Company

The large Israeli nonprofit Yad Sarah, which lent medical equipment and services to disabled and elderly citizens, undertook a collaboration with a major pharmaceutical company.[12] The collaboration aimed to use the company's volunteers to perform a variety of services. The most valuable services for the nonprofit involved the efforts of the company's medical sales representatives, who were able to introduce and promote the nonprofit's services to doctors and make the doctors aware of the nonprofit's needs. This access and this network were very complementary and therefore proved quite useful. In contrast, company volunteers who provided computer training added very little value, because the nonprofit could obtain that service from existing and even more skilled volunteers. Volunteers in a third group, who were working directly with Yad Sarah clients, were not well equipped to provide any distinctive service, and the transaction costs of managing them were higher than the benefits derived.

Resource Nature: What Kinds of Resources Are Deployed?

The directionality of the flow and the complementarity of the resources are important sources of value creation, but value creation also depends on what kinds of resources the partners are mobilizing and applying to the collaboration. We place resources into three categories:

1. *Generic* resources
2. *Organization-specific* resources
3. *Key success-related* resources

Each type of resource has a distinct role, but they can all fulfill complementary functions, and they can all be mobilized in any collaboration.

Generic resources are those that are common across organizations. All businesses, for example, have and generate financial resources, and almost all nonprofits have a social service function and a positive social image. Thus a cash donation can be made by a business to a homeless shelter, and the shelter can continue to provide care for its clients; in this case, a generic cash donation goes to the nonprofit, which then provides a social service. Such resources are valuable inputs to a collaboration. Because such resources are common, however, the source of the value creation is fungible; the exchange can take place between almost any business and almost any nonprofit, and there is no differentiation of these resources according to the unique characteristics of the nonprofit organization. Therefore, in terms of quantity, one business might donate more funds than another; but in terms of quality, money is money, regardless of the source.

Organization-specific resources are particular to a company or a nonprofit. They are tangible or intangible resources that significantly differentiate one organization from others. Consequently, these resources are scarcer and potentially more valuable, if they can be appropriately engaged in the collaboration. For example, a company might have particular technical services or infrastructure, and a nonprofit might have access to and credibility with a specific population group. The mobilization of these resources holds the potential for designing collaborative undertakings that have richer value-creating possibilities because these resources are more differentiated than generic resources. For example, a bus company could provide transportation services to the residents of an elderly-housing community.

Key success-related resources constitute a smaller subset of organization-specific resources and include those that constitute the distinctive capabilities central to the company's or nonprofit's success. This is the constellation of drivers that enable the organizations to excel. For example, a company's distribution network or its technology, like a nonprofit's knowledge of a social problem or its service-delivery configuration, may be a key determinant of success. When these most valued resources are deployed, the collaboration is leveraging the organizations' most powerful assets, thereby opening the door to even higher levels of value creation.

As one applies different kinds of resources to the collaboration, value creation is ratcheted upward to higher levels; generally, generic resources are the most prevalent, with organization-specific assets less prevalent and key success-related assets least prevalent; but their importance is inversely related to their prevalence, as shown in the tangent and inverted triangles in Figure 2.4. The deployment of these resources is not mutually exclusive. All three types are to some degree reinforcing and can be mobilized simultaneously. The case examples that follow illustrate resource nature, the third source of value, through the three types of resources.

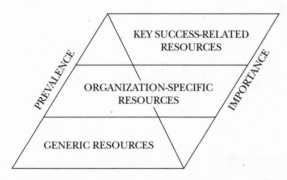

Figure 2.4.   The Collaborative Value Creation Spectrum: Resource Nature

---

Resource Nature: Case Examples

Yad Sarah and the Pharmaceutical Company

In this previously described collaboration, the first resource—the medical sales representatives—represented a distinctive competency of the company, whereas the other two resources did not. Probing which type of resources the collaborative value will come from helps partners construct a more productive and mutually beneficial exchange.

(continued)

Resource Nature: Case Examples (*continued*)

A British Retailer and a Breast Cancer Nonprofit

An evolving collaboration between a British retailer and a nonprofit focused on breast cancer also shows the value of combining distinct types of resources.[13] In the initial relationship, the retailer's lingerie department selected the nonprofit as the recipient of its annual charitable donation. This philanthropic donation simply contributed to the nonprofit's ongoing work. Any company could have made a similar cash donation. Two years later, the company moved from this disbursement of generic resources to leveraging its sales and branding skills—two organization-specific resources—so as to create a special brand of several lingerie products to be put on sale during Breast Cancer Awareness Month, with proceeds benefiting the charity. This marketing effort dramatically increased revenues for the charity, by comparison with the company's earlier cash donation. As a next phase in this collaboration, the two partners combined their core competencies to enable an even higher level of value cocreation: they joined together to create a new product line of postoperative lingerie for women who had undergone breast surgery. The store used its distinctive capacities for product design and marketing, and the nonprofit contributed its unique access to and bonds with the target consumers by holding focus groups, offering design recommendations, and testing out prototypes. Thus we see how the partnership was able to advance to higher levels on the Collaborative Value Creation Spectrum by shifting from generic to organization-specific to key success-related resources.

Linked Interests: What Interests Do We Share?

Another source of value is rooted in the linkages between the partners' respective interests. The greater the partners' perception that their interests are linked to the creation of value for each other, the greater their underlying, driving motivation for co-generating value. Understanding value linkages across organizations is complicated because of varying perceptions of interests and value. Partners in cross-sector collaborations do not necessarily have the same objectives. They may be seeking different things from the partnership. There is not necessarily a common currency with which to measure value created or the fairness of its division. It depends on each partner's perception of what is valuable. Consequently, it is very important that each partner gain a clear understanding of what the other values and is seeking from the collaboration. A vital partnering process is the reconciliation of divergent views so as to achieve fusion of value frames.[14] In effect, the greater the clarity of perceived mutuality of interests and joint opportunity, the greater will be the potential for realizing the co-creation of value.[15]

The potential value residing in linked interests can be assessed in terms of breadth and depth.[16] The partners may have a broad range of connected interests, which would increase the value potential, but the connections may be weak. In contrast, there may be relatively few connections, but they may be quite deep, which could be a powerful motivating force. As depicted in Figure 2.5, the lowest value potential exists when the linked interests are narrow and shallow, which means that there are a few superficial connections. There is moderate potential if there is greater breadth, although little depth; many trees are good, but shallow roots cannot always withstand adverse winds. There is also

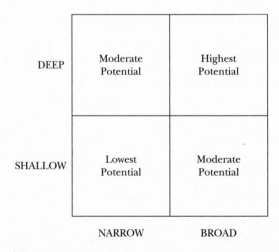

Figure 2.5.   The Collaborative Value Creation Spectrum: Linked Interests

moderate potential if there is depth, but only in a narrow range of interests; deep roots give strength, but lightning can topple that single tree. A broad set of deeply linked interests is the most robust value configuration because of the amplitude of possibilities and the durability of the engagement. If each partner perceives its self-interest as linked not only to the other's but also to creating value for the larger society, then the potential is even greater for moving across the Collaborative Value Creation Spectrum to higher co-creation at the societal level. The case examples that follow illustrate linked interests, the fourth source of value.

Linked Interests: Case Examples

The British Retailer and the Breast Cancer Nonprofit

These two partners' linked interests were focused on the same group of stakeholders—women in the at-risk age group. Although this was a narrow bond, there was depth to both partners' linked interests in this group.

Ralston Purina and the American Humane Association

This pet food manufacturer teamed up with a humane society because of both partners' deeply shared interest in promoting pet adoptions in order to reduce animal euthanasia.[17]

Rainforest Expeditions and an Amazon Community

Breadth and depth of interests were present in the partnership between the ecotourism company Rainforest Expeditions and the indigenous Ese'eja community in the Peruvian Amazon, a partnership formed to jointly create and operate a nature resort.[18] Shared interests across a broad range of educational, cultural, conservational, managerial, and financial activities were essential to the success of the venture. The depth of these shared commitment is revealed by the twenty-year term of the partnership agreement.

How to Analyze Potential Sources of Value

By delineating the four sources of value, the Collaborative Value Creation Spectrum provides a path for systematically identifying and analyzing where collaborative value can be derived from. This allows us to think more strategically about the sources, their combinations and interactions, and the resultant value they produce. Although the four sources are interrelated, each is distinctive and addresses different dimensions of value creation. One should therefore examine each one to assess the potential that it holds for building a new collaboration or strengthening an existing alliance. One is addressing the question "Are we tapping to the fullest the value potential embedded in each possible source?" In addition to a focused analysis of specific sources, one should then examine the entire constellation to understand the interconnections. One should assess the relative availability of each source, since this can vary by collaborating context. The next analytical step is to identify the possibilities of combining the different sources to determine the answer to the question "Have we created the optimum value-source mix to move the collaboration toward the highest level on the Collaborative Value Creation Spectrum?" In a high-performance collaboration, for example, the resources would be flowing from both partners and would move beyond a bilateral exchange to enter into a conjoined fusion of resources. The resources would be complementary, and the organizational fit would be compatible, thereby adding new capabilities to the integrated effort. Key success-related resources would be deployed so as to leverage the distinctive competencies of each partner. The collaboration would be propelled by broad and deep linkages between each partner's self-interest and the creation of value for the other partner and for the larger society.

Figure 2.6 summarizes how the sources of value evolve as they move across the Collaborative Value Creation Spectrum from low to high value. In effect, we are filling in the cells of the *sources* portion of the VCS shown in Figure 2.1. *Resource directionality* ranges from sole creation, with unilateral resource flows, to dual creation, with parallel and bilateral resource exchange, to co-creation, with resources conjoined. *Resource complementarity* has low value when the resources are unconnected and misfit, but

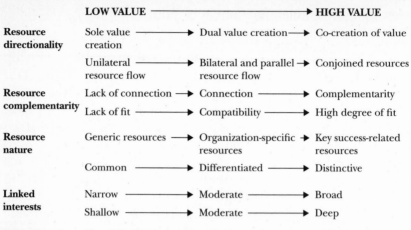

	LOW VALUE ————————————————→ HIGH VALUE		
Resource directionality	Sole value ————→ creation	Dual value creation—→	Co-creation of value
	Unilateral ————→ resource flow	Bilateral and parallel —→ resource flow	Conjoined resources
Resource complementarity	Lack of connection —→	Connection ————→	Complementarity
	Lack of fit ————→	Compatibility ————→	High degree of fit
Resource nature	Generic resources —→	Organization-specific —→ resources	Key success-related resources
	Common ————→	Differentiated ————→	Distinctive
Linked interests	Narrow ————→	Moderate ————→	Broad
	Shallow ————→	Moderate ————→	Deep

Figure 2.6.   The Collaborative Value Creation Spectrum and Sources of Value

then value increases when they are connected and compatible; highest value comes when they attain a highly complementary fit. *Resource nature* reveals modest value with generic resources commonly available, but it increases in worth as differentiated organization-specific assets are mobilized, and it attains highest value when the partners' distinctive core competencies, the keys to their individual success, are deployed for the collaboration. *Linked interests* are weak when they are narrow and shallow, and they grow in value as they broaden and deepen.

Types of Value

The four *sources* of value give rise to different *types* of value. In the literature as well as in practice, the benefits of collaboration are generally categorized in terms of economic, social, and environmental value. These are useful aggregate categorizations because they demonstrate the predominant types of value created. Nevertheless, we can gain a more refined understanding of value creation by identifying and examining more precise types of collaborative value. The Collaborative Value Creation Spectrum disaggregates economic, social, and environmental benefits into four underlying precursor types of value in relation to co-creation:

1. Associational value
2. Transferred-asset value
3. Interaction value
4. Synergistic value

Each of these interrelated types of value has multiple manifestations, and so we will also specify those value subsets. The more specific we can be, the more robust will be our analytics of value creation. Too often the full value of a collaboration is unrecognized because such specificity is lacking. A collaboration can produce some or all of these types of value, but in differing amounts. Therefore, it is important for partners to know or project the value configuration, that is, the mix of types of value that the collaboration will produce. The value function of each type can vary; not all types of value and their subsets are equally significant to a partner. For example, obtaining associational value that could enhance the organization's reputation may be most important to one partner, whereas obtaining a particular transferred asset, such as technology, may be most important to the other. We will now examine each of these four types of value.

Associational Value

The first type of value is that which arises from being seen by others as associated with your partner. The mere act of cross-sector collaboration can generate reputational enhancement, a subset of associational value. Over two-thirds of the respondents in a global survey agreed with the statement "My respect for a company would go up if it partnered with an NGO to help solve social problems."[19] The positive association is fundamentally related to the production of value for society, with the nonprofit being a vehicle for achieving that. Analogously, a nonprofit's image can be enhanced simply because it was selected as a partner by a well-regarded company, a signal that the nonprofit is an organization worth supporting. This basic form of associational value is intrinsic to collaborating; it represents a minimum base level of value accruing to most collaborations.

To understand this value further, one needs to move from the generic act of partnering to the specifics of the partnering relationship, which reveal the subsets of associational value. Each organization brings to the partnership its particular reputation, in terms of how well known it is, what it is known for, and whom it is known by. This represents the potential associational value. How fully that potential is realized will be shaped by the degree of complementarity and fit between the partners.[20] The partners harvest associational value in many forms—that is, value subsets, such as enhanced projected credibility and desirability in the eyes of their respective stakeholders—because of the association. These stakeholder perceptions in turn can manifest themselves as multiple additional subsets of associational value, such as greater affinity for the organizations; better employee recruitment, retention, and motivation; higher client patronage of their products and services; stronger community and governmental support; and additional attractiveness to investors and donors.[21] One survey confirmed this signaling effect of collaboration, finding that respondents indicated that a company's commitment to social issues was important when they decided which companies they wanted in their communities (84 percent of respondents), where they wanted to work (77 percent), and which stocks and mutual funds they would invest in (66 percent).[22]

To realize this value, partners need to communicate effectively to stakeholders (see Chapter Five). As a collaborative relationship becomes closer, the partners' employees as well as the public at large and other outside stakeholder groups increasingly see the identity of each partner as interrelated. Associational value magnifies as the collaboration moves from sole creation to co-creation across the Collaborative Value Creation Spectrum. Nevertheless, just as there is imputed pride of association, there can also be presumed guilt by association: one partner can be exposed to negative associational value because of the inappropriate behavior of the other partner in activities outside the partnership. For example, if one partner comes under attack for some perceived negative practice, then the other partner's stakeholders may question the organization's judgment or its desirability on account of the affiliation with the criticized partner. The case examples that follow illustrate the concept of associational value.

Associational Value: Case Examples

ANZ Bank and the Cancer Society of New Zealand

These parties found significant associational value. The widespread and longstanding Daffodil Day fund-raising event assured the partners of high visibility for their collaboration, thereby enhancing their reputations as caring organizations contributing to the community. This relationship, and their identification with each other as important institutions and with the cause, provided reinforcing associational value by signaling both their worthiness as partners and their community responsibility.

Unilever and the World Wildlife Fund

In 1996, Unilever, the leading buyer of seafood products, and the World Wildlife Fund, a major international conservation organization, were drawn together by linked interests in ensuring healthy oceans and sustainable fisheries.[23] Their collaboration resulted in the creation of the Marine Stewardship Council (MSC) and the subsequent certification system for sustainable seafood products. The MSC's eco-labeling—along with other, analogous, nonprofit-endorsed certification labeling for sustainable forestry products, fair trade products, and other types of products—fundamentally represents associational value for collaborating companies. The collaborating organizations' brands and reputations are enhanced by the eco-labels, which signal underlying social or environmental value creation.[24]

British American Tobacco and Earthwatch Europe

The British American Tobacco (BAT) Company sought a partnership with Earthwatch Europe as a collaborative

(*continued*)

Associational Value: Case Examples (*continued*)

pathway into the larger NGO and public policy communities.[25] The company was already participating in the NGO's workshops for its Corporate Environmental Responsibility Group and desired a deeper relationship that would give it projected credibility and access to the nonprofit's networks. The partners entered into a three-year contract, with funding that would enable the nonprofit to carry on important field research and have a positive influence on BAT's conservation practices in its agricultural production in developing countries. The controversial nature of the tobacco industry made such a relationship risky for Earthwatch Europe, exposing it to the possibility of criticism from some of its stakeholders, that is, the possibility of negative affiliation value. Consequently, the nonprofit, with the agreement of the company, kept the collaboration at a low visibility level with the general public but did communicate about it with policymakers and certain other NGOs. This selective visibility generated associational value for the company with these specific stakeholder groups of interest.

Transferred-Asset Value

The second type of value is the benefit represented by the receipt of an asset that has been transferred by one partner to the other. The significance of the transfer will depend on the magnitude and nature of the asset and how it is used. We have seen from our discussion of sources of value that, for example, the transfer of key success-related resources that are highly complementary and conjoined will produce a more valued benefit. And, generally, more is better.

There are important additional dimensions for understanding and assessing these transferred assets. They can be depreciable assets; these get used up. For example, a company's cash donation gets spent, or a nonprofit's service gets delivered. Other transferred assets are durable assets, such as equipment or buildings;

they last longer and continue to produce benefits. Durable assets can also be intangible. For example, a nonprofit can learn a new skill from a company, or the company can gain new knowledge about a community or a social problem from the nonprofit. The partner absorbs this new understanding and begins to use it. In effect, such capacity-enhancing assets become internalized by the recipient and enable an ongoing stream of benefits. Depreciable and durable assets are both valuable, but the recipients need to assess the functions that both are serving, relative to needs, and determine the optimum mix.

What is even more fundamental is the importance of recognizing that once an asset has been transferred, it is no longer part of the value exchange of the collaboration. Those assets and their value-creating capacity are now in the hands of the recipient and are not dependent on the other partner. Consequently, for asset transfer to continue to be valuable, the partners must renew the value proposition of their partnership. They can do this either by providing more assets of a similar kind or new types of depreciable or durable assets that would be deemed valuable by the partner. Renewability of transferred assets is a prerequisite for a collaboration's longevity. The case example that follows illustrates the concept of transferred-asset value.

Transferred-Asset Value: Case Example

A British Energy Supplier and an NGO Focused on Learning Disabilities

In 2005, a British energy supplier made its charity of choice a nonprofit that specialized in assisting people with learning disabilities. The asset transfer was a cash donation of funds raised by company's employees.[26] The employees' fundraising activity finished, and the funds were spent. In effect, the value of the depreciable assets was used up. To renew the collaboration, the nonprofit created a new value proposition

(continued)

Transferred-Asset Value: Case Example (*continued*)

in the form of providing training on disability awareness to all the company's employees, and specialized training on dealing with skill-challenged customers for select staff servicing this group. This training, in turn, led to the development of improved protocols for the company's communication with its customers. This was a transfer of durable assets in the form of new capabilities. Subsequently, the nonprofit trained the company's trainers, thereby completing the asset transfer and the partnership cycle, since there was no further asset base to be transferred and with which to renew the value proposition.

Interaction Value

The third type of value results from the partners' interactions. The interaction processes in question consist of the set of intangibles that constitute a type of value. What is particularly distinctive about these intangibles is that they are not just outputs of the value-creation process but also inputs to it. Co-creating value both produces and requires these intangibles. Whereas conventional economic analysis considers interactions to be a transaction cost, our framing views interactions as a source of benefits.

Like the other types of value, interaction value has multiple value subsets, and each can carry differing worth for different partners. For example, *relationships* are one subset of interaction value. Some researchers of the collaborative relationships involved in the implementation of programs for corporate social responsibility (CSR) contend that the actual value of CSR "transcends any single transaction" and instead "stems from the deep, meaningful and enduring relationships" that CSR entails.[27] This relational capital is embedded in the intangible of *trust*, another subset of interaction value. A trustworthy relationship serves as a mechanism for risk mitigation because it enables the partners to assume greater risks in their joint value-producing endeavors, thereby extending the frontiers of collaborative creativity.[28] Interaction intangibles can become capabilities that not only enhance the existing collaboration but also are applicable to the individual activities of the partners, beyond the specific collaboration, either in other alliances or within each organization. Other broadly applicable capabilities related to interaction value include understanding and valuing differences, joint problem solving, communication, coordination, trust building, and conflict resolution. As more complex, deeper, and integrated relationships develop through alliances, the interactions intensify accordingly, and greater and more valuable intangibles emerge. The case examples that follow illustrate the concept of interaction value.

Interaction Value: Case Examples

Natura and a Public School

Natura, Brazil's leading cosmetic company, initiated its first cross-sector alliance with a nearby public school.[29] Through this experience, the company learned how to interact and build deep relations with an external social organization. These interaction capabilities gave it the confidence and skills to undertake much larger and much more complex collaborations.

Farmacias Ahumada and la Fundación Las Rosas

Farmacias Ahumada, one of Chile's leading pharmacy chains, had a collaboration with a nonprofit that provided care to elderly people in need; in this collaboration, the company collected donations from customers in its stores.[30] The company discovered that the employees who were most successful in collecting donations became the most productive salespeople, and this discovery led the company to develop with the nonprofit a training program to strengthen communication skills that incorporated emotional connection with clients.

(*continued*)

Interaction Value: Case Examples (*continued*)

Stora Enso and the Association for Nature Conservation

Stora Enso, a Finnish company manufacturing paper, packaging, and forestry products, used a dialogue strategy as one of its main vehicles for engaging with such NGOs as the Finnish Association for Nature Conservation.[31] The interaction value being sought through such two-way communication included greater mutual understanding of perspectives, learning, and conflict management, all of which can serve as contextual risk-reduction mechanisms.

Tiffany, Global Witness, and Amnesty International

In 1998, Global Witness and Amnesty International, two advocacy organizations, fought against the flow of "conflict diamonds" by protesting against Tiffany & Co., whose CEO reacted by first ensuring that his suppliers were handling only legitimate diamonds. Then he engaged with the two NGOs, other companies, and government officials to create, in 2000, the Kimberly Process Certification Scheme.[32] This engagement produced interaction value in the form of trust and credibility, subsequently leading Global Witness to praise rather than criticize Tiffany, which for Tiffany became a form of associational value. Collaborations can simultaneously produce multiple types of value.

A UK Financial Services Company and a Money-Management Education Nonprofit

A UK financial services company collaborated with a nonprofit to provide educational materials to first-year university students. This collaboration was an example of how the relational dimensions of trust, sympathy, goodwill, and solidarity fostered collaborative behavior in the partnership.[33]

Synergistic Value

The fourth type of value is rooted in the basic collaboration rationale that partners, by combining their resources, are able to accomplish more together than they can separately. The synergism of the resources enables innovation. The more specific focus is on value interaction. At the level of the aggregate value categories, the core premise is that collaborative creation of social or environmental value can generate economic value, and vice versa. There is a synergistic relationship, whereby the generation of one type of value gives rise sequentially or simultaneously to other types of value, creating a virtuous value circle.

Innovation is the highest form of synergistic value. When collaborators' resources combine in unique ways to produce completely new forms of change, then there is the potential for significant organizational and systemic transformation and advancement at the microlevel, the mesolevel, and the macrolevel. In addition to creating such specific innovations, the partners develop processes and pathways to synergism. The case examples that follow illustrate the concept of synergistic value.

Synergistic Value: Case Examples

A TV Broadcaster and a Disabilities-Related Nonprofit

In anticipation of possible governmental regulations, a pay-television broadcaster in the United Kingdom collaborated with a nonprofit to address the special needs of physically impaired viewers.[34] The nonprofit organized focus groups from among its clients, generating recommendations for the broadcaster, and this activity led to the creation of a special call center and a new type of remote control handset. These innovations provided social benefits for the users and generated economic benefits for the company by solidifying the company's relationship to and retention of a customer base of 40,000 viewers.

(*continued*)

Synergistic Value: Case Examples (*continued*)

The British Retailer and the Breast Cancer Nonprofit

The earlier cited collaboration between the British retailer and the cancer society reveals that the evolving interaction can migrate toward synergistic value. The initial charitable donation established the relationship, which then developed into the partners' combination of their competencies to co-create an innovative product for postoperative breast cancer patients. This collaboration resulted in the synergistic creation of social value and economic value, emanating from the addition of an expanded product line that fulfilled a social need and deepened the client relationship with the business and the nonprofit.

Bell Atlantic and the New Jersey Schools

An example from the technology arena is Bell Atlantic's partnering with the New Jersey public school system to introduce and test its high-bit-rate digital subscriber line (HDSL) fiber optics and Internet connectivity.[35] The company was mobilizing its distinctive competencies, and the school system created a new technology school as the implementation site. The Stevens Institute of Technology was brought in to create an Internet-based set of curricula with the teachers. Students and parents were given access to computers, and the staff learned how to utilize the technology while also becoming more efficient and effective in managing innovative processes. This enriched educational environment simultaneously produced significant learning improvement, tested the new technology, and increased the company's knowledge of how to serve the larger educational market, thereby broadening social value creation as well as the firm's revenue opportunities. An even more powerful synergistic value was the subsequent technological innovation, in the form of a patent that enabled the company to create a new high-speed DSL product line in 1999.

How to Analyze Value Types

The first path of analysis is to examine the nature of each of the different types of value and their respective subsets, as created by the collaboration. The following list shows the usually associated subsets of associational value (emerging from the perceived worthiness of the relationship in the eyes of the partners' internal and external stakeholders), transferred-asset value (emerging, as this phrase implies, from the exchange and sharing of resources), interaction value (emerging from the partners' interactions), and synergistic value (emerging from the reciprocal and continuing co-generation of value):

Associational Value

- Reputational enhancement
- Credibility
- Desirability
- Affinity toward organization
- Employee recruitment, retention, and motivation
- Client patronage and loyalty
- Community support
- Government support
- Investor and donor attractiveness

Transferred-asset Value

- Depreciable assets
- Durable assets
- Renewable assets

Interaction Value

- Relational capital
- Trust building
- Diversity management
- Empathy
- Solidarity
- Joint problem solving
- Conflict resolution
- Communication
- Coordination
- Collaborative leadership

Synergistic Value

- Virtuous value circle
- Synergistic resource combinations
- Innovative solutions
- Synergism processes and pathways

Of particular interest is the form in which a type of value manifests itself across the Collaborative Value Creation Spectrum, as illustrated in Figure 2.7. The positioning on the VCS is a first approximation of value for each type. One then moves to a more detailed analysis of the aforementioned value subsets that emanate from each type of value, given its position. For example, associational value that has reached the level of deep identification between the partners can be examined in terms of the affinity and reputational benefits manifested by better employee recruitment and turnover rates, or by client or donor patronage, or by community or governmental support. Similar analyses can be carried out for each type.

The second path of analysis entails taking a holistic view and examining the values just estimated for each type, as elements of a collaborative value portfolio. From the perspective of portfolio management, one recognizes that each type of value and each subset of that value in a specific collaboration will serve a distinct function, although all these values are interrelated to some degree. The goal is to find the mix that best meets the individual and collective goals of the partnership. Consequently, there is no uniformly applicable target mix; each is collaboration-specific. In the portfolio assessment, one is estimating the relative contributions from the value types and their subsets. Such analysis, even if it yields only rough approximations, can be helpful in revealing

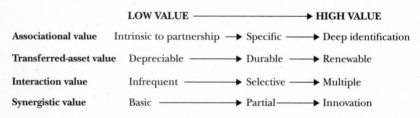

Figure 2.7.   Value Creation and Types of Value

imbalances among the types of value, in terms of the partners' needs. For example, the left side of Figure 2.8 shows, in simplified form, a portfolio mix in which associational value has an overwhelming presence, which would raise the question of whether this "univalue" collaboration is relying too much on a single value type and leaving other forms of potential value untapped. In contrast, the right side of the figure shows a symmetrically balanced multivalue portfolio, which broadens the value mix. Equal is not necessarily optimal, however. The partners need to determine what will be, for them, the relative strategic importance of the different types of value. In some cases, emphasizing one type more than others may make sense; imbalance may be optimal. In addition, it is not just the shares but the absolute size of the value "pie" that counts; different mixes can affect the aggregate value of the portfolio. For example, a portfolio containing a dominant mix of synergistic value may create a larger aggregate value than one that is heavy on associational value, since innovations may create novel solutions that generate more significant benefits for individuals, for the collaborating organizations, and for society in general.

Reviewing the Collaborative Value Creation Spectrum

The core question is not whether we are collaborating but whether we can produce more collaborative value for individuals, organizations, and society. The collective pursuit should focus on the realization of the partnership's full potential for creating value.

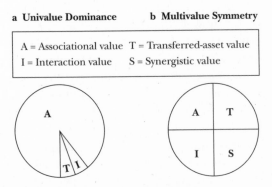

a **Univalue Dominance**   b **Multivalue Symmetry**

A = Associational value   T = Transferred-asset value
I = Interaction value   S = Synergistic value

Figure 2.8.   The Collaboration Value Portfolio

The Collaborative Value Creation Spectrum provides a starting point in visualizing this aspiration. It provides a way of acknowledging that collaborations can ratchet up their value production as a function of their value sources and types. It gives us a conceptual mapping tool for identifying where a partnership's value creation resides on the spectrum, from low-performing to high-performing collaborations. The figures throughout this chapter illustrate how sources and types of value differ across the spectrum.

Such value analysis can be made more systematic with scrutiny of the four core sources of collaborative value. First, *resource directionality* has to do with the question of who provides value-generating resources, and how. Resource flows hold greater value potential as resources move from sole creation to dual creation to co-creation. Second, *resource complementarity* has to do with how productive the fit is between the collaborators' respective resources. The key is to preserve value-creating differences while achieving compatibility between the partners. Third, *resource nature* has to do with the kinds of resources deployed. Greater value can be generated through movement from generic resources to differentiated, organization-specific resources to key success-related resources. Fourth, *linked interests* have to do with the value-creating linkages that the partners have in common. The broader and deeper the shared interests, the greater the value potential. Value analytics dictate that partners assess whether they are tapping the full potential of each source and achieving the optimum combination of sources.

Broadly speaking, these four sources of value give rise to economic, social, and environmental value. A more refined value analysis examines the four underlying types of value. The first, *associational value*, is the most common form of value, derived simply from being related to the partner and the social cause. Greater associational value accrues as the relationship intensifies and the identities mesh. *Transferred-asset value*, the second type of value, has to do with benefits accruing to the receipt of depreciable or durable assets. Once the asset has been transferred, the partners need to renew the value proposition, with more of the same asset or with different valued assets, in order to ensure the longevity of the collaboration. The third type of value, *interaction value*, emerges in the form of those intangibles (social capital, trust, communication, and so forth) that are due to the processes of the two organizations' collaboration. These intangible

outputs are valuable capabilities applicable outside the specific collaboration, and they are also necessary value-enhancing inputs to
the specific partnership. Rather than transaction costs, interaction
constitutes benefits. The fourth type of value, *synergistic value*, is the
highest manifestation of complementarity, whereby one form of value
produces another form of value and creates ongoing processes and
pathways for capturing the benefits of synergism. The most productive synergism is innovation, particularly when it has transformative
effects on individuals, organizations, and societal systems. Value analytics requires that one view the foregoing types of value as a portfolio
to be assessed and managed so that the mix is strategically optimal.

With the Collaborative Value Creation Spectrum showing the
way to a deeper and more systematic method of understanding the sources and types of collaborative value, we are now
ready to move on to the next chapters and learn about how the
other four components of the CVC Framework enable collaborations to advance across the VCS and co-generate ever-higher
levels of value. We begin in the next chapter by examining the
Collaborative Value Mindset.

Questions for Reflection

1. This chapter has suggested that to achieve higher lev-
    els of collaborative value, it is important to understand
    the two main components of the Collaborative Value
    Creation Spectrum: the sources of value, and the types
    of value. Use one of your organization's cross-sector col-
    laborations as a case study, and answer the following
    questions that focus on the sources of value:
    a. Is the exchange of resources unilateral, bilateral, or
        conjoined?
    b. How complementary are the resources exchanged
        between your organization and your partner?
    c. Does your organization deploy generic resources,
        organization-specific resources, or key success-related
        resources?

    d. What is your partner's fundamental interest in the collaboration, and how does that link with yours?

2. The second component of the Collaborative Value Creation Spectrum focuses on the types of value produced as a result of the interactions and deployment of the sources of value. Using the same cross-sector collaboration case study, answer the following questions that focus on the types of value:

    a. What is the potential for associational value? That is, how well is your partner known, what is your partner known for, and by whom is your partner known?

    b. Has your organization transferred depreciable assets or durable assets to your partner?

    c. For your organization and your partner, what forms of intangible interaction value are the result of your collaborative activities?

    d. What are the synergies with respect to the collaboration's generation of economic, social, and environmental value, and to what extent have you produced system change and innovation?

3. Use the perspective of a collaborative value portfolio to map the types of value produced by all the cross-sector collaborations of your organization. Are you leaving some types of potential value untapped?

4. The Collaborative Value Creation Spectrum provides new terms of reference for defining and analyzing value creation. How do these new terms assist the development of theory and practice?

5. As noted in Chapter One, we have defined collaborative value as "the transitory and enduring multidimensional benefits relative to the costs that are generated due to the interaction of the collaborators and that accrue to organizations, individuals, and society."[36] How do the different elements of this definition guide the analysis of the co-generation of value?

Chapter Three

The Collaborative Value Mindset

Equipped with our new understanding of sources and types of collaborative value, we now examine the important issue of how business and nonprofit partners think about creating value through collaboration. The partners' mental frameworks fundamentally shape the collaborative co-creation of value. An underlying primary conditioning factor for co-creating value is the mindset that the business and the nonprofit hold regarding value and collaboration. Because mindsets emerge from the evolution of theory and practice, this chapter fosters understanding of mental frameworks by examining the second component of the Collaborative Value Creation Framework: the evolution of the business's and the nonprofit's thinking about and management of value and collaboration with respect to three basic questions:

1. What is value?
2. Who is served by what concept of value?
3. How can value be created collaboratively?

The journeys of the business and nonprofit sectors toward co-generation of value have been distinct and converging. An important ingredient of achieving a collaborative value mindset is comprehension of your own and your partner's evolving thinking, practices, and trajectory regarding value creation and collaboration. In addressing the three questions just listed, we will identify various key dimensions that characterize weaker versus stronger collaborative value thinking. We will specify a series of mindsets that correspond to these dimensions. Together, these are the building blocks for the collaborative value mindset. While reading the following sections, readers should reflect on where their own mindsets, their organizations' mindsets, and their partners' mindsets are located on these evolutionary paths.

Business Mindsets: Five Central Themes

In recent decades, the question of what value is has been newly framed in the business world in terms of corporate social responsibility (CSR), which has been defined as a business's discretionary actions aimed at increasing social well-being. CSR has been in a state of continuing conceptual evolution,[1] as reflected by the variety of additional labels that have emerged, such as *corporate social performance, corporate citizenship, triple bottom line*, and *sustainability*.[2] Bibliometric analysis of three decades of CSR research has provided a comprehensive view of the evolving theoretical, prescriptive, and descriptive work in this field.[3] CSR theories and approaches have been categorized as instrumental, political, integrative, and ethical[4] and have also been depicted in terms of evolutionary stages.[5] Many recent reviewers have concluded that CSR, although deeply established as a field of study and practice, still suffers from a lack of definitional and theoretical consensus.[6] The 2012 review by Aguinis and Glavas[7] moves toward greater systemization through their multilevel, multidisciplinary model, which includes mediating processes, moderating conditions, and predictors of outcomes. The field continues to evolve in terms of both conceptualization and implementation. In our focused review of how the CSR literature deals with economic, social, and environmental value creation and collaboration, we have identified five central themes and a number of mindsets:

1. Theme 1: A focus on the question of whether value will serve shareholders or stakeholders
2. Theme 2: Empirical emphasis in assessing the business's social and financial performance

3. Theme 3: The existence of multiple motivations
4. Theme 4: A focus on value integration
5. Theme 5: A focus on cross-sector collaboration

These five themes reveal how the business community's collective mental framework has evolved. For each theme, we will identify the emerging key mindsets regarding value and collaboration. Readers particularly interested in collaborative self-diagnosis should ponder the extent to which each of the mindsets discussed in this chapter represents their own and their partners' mental frameworks.

Theme 1: Value for Shareholders or Stakeholders?

The most frequently referenced anchor argument against CSR is the one first set forth by Milton Friedman in 1962 and reprised in 1970, which holds that social actions (and their moral justification by managers) are contrary to the primary function of generating profits and returns to shareholders. According to Friedman, there is "one and only one social responsibility of business—to use its resources and engage in activities designed to increase its profits so long as it stays within the rules of the game, which is to say, engages in open and free competition without deception or fraud."[8] In this conception, the value mindset is focused on economic returns to a single group. This highly and narrowly focused conception is what we identify with the *shareholder mindset.* From this perspective, there is no perception of linked interests between economic performance, on the one hand, and social actions and actors, on the other.

In the years since Friedman offered this formulation, academic thinking and management practice have broadened the conceptualization of a company's relevant stakeholders beyond investors. The group of stakeholders is now considered to include consumers, employees, communities, governments, the environment, and nonprofit organizations.[9] As the management pioneer Peter Drucker is reported to have said, "Every organization must assume full responsibility for its impact on employees, environment, customers, and whomever and whatever it touches. That is social responsibility. But we also know that society will increasingly look to major organizations, for-profit and nonprofit alike, to tackle major social ills."[10] Thus this mindset has shifted from exclusivity toward inclusivity (that is, it has become the *inclusionary mindset*). For some, this development has positioned stakeholders as alternative claimants on a company's value (by way of wealth redistribution). Nevertheless, also embedded in an approach that takes account of stakeholders other than investors is the argument that attending to these stakeholders is not incompatible with profitability and even contributes to profitability in many ways. Various researchers[11] have stressed the instrumental and practical value of engaging stakeholders. In effect, creating social value—that is, benefits for these other stakeholders—has been seen as producing various kinds of business value. These have included, for example, associational value (enhanced reputation, legitimacy, and license to operate; improved employee recruitment, motivation, retention, skill development, and productivity; consumer preference and loyalty) and synergistic value (product innovation and market development as well as preferential regulatory treatment).[12] Thus the value mindset has shifted from one of incompatibility between economic value, on the one hand, and social or environmental value, on the other, to a mindset focused on synergistic relationships (the *synergy mindset*).

Aguinis and Glavas, after reviewing 508 journal articles and 110 books and chapters, conclude that "the actions and influence of stakeholders serve as an important predictor of CSR actions and policies."[13] In practice, there has been a clear shift from the shareholder mindset to the stakeholder mindset, which opens the door to collaborative interaction and value creation. Bill George, former CEO of Medtronics, has stressed the importance of seeing stakeholders in terms of an interdependent "virtuous circle."[14] The shift in mindsets that has propelled the evolution of thinking about the nature and scope of corporate social responsibility has often been a result of distinctive leadership.[15]

According to Michael Jensen, a pioneering thinker on agency theory, "We cannot maximize the long-term market value of an organization if we ignore or mistreat any important constituency," but Jensen also specifies that under

> enlightened value maximization . . . managers can choose among competing stakeholder demands [with] an additional

dollar [spent] on any constituency to the extent that the long-term value added to the firm from such expenditure is a dollar or more . . . Enlightened stakeholder theorists can see that although stockholders are not some special constituency that ranks above all others, long-term stock value is an important determinant . . . of total long-term firm value. They would see that value creation gives management a way to assess the tradeoffs that must be made among competing constituencies, and that it allows for principled decision making independent of the personal preferences of managers and directors . . . None of the above arguments depend on value being easily observable. Nor do they depend on perfect knowledge of the effects on value of decisions regarding any of a firm's constituencies.[16]

Furthermore, from a legal standpoint, managers are not prohibited from taking actions to benefit the company's broader constituencies.[17]

A collaborative value mindset thinks of resources allocated not as expenses but as investments that will generate returns in multiple forms of value over a longer time frame. Business and academic leaders have increasingly emphasized the need for business to escape the narrow-sightedness caused by fixation on short-term financial results and shift to a longer-term orientation within which to build mutually reinforcing social and economic value. Dominic Barton, McKinsey & Company's global managing director, has called for a "shift from what I call quarterly capitalism to long-term capitalism . . . thinking and acting with a next-generation view . . . rewiring the fundamental ways we govern, manage, and lead corporations . . . changing how we view business's value and its role in society."[18] Rosabeth Moss Kanter observes, "Thinking of the firm as a social institution generates a long-term perspective that can justify any short-term financial sacrifices required to achieve the corporate purpose and to endure over time."[19] Generating multiple kinds of value, particularly collaboratively, requires a mindset with a longer time frame (that is, the *long-term mindset),* even though some benefits can start accruing quickly.

Although there has been this broadening view of the business value derived from benefiting other stakeholders, many see it as primarily instrumental or self-serving,[20] with Halal asserting that "corporations still favour financial interests rather than the balanced treatment of current stakeholder theory."[21] Margolis and Walsh express concern that "if corporate responses to social misery are evaluated only in terms of their instrumental benefits for the firm and its shareholders, we never learn about their impact on society, most notably on the intended beneficiaries of these initiatives."[22] Shamir expresses concern that the "moralization of markets" also brings with it the risk of the "economization of morality."[23] That there are benefits accruing to the firm is good. The concern is that the mindset's benefit scope is only internal rather than also encompassing external effects and beneficiaries (that is, by way of the *external-benefits mindset*).

Theme 2: Empiricism in Assessing Social and Financial Performance

As some researchers began postulating the "business case" for CSR,[24] others began empirically testing whether, in the aggregate, corporate social performance (CSP) contributes positively or negatively to corporate financial performance (CFP).[25] The results of these analyses of social and economic value links have often been ambiguous or contradictory. Some researchers contend that multiple bottom lines cannot be meaningfully measured.[26] Nevertheless, a comprehensive meta-analysis of fifty-two studies found a positive association.[27] A recent matched-sample analysis of two sets of 180 very similar firms, one set characterized by high-sustainability practices and stakeholder engagement and the other set by low sustainability and engagement, revealed that the high-sustainability set had significantly superior performance in terms of the stock market and financial returns.[28] This finding is also supported by the analysis of another study of 400 firms that found "a positive relationship between sustainability and financial performance, as measured by stock returns."[29]

Various researchers have posited explanations for ambiguous results, as they depend on the specific historical relationship pathways between companies and their stakeholders and thus will vary across firms and time. Barnett asserts that results depend on the special capabilities of a firm "to identify, act on, and profit from opportunities to improve stakeholder relationships through CSR."[30] Other researchers point to the importance of picking appropriate key stakeholders.[31] Stakeholders, including consumers, have perceptions of and responses to new CSR actions, and these perceptions and responses produce unique value outcomes.[32] A Goldman Sachs analysis has concluded that "it takes some time for superior performance on [economic, social, and governance] metrics to feed through into financial performance and stock market recognition."[33] It may also be that the four sources of value—resource directionality, resource complementarity, resource nature, and linked interests—were not fully tapped or optimally managed. Barnett, looking at the macrolevel of value creation, raises the issue of whether CSR improves social welfare and notes that "oddly enough, this question is seldom asked or answered,"[34] an observation that exposes the absence of the external-benefits mindset (we address this void in Chapter Six).

The empirical analyses of CSR did not disaggregate and identify the value contributed from collaborative activities in particular, but these analyses were important in moving the debate from the perspective of *Should we?* to those of *How?* and *So what?* And this is where collaborations enter the socioeconomic value equation. According to Margolis and Walsh, "The work leaves unexplored questions about what it is firms are actually doing in response to social misery and what effects corporate actions have, not only on the bottom line but also on society," but they also state that examples of partnering with nonprofits abound, are increasing, and "may be the option of choice when the firm has something to give and gain from others when it makes its social investments,"[35] and here we see the *collaborative* and *investment mindsets.*

Theme 3: Multiple Motivations

Even in advance of researchers' empirical validation, practitioners perceived value in CSR and broadly and increasingly have been taking actions to implement it, although the degree and form vary across firms and over time. Recent surveys of more than 100,000 executives by Boston College's Center for Corporate Community Relations revealed that over 60 percent saw "as very important that their company treat workers fairly and well, protect consumers and the environment, improve conditions in communities, and, in larger companies, attend to ethical operation of their supply chain."[36] In a McKinsey & Company survey of over 4,000 managers in 116 countries, 84 percent agreed that companies should "generate high returns to investors but balance that with contributing to the broader public good."[37]

Research exploring the motivations behind this increased practice suggests that it is not entirely instrumental but rather is a varying mix of altruism ("doing the right thing" to benefit others) and utility to the company.[38] Aguilera, Rupp, Williams, and Ganapathi, presenting an integrative theoretical model, contend that "organizations are pressured to engage in CSR by many different actors, each driven by instrumental, relational, and moral motives."[39] Among these actors are nonprofit organizations acting as societal watchdogs to counter adverse business practices and agitate for positive corporate social actions. Others point to institutional pressures at the community level[40] and to economic and competitive conditions[41]as key shapers of the nature and level of corporations' social actions. The growing societal expectation[42] for business to assume more significant responsibility for solving social problems has created, according to Lynn Paine, a "new standard of corporate performance—one that encompasses both moral and financial dimensions."[43] The contention is that personal and corporate values have intrinsic social worth but also business value.[44] It has also been asserted that the potential for value creation is greater when motivation is intrinsic (coming from internalized values) rather than instrumental.[45] The *motivational mindset* broadens from unidimensional to multidimensional.

Theme 4: Focus on Value Integration

This movement toward a merged value construct requires a mindset that moves value relationships from a segregated to an integrated position (the *integrative mindset*). This has recently been extended into a repositioning of the very purpose of corporations and capitalism. Porter and Kramer's concept of "shared value,"[46] while setting forth the same premise of producing economic and social value previously discussed extensively in the literature[47] and referred to in our CVC Framework as *synergistic value creation*, emphasizes this as central to corporate purpose, strategy, and operations. It is asserted that such an approach will stimulate and expand business and social innovation and value in addition to restoring credibility in business and, in effect, reversing Milton Friedman's "thou shalt not" to "thou must." Social value is seen as essential rather than antithetical to achieving profitability in business. Kanter's study of highly successful companies led her to observe, "The need to cross borders and sectors to tap new business opportunities must be accompanied by concern for public issues beyond the boundaries of the firm, requiring the formation of public-private partnerships in which executives consider societal interests along with their business interests."[48] According to Lee Scott, CEO of Wal-Mart, "Environmental problems are *our* problems . . . being a good steward of the environment and in our communities, and being an efficient and profitable business, are not mutually exclusive. In fact, they are one and the same."[49]

Walsh, Weber, and Margolis have also signaled the growing importance of double value: "Attending to social welfare may soon match economic performance as a condition for securing resources and legitimacy."[50] Zadek conceptualizes corporations' learning about CSR as reaching a "strategic stage" at which they integrate the societal issue into their core business strategies.[51] Quelch and Jocz argue that CSR programs "are more relevant than ever in the face of economic recession."[52] A recent U.S. survey reported that 31 percent of the respondents had even higher expectations of company assistance during an economic downturn.[53] An earlier U.S. survey revealed that only 5 percent of respondents thought that companies were doing an excellent job of acting responsibly, whereas over 75 percent rated U.S. companies' social responsibility (defined as commitment to communities, employees, and environment) as either fair or poor, with 52 percent actively seeking information on corporate CSR primarily through the Internet.[54] And a McKinsey & Company survey of 391 companies revealed that over 90 percent of CEOs believed that public expectations were higher than ever and rising, with many of the CEOs emphasizing that not fulfilling their CSR obligations would lead to declining market share and loss of talent; the likely effect on employees had the greatest influence on how they managed CSR, and consumers' reactions were a close second.[55]

Investors' growing interest in social and environmental benefits in addition to economic returns is indicated by the emergence of several social-responsibility rating indicators, such as the Dow Jones Sustainability Indexes, the FTSE4Good Index Series, the Calvert Social Index, and the Social Investment Index. More than 180 institutions representing $8 billion have signed up for such initiatives as the United Nations Environment Programme Finance Initiative and the United Nations Principles for Responsible Investment, whereas the Enhanced Analytics Initiative for responsible investing research recently reported the participation of twenty-seven institutions representing $2.4 billion in assets.[56] In 2013, the World Federation of Exchanges was considering a standard for integrated sustainability reporting by listed companies.[57] This integrative, multivalue mindset is increasingly found in companies around the world, as in FEMSA, a Mexican-headquartered multinational whose acronym stands for Fomento Económico Mexicano, Sociedad Anónima (Mexican Economic Advancement, Inc.), and whose website[58] includes a pledge to preserve the planet for future generations by honoring the commitment to social responsibility as an integral part of the corporate culture and by recognizing the importance of operating the corporation's businesses in such a way as to create economic and social value for its employees as well as for the communities where the corporation does business. The chairman of the DeBeers Group has commented on the search for the "new normal," which will stem from exploiting the synergies that exist between "running a sustainable and responsible business, and a profitable one," an endeavor that, in some cases, will admittedly represent a departure from past practices.[59] McKinsey & Company's 2007 CEO survey found that 90 percent of CEOs were incorporating more environmental, social, and governance elements into corporate strategy than had been the case five years earlier, and that 72 percent thought these elements should be fully embedded, whereas only 51 percent saw their firms as having achieved this goal, partially because of a failure to recognize the links to value drivers.[60] Kanter's research on highly successful companies led her to conclude, "Service to society, guided by well-articulated values, is not just 'nice to do' but an integral part of the business models of companies that I call *the vanguard*. They use their unique strengths to provide innovative new solutions to societal challenges . . . Societal initiatives undertaken largely without direct profit motives are part of the culture that builds high performance and thus results, ironically, in profits."[61]

Porter and Kramer see this happening through (1) development of new and profitable products, services, and markets that meet societal needs in superior ways; (2) improvements in processes related to such elements as workers' welfare, the environment, and resource use in the value chain, improvements that simultaneously enhance productivity and social well-being; and (3) strengthening of the surrounding community's physical and service infrastructure, a strengthening that is essential to the competitiveness of clusters and companies. According to Porter and Kramer, "Not all profit is equal. Profits involving social purpose represent a higher form of capitalism, one that creates a positive cycle of company and community prosperity."[62] Although this point of view represents an *integrative mindset*, there remains the question of prioritization—that is, does profit take precedence over community welfare?

This approach and mindset of integrating social, environmental, and economic value generation into business strategy and operations is also a central premise of the Base of the Pyramid (BoP) movement that has emerged over the last decade. BoP strategies aim to incorporate the low-income sector into the value chain as consumers, suppliers, producers, distributors, and entrepreneurs.[63] The fundamental socioeconomic value being sought is poverty alleviation through market-based initiatives. Recent research has shifted the focus from "finding a fortune" *in* the business opportunities of the mass low-income markets to "creating a fortune" *with* low-income actors.[64] This involves combining complementary key assets to leverage linked interests through an *interdependence mindset*. As London and Anupindi put it, "This perspective relies on the proposition that the [more] the enterprise is able to meet the needs of the poor, the greater the return to the partners involved. This relationship clearly suggests that the ability to understand and create [the] value desired by different stakeholders is critical to successful venture performance."[65] In a survey of fifty-six Australian businesses, 93 percent of the respondents expressed the belief that business can play a role in poverty alleviation; factors reported to have driven these companies to engage in poverty-alleviating actions were brand, trust, and reputation (66 percent), employee engagement and recruitment (38 percent), personal motivation (30 percent), the governmental regulatory environment (21 percent), and demand and revenue growth (20 percent), and half of the respondents also indicated that they would partner with nonprofits and communities.[66]

Theme 5: Focus on Cross-Sector Collaboration

As companies have entered more deeply into an integrative value approach, the imperative of collaborating with the nonprofit and governmental sectors has become increasingly clear. According to Salamon, "Few corporations acting on their own can get real traction on the kind of social and economic problems that confront their societies. To go beyond symbolic public-relations efforts and make meaningful inroads on significant societal problems, corporations must join forces with other corporations, and with other social actors—in government and civil society."[67] And according to the statement of the CEO Task Force on Global Corporate Citizenship, "We believe we have an important role to play, in partnership with others in the public and private sectors and civil society, to help spread the benefits of development more widely by the manner in which we pursue our business activities. A commitment on our part to listen to and work with these other groups makes sound business sense and will enable us to better serve the interests of our shareholders and other key stakeholders, especially over the longer term."[68] This statement reflects the *interdependence mindset* and the *long-term mindset*. Some problems, such as climate change, inherently elicit more interconnected and longer-term perspectives.[69]

Over 90 percent of the CEOs just cited judged that such cross-sector partnerships would play a significant role in addressing development challenges.[70] Andrioff and Waddock stress mutual dependency in defining engagement and partnerships with stakeholders, characterizing such relationships as "trust-based collaborations between individuals and/or social institutions with different objectives that can only be achieved together."[71] Others emphasize how stakeholder strategies can create collaborative advantage.[72] In effect, the mindset shifts from independence to interdependence and to an attitude of openness to participative interaction.[73] A survey of the top 500 companies in the Netherlands found that collaboration with nonprofits was influenced by the firms' commitment to CSR, by strategic resource fit, and by contact and experience with and pressure from NGOs.[74]

Success in BoP terms most often requires critical inputs and collaboration from community organizations and sometimes from the public sector.[75] One example is the joint venture in Bangladesh created in 1997 between GrameenPhone and the Norwegian firm Telenor, as documented by Seelos and Mair.[76] The partners formed two separate but linked organizations. GrameenPhone was staffed by Telenor managers with technical and management expertise. Grameen-Telecom was the administrative interface to the existing Grameen Bank, founded by the Nobel Peace Prize winner Mohammed Yunnus. It provided microfinance and ran microenterprises to create jobs for millions of poor people through its network in 60,000 villages. As Tormod Hermansen, then CEO of Telenor, noted, "GrameenPhone and GrameenTelecom have a very neat form of collaboration. [Grameen-Telecom] recruit[s] the [village microentrepreneurs], . . . organize[s] the telephone shops, the debt collection, and buy[s] discounted air time in bulk. GrameenPhone extends the network, base station after base station, to increase the capacity to allow taking on new customers."[77] By 2006, the joint venture had generated more than 250,000 jobs for village microentrepreneurs.

Companies are realizing that the ability to anticipate, manage, and mitigate long-term risks in turbulent times[78] will be achieved through deepening their collaboration with stakeholders, including employees, customers, governments, local communities, and nonprofits.[79] Nonprofit organizations are key actors with deep expertise in social fields, and they are embedded in local communities[80] as well as in global networks.[81] Therefore, engagement with nonprofits represents substantial opportunities for corporations to co-create local and potentially global value by providing solutions to social problems[82] or by designing social innovations that will deliver social betterment.[83]

Although businesses and nonprofits may have different approaches to value creation, the research of Le Ber and Branzei reveals that "frequency, intensity, breadth, and depth of interactions may afford frame alignment."[84] Bob Thust, head of corporate responsibility at Deloitte, sums it up this way: "The bottom line is that there is considerable opportunity for longer-term and more strategic partnerships between corporate and third sector organizations which deliver significant impact and benefit on both sides of the relationship."[85] These benefits can accrue not only to the partnering institutions but also to society and to other individuals and organizations that are affected by a collaboration.

Porter and Kramer emphasize that the "ability to collaborate across profit/nonprofit boundaries" is a critical element of producing shared value.[86] Roger Polman, CEO of Unilever, has called for a shift to "collaborative capitalism."[87] Earlier, Halal urged "viewing stakeholders as partners who create economic and social value through collaborative problem solving."[88] Similarly, Zadek called for collaboration with the increasingly important nonprofit sector as the way to move beyond traditional corporate philanthropy.[89] Ryuzaburo Kaku, former chairman of Canon, has stated that the way for companies to reconcile economic and social obligations is *kyosei*, or the "spirit of cooperation," whereby "individuals and organizations live and work together for the common good."[90] Recent research on inclusive business development from the BoP perspective has also highlighted the critical roles that not-for-profit organizations frequently play in building these ventures and co-creating value.[91] Social partnerships with informal agreements and donations have been cited as more appropriate governance mechanisms for subsistence markets than formal contracts and equity investments.[92]

Googins, Mirvis, and Rochlin assert that for the emerging generation of partnerships between businesses and nonprofits, "the next big challenge is to co-create value for business and society."[93] According to a recent survey of members of Business in the Community, 72 percent of the respondents saw collaboration as the most effective way to address sustainability issues.[94] In effect, at higher levels of CSR, collaboration becomes more important in the value-creation process. As creating synergistic value becomes integrated and institutionalized into a company's mission, values, strategy, and operations, engaging in the co-generation of value with nonprofits and other stakeholders becomes an imperative.

If a company's CSR platform is weak, its collaborative capacity will also be weak. Hence, co-creating value indicates and requires a higher degree of CSR development and institutionalization. Thus the *collaborative mindset* becomes an essential ingredient of CSR implementation.[95]

The Evolving Nonprofit Mindset

Just as businesses have increasingly turned to nonprofits as collaborators to implement CSR and produce social value, several factors have also been moving nonprofits toward a mindset shift favoring greater engagement with companies. Grant and Crutchfield found that "becoming a high-impact nonprofit is not just about building a great organization and then expanding it to reach more people. Rather, high-impact nonprofits work with and through organizations and individuals outside themselves to create more impact than they ever could have achieved alone."[96] In other words, this is a shift toward the *interdependence mindset.* In the 1990s there was growing recognition that corporations might be part of the solution for nonprofits. In the words of one representative from an international environmental nonprofit, the World Wildlife Fund, "While industry represents perhaps the biggest single threat to society and the natural world, it can also represent one of our greatest allies in our mission to safeguard it and to provide for its sustainable development."[97]

Parallel to the increasing integration of social value into business strategy, there has emerged a growing and analogous emphasis in nonprofits on incorporating business disciplines and economic value into their orientation—that is, an *integrative mindset.* In the same vein, the field of social marketing has emerged as the application of marketing concepts and techniques for changing behavior so as to achieve social betterment.[98] It is a set of tools that can be used independently by either businesses or nonprofits as part of their strategies, but researchers have highlighted the importance of cross-sector collaboration in its application.[99] Social enterprise and social entrepreneurship arose as an organizational concept. Some conceptualizations have referred to the application of business expertise and market-based skills to the social sector, such as when nonprofit organizations operate revenue-generating enterprises.[100] Conceptualizations of social entrepreneurship point to innovative activity with a social purpose in either the business or the nonprofit sector or as hybrid structural forms that mix for-profit and nonprofit activities.[101] Social entrepreneurship has also been applied to corporations and can include cross-sector collaborations.[102] Emerson has emphasized the generation of "blended" social and economic value,[103] as a consequence of which nonprofits have broadened their views of value and value creation, a broadening that is fostered by the *innovation mindset.*[104]

Many academics and practitioners have commented on the blurring of boundaries between the sectors,[105] and some researchers have empirically documented this convergence.[106] Although this overlap of purposes reflects an increasingly common appreciation and pursuit of social and economic value creation and fosters collaboration across the sectors, this is an uncomfortable direction for some nonprofits. Many advocacy nonprofits oppose business practices that they consider socially harmful, and they fear being co-opted by collaborating with companies.[107] Cloaking corporate malfeasance is no longer a feasible option. Global connectivity through the Internet has accelerated transparency and communications. Businesses and nonprofits alike have engaged in information warfare, as Exxon Mobil and Greenpeace have done in their dispute over climate change.[108] Negative practices are soon revealed and broadly and instantaneously communicated. Such checks and balances and accountability mechanisms are integral elements of a healthy society. At any rate, increasing numbers of advocacy nonprofits and opposing companies have discovered linked interests and complementary resources, and these discoveries have led to mutually beneficial partnerships.[109]

Conflict management represents an intangible form of interaction value. For example, activist NGOs, labor unions, and management at Chiquita Brands overcame historic conflicts and learned to work together to bring about significant transformations that produced benefits for all the parties.[110] The CEO of a consumer packaged-goods company put it this way: "I think we are entering a new era here. The NGOs and businesses know that the confrontational ways of the past that were used to bring attention to the issues are behind us. The issues are out there. Now it's about solutions. Now we're saying we can do more by working together than by not working together."[111] The mindset has been shifting from confrontation to collaboration.

Many business leaders have adjusted their conflictive posture toward activist nonprofits and now view them as important stakeholders with whom constructive interaction is possible and desirable.[112] For example, John Mackey, founder and CEO of Whole Foods Market, says he "perceived them as . . . enemies" but now believes that "the best way to argue with your opponents is to completely understand their point of view" and that "to extend our love and care beyond our narrow self-interest is antithetical to neither our human nature nor our financial success. Rather, it leads to the further fulfillment of both."[113] In his most recent thinking, Mackey and his co-author Raj Sisodia put forth the case for "conscious capitalism," whereby companies can "reinvent themselves as agents of creation and collaboration, magnificent entities capable of cross-pollinating human potential in ways nothing else can, creating multiple value for everyone they touch."[114]

Porter and Kramer contend that "leaders in both business and civil society have focused too much on the friction between them and not enough on the points of intersection," and they further assert, "The mutual dependence of corporations and society implies that both business decisions and social policies must follow the principle of shared value. That is, choices must benefit both sides. If either a business or a society pursues policies that benefit its interests at the expense of the other, it will find itself on a dangerous path. A temporary gain to one will undermine the long-term prosperity of both."[115] In effect, the mindset needs to be one of being a value adder rather than just a value extractor. Seelos and Mair's analyses of BoP partnerships in Bangladesh led them to conclude that "organizations with primarily social strategic objectives can constitute a source for economically undervalued resources and capabilities. The cases show that providing scale to these organizations creates more social value from their resources and at the same time may enable company partners to leverage economic value."[116]

A recent illustration of this interface is Greenpeace's attack on the outdoor-apparel maker Timberland with the accusation that leather for the company's boots came from Brazilian cattle ranchers who were deforesting the Amazon. Jeff Swartz, Timberland's former CEO, received 65,000 e-mails from Greenpeace supporters, engaged with the nonprofit, and worked with Timberland's suppliers to ensure that none of the company's leather would be sourced from the Amazon area. Reflecting on Timberland's experience with the activist NGO, Swartz observed, "You may not agree with their tactics, but they may be asking legitimate questions you should have been asking yourself. And if you can find at least one common goal—in this case, a solution to deforestation—you've also found at least one reason for working *with* each other, not against."[117] Eccles, Newquist, and Schatz's advice on managing reputational risk echoes Swartz's perspective: "Many executives are skeptical about whether such organizations are genuinely interested in working collaboratively with companies to achieve change for the public good. But NGOs are a fact of life and must be engaged. Interviews with them can also be a good way of identifying issues that may not yet have appeared on the company's radar screen."[118]

Seitanidi, in keeping with Covey and Brown,[119] asserts that such "overt functional conflict," although often lacking in partnerships, can play an important role in enabling changes of "perceptions, policies and actions."[120] Koschmann, Kuhn, and Pfarrer concur, stating that "a simultaneous ethic of inclusiveness and confrontation is more likely to generate the meaningful participation needed for the creative, integrative, and legitimate solutions participants seek."[121] In a similar vein, other research documents the valuable types of resources that nonprofits can bring, such as legitimacy, awareness of social forces, distinct networks, and specialized technical expertise that can head off trouble for the business, accelerate innovation, spot future shifts in demand, shape legislation, and set industry standards.[122] One study of 214 business managers revealed that cross-sector partnerships with environmental NGOs increased companies' perceived legitimacy and enabled the development of a more proactive and deeper commitment to environmental betterment.[123]

One of the bridging areas between nonprofit advocacy and collaboration with businesses has been corporate codes of conduct. Nonprofits have often compelled the adoption of such codes, but they have also helped corporations by providing knowledge that enables compliance.[124] Conroy labels this phenomenon the "certification revolution," whereby nonprofits and companies establish standards and external verification systems across a wide array of socially desirable business practices and sectors (for example, forestry, fishing, mining, textiles, and apparel).[125] The resultant fair trade movement has experienced rapid and significant growth, generating improved economic and social benefits for producers and workers. Simultaneously, it has given companies a vehicle for differentiating and enriching their brands in terms of the social value they are co-creating. Providing consumers with more information about a company's social practices (such as those involving labor conditions in the production of apparel) can positively affect consumers' willingness to pay for those products.[126] Various other, more general standards and social reporting systems have emerged from consultative dialogue among multiple stakeholders.[127] These collaborative certification arrangements produce associational value that enhances company credibility, and they lead to socially beneficial changes in business practices. The *collaborative mindset,* the *integrative mindset,* and the *interdependency mindset* enable the creation and operation of these certification systems and codes.

Even when the relationship is more adversarial, the advocacy NGOs can trigger a process of reflection and adjustment of business practices that, in the end, can be beneficial to the company and to society. For example, several advocacy NGOs targeted the project-financing practices of various leading banks, which responded by promulgating the Equator Principles, a new set of lending standards aimed at eliminating adverse societal impacts of development projects. Over a decade, the NGOs continued to monitor the banks and to pressure them to walk their talk. Researchers have found that the decoupling of companies' stated policies from their actual implementation is not generally a "calculated deception" but rather "can be the outcome of organizational learning efforts that are fraught with complexity under conditions of inconsistent, and rapidly changing, stakeholder pressures."[128] The ongoing advocacy process of the NGOs led the banks to a gradual deepening of their commitment and to institutionalization of new and significant process changes that led one group of researchers to conclude that "it might pay off to tolerate their gradual transformation and encourage experimentation informed by mutual learning and dialogue."[129] Heugens found that even from adversarial relationships with NGOs a company could develop "integrative and communication skills."[130]

Consequently, one can even consider that what may seem to be a conflictive relationship between antagonists may actually be a form of what we call *adversarial collaboration*. The benefits accruing to the businesses, to the NGOs, and to society would not have been achieved without the communicative interaction.[131]

Reviewing the Collaborative Value Mindset

From the foregoing examination of evolving thinking and practice with respect to value and collaboration among businesses and nonprofits, we have identified a constellation of mindsets that, in effect, constitute thirteen dimensions of the mental framework for collaborative value creation. How these thirteen mindsets manifest themselves—weakly or strongly, as depicted in Table 3.1—can make a difference in how they contribute to the collaborative creation of value.

Let us conclude by reexamining the thirteen dimensions of the Collaborative Value Mindset listed in Table 3.1. Throughout the chapter, we have identified the constellation of component mindsets that together constitute the overall Collaborative Value Mindset. In effect, how one thinks about each of these dimensions can make the collaboration weaker or stronger. Here, we highlight each of these dimensions and the characteristics of the corresponding mindsets as each is associated with strength rather than weakness. Readers can assess where their own and their partners' mindsets fall more on the side of strength or on the side of weakness. This exercise can identify areas of difference as well as opportunities for strengthening the partners' individual and collective mindsets.

1. *Value concept.* The starting point is to conceive of value broadly as economic, social, and environmental rather than narrowly focusing on just one category. Drawing on the more refined value types delineated in the Collaborative Value Creation Spectrum (see Chapter Two) would mean including associational value, transferred-asset value, interaction value, and synergistic value.

2. *Value compatibility.* Instead of viewing economic, social, and environmental values as trade-offs, one recognizes them as compatible. Furthermore, it is not simply that they can coexist but rather that they are synergistic.

Table 3.1. Thirteen Dimensions of the Collaborative Value Mindset

Dimension	Weak Manifestation	Strong Manifestation
1. Value concept	Concept is narrow	Concept is broad
2. Value compatibility	Compatibility requires trade-offs	Compatibility promotes synergy
3. Value relationships	Relationships are segregated	Relationships are integrated
4. Value role	Focus is on extracting value	Focus is on adding value
5. Participation	Participation is exclusive	Participation is inclusive
6. Benefit scope	Scope is limited to internal benefits	Scope includes external benefits
7. Outlays	Outlays are seen as expenses	Outlays are seen as investments
8. Time frame	Time frame is for the short term	Time frame is for the long term
9. Dependency	There is independence	There is interdependence
10. Motivations	Motivations are unidimensional	Motivations are multidimensional
11. Attitude	Attitude is conflictive	Attitude is cooperative
12. Compatibility	Multiple core organizational elements diverge	Multiple core organizational elements converge
13. Change	Change is minimal	Change is characterized by innovation

3. *Value relationships.* Rather than segregating value relationships, one integrates them. Instead of placing them in hierarchical order, one views them together as a value package. One does not say, "First I have to have this type of value, and then we'll see about the rest." Thinking holistically can better reveal the fullness of potential value.

4. *Value role.* The collaborative value process involves both creation and capture. Even though all partners should expect to harvest benefits, the collaborative mindset is not fixated on extraction but rather on how to add value to the partnership. Creating value for a partner triggers reciprocity and can lead to a virtuous value circle.

5. *Participation.* One needs to move from being exclusionary and internally focused to becoming inclusive. In this way, one sees the shift from a fixation on shareholders to engagement of stakeholders.

6. *Benefit scope.* One is externally oriented in terms of who benefits from the collaboration. It is not just what gains each partnering organization garners but how benefits are extended to outside groups and the larger society.

7. *Outlays.* One thinks of resource expenditures not as expenses but as investments, with the returns being multifaceted benefits accruing to multiple groups. Rather than thinking in terms of transaction costs, one recognizes interaction as a form of value.

8. *Time frame.* Fixation on the short term crowds out collaborative creativity and forgoes the success of sustainability. The stronger mindset thinks in terms of long-term value creation. Collaboration benefits can and do get generated in the short run, but the strategic perspective requires a longer vision.

9. *Dependency.* There is a recognition that organizations and individuals are inescapably interdependent rather than isolated and independent. In the words of Visser, "Being responsible . . . does not mean doing it all ourselves. Responsibility is a form of sharing, a way of recognizing that we're all in this together. 'Sole responsibility' is an oxymoron."[132]

10. *Motivations.* Collaboration motivations are multifaceted and complementary. "Doing the right thing" does not preclude "doing good and doing well." Value-based motivations contribute to collaborative sustainability, but so do results that concretely benefit the partners.

11. *Interaction attitude.* The orientation is toward constructive cooperation rather than antagonistic conflict.[133] There is an openness to interactions, and there is the belief that it can lead to mutual benefits. Nevertheless, there is also a recognition

that disagreements will and should arise and can be beneficial. Constructive conflict emerges from and reinforces mutual respect.

12. *Compatibility.* Multiple core elements of the organizations (such as mission, strategy, and values) are perceived as converging rather than diverging. There is a shared perception of linked interests and mental alignment.

13. *Change.* There is a shift away from a perspective of minimal change and toward innovation. Collaboration is viewed as a vehicle enabling meaningful change. There is a recognition that creating value collaboratively will require internal change before external change can be achieved.

One's mental framework molds everything else. There is a fundamental way in which the appropriate collaborative value mindset shapes the value-creation potential of a partnership. The stronger the collaborative mindset, the farther the partnership will advance across the Collaborative Value Creation Spectrum. We turn our attention in the next chapter to the nature of collaborative relationships and how their evolution affects the generation of value.

Questions for Reflection

1. What constitutes value for your organization and your partner organization?
2. For each of the thirteen categories listed in Table 3.1, how would you judge your organization's and your partner's mindsets?
3. By examining your organization's cross-sector collaborations, can you provide examples demonstrating compatibility among economic, social, and environmental value (that is, a synergy mindset)?
4. Why, in your opinion, do companies increasingly embrace the integrative mindset?
5. When organizations from different sectors aim to co-create value, how should potential or actual incompatibilities between mindsets be dealt with?

Chapter Four

Collaboration Stages and Value Relationships

Cross-sector relationships come in many forms and evolve over time. They can pass through collaboration stages that vary in terms of degree of intensity of the relationship, form of interaction, and structural arrangement between the non-profit and the corporation. It is important to note that each stage has distinct dynamics and potential for collaborative value creation. This provides us with another window through which to view and understand collaborative value creation. We will explore this third component of the Collaborative Value Creation Framework first by explaining the concept of the Collaboration Continuum and then by examining how value is created at each stage along the continuum.

The Concept of the Collaboration Continuum

Austin's Collaboration Continuum, or CC,[1] has been widely cited in the literature on cross-sector partnering[2] and is in wide use among practitioners. We will elaborate and expand on the CC in this chapter, with particular focus on the nature of value creation at each collaboration stage. The conceptualization of collaborative relationships as lying along a continuum is important because value creation is a dynamic process that is shaped by the evolving nature of the partnering relationship. Other scholars have also found the concept of a continuum useful, and we have analyzed their similarities and differences elsewhere.[3]

The original CC identified three relationship stages, and we added a fourth stage (Austin and Seitanidi, 2012a):

1. The *philanthropic* stage, characterized by charitable corporate donors and NPO recipients, and largely constituting a unilateral transfer of generic resources
2. The *transactional* stage, characterized by bilateral reciprocal exchanges of more valuable resources through structured activities, sponsorships, cause-related marketing, and personnel engagements
3. The *integrative* stage, when missions, values, strategies, personnel, processes, and activities become organizationally integrated and lead to greater co-creation of value
4. The *transformational* stage, which is emerging as a more advanced form of collaborative relationship, with even greater potential for value creation, and with a greater degree of interdependence, collective action, and social innovation producing synergistic value and transformative effects on the partnering organizations and on society as a whole

Enterprises of all sizes engage in these various forms of collaboration. In Europe, for example, 48 percent of microenterprises and 65 to 70 percent of small and medium enterprises (SMEs) are involved in external actions having to do with social responsibility. In Italy, 51 percent of SMEs have relationships involving philanthropic donations, 83 percent have activities involving employees' social involvement, and 75 percent engage in transactional sponsorships.[4] In Romania, 67 percent of SMEs have formed partnerships with NGOs.[5] SMEs are particularly embedded in local communities. Their success is often rooted in collaborative relationships and engagements that foster reputational enhancement, legitimacy, and trust, which are all elements of social capital vital to the success of these enterprises.[6]

The concept of a continuum enables one to have a more refined understanding of the development of collaborative relationships. The stages along the continuum allow us to characterize four basic types of collaborative relationships, whereas the continuum itself helps us to recognize that relationships do evolve. Some characteristics of a collaboration may more closely resemble the features of one stage, and others may more closely resemble the features of the next. Stages are not discrete points or rigid cells. Therefore, one can analyze the constellation of multifaceted characteristics of a collaboration to identify which characteristics need closer attention and further development in order for the collaboration to move to a later stage along the continuum. The CC is not just an identifier of relationship stages but also a value continuum; the potential for co-creation of value increases as a partnership moves toward the next stage.

There is nothing automatic about progressing along the continuum. In fact, a collaboration can even regress. The collaboration's movement depends on the actions that the partners take and do not take. Nor is it necessary for a relationship to pass sequentially through all the stages. For example, a business and a nonproft might start with a transactional collaboration rather than with a philanthropic one. Moreover, even at a particular stage there is a range of value-creation potential, and so it is important to identify the value drivers. Our examination of multitudes of cross-sector collaborations has identified three salient value drivers—*alignment, engagement,* and *leverage*—each encompassing a constellation of value contributors that are tied to the sources and types of value discussed in the previous chapters. The matrix shown in Figure 4.1 depicts each of these four collaboration stages along with the three value drivers, which we will now proceed to analyze in more detail.

	STAGE I	STAGE II	STAGE III	STAGE IV
NATURE OF RELATIONSHIP	Philanthropic	Transactional	Integrative	Transformational
Value Driver				
• Alignment				
• Engagement				
• Leverage				

Figure 4.1.   The Collaboration Continuum Matrix

Stage 1: Philanthropic Relationships

The traditional and most common relationship is the one between a philanthropic corporate donor and a grateful nonprofit recipient. Corporate philanthropy is significant: in the United States, donations in cash and kind amounted to $14.6 billion in 2011.[7] In Brazil, a 2000 study estimated corporate contributions to social projects at $2.3 billion, equivalent to 4 percent of gross domestic product.[8] There is no doubt that these flows are important to cash-starved nonprofits and beneficial to donor companies, but the relevant issue to be examined is how a relationship at the philanthropic stage could produce even more value.

Using the CVC analytical elements of sources and types of value, we can characterize a traditional and relatively underdeveloped philanthropic relationship as follows. The resource flow is the company's unilateral transfer of cash, a generic resource. There is basic resource complementarity in that the company has money that the nonprofit needs, and the nonprofit has the ability to deliver some social good or service that the company deems worthy. Each partner provides inputs, but largely independently of the other. Engagement tends to be infrequent, and interactions are procedural rather than substantive. There is sole creation rather than co-creation of value. The resource transfer enables the nonprofit to sustain or do more of what it has been doing, and this produces some social value. There are some linked interests, but they are few and relatively shallow. A Deloitte survey in the United States indicated that 92 percent of the respondents thought that it is important for companies to make charitable contributions or donate products and/or services to nonprofit organizations in the community.[9] Therefore, the mere act of donating will provide some associational value, in the form of reputational enhancement, and can even serve as risk insurance to mitigate negative events that may occur.[10] Similarly, having been vetted and selected as a donation recipient can increase a nonprofit's image in the eyes of other donors.[11] The corporation and perhaps the nonprofit harvest some associational value, but it is not necessarily strategically important, and of course those benefits need to be weighed against the costs that both partners will incur in generating them.

The company's enhanced reputation and goodwill with various stakeholders, including communities and regulators, can positively affect its "license to operate," which may be at risk in some situations. Reputational enhancement is in part due to the generally higher levels of trust associated with nonprofits, and with the value created for the business when that asset is transferred through association. A McKinsey & Company survey found that 82 percent of European respondents and 84 percent of U.S. respondents trusted NGOs to act in the best interests of society, a level of trust that was twice what the respondents had in companies.[12] A survey for the United Kingdom's Commission on Charities found a mean trust score for nonprofits of 6.3 on a scale of 0 to 10.[13] A World Economic Forum study found that almost half the executives surveyed indicated that "protecting reputation and brand" was their reason for partnering.[14] The Reputation Institute has calculated that 14 percent of U.S. companies' reputations are attributable to citizenship efforts.[15]

The 1992 riots in Los Angeles destroyed a multitude of businesses, but not a single one of the sixty McDonald's restaurants. Because of the company's donations to community causes and the good reputation and work of the Ronald McDonald Houses, the community shielded the business from harm.[16] A top executive at Duracell has described community service as a form of goodwill banking: "What you're always most fearful of is bad publicity. Community involvement builds a little bit of a bank account. The benefit will come the day that something unforeseen happens, an environmental accident or a strike, or something that is going to thrust Duracell into the forefront, when we are going to have to start making some withdrawals from that bank of goodwill that hopefully we have built up over a period of years."[17]

The key question is this: How can we make the value relationship more robust at the philanthropic stage? The challenge is, in effect, that of achieving progressive value creation as one moves along the Collaboration Continuum, at particular stages as well as across the four stages. Both in the academic realm and in practice, this goal at the philanthropic stage has been characterized in terms of moving toward strategic philanthropy.[18]

Alignment at Stage 1 (Philanthropic Relationships)

Alignment has linked or linkable interests as its main source of value. The greater the alignment between the partners' missions, strategies, values, and motivations, the greater the value-creation potential. Alignment does not mean that these elements are identical but rather that they mesh together productively. To begin with, the social or environmental mission focus of the nonprofit should be clearly relevant to the company. For example, several beverage companies, such as Coca-Cola, Nestlé, and Diageo,[19] have focused their philanthropy on water conservation. Fomento Económico Mexicano, Sociedad Anónima (FEMSA), the largest distributor of Coca-Cola in Latin America, worked with nonprofits and other community and governmental organizations in Mexico to preserve watersheds by planting 31 million trees between 2008 and 2011. Furthermore, FEMSA established a corporate foundation with an exclusive focus on water conservation. In 2009, Coca-Cola Mexico signed a five-year partnering agreement with a conservation NGO and the government forestry commission to reforest almost 62,000 acres.[20]

Porter and Kramer would label such an effort "context-based giving,"[21] whereby a firm's donations address some phenomenon with importance to society that is also of strategic importance to the company—in this case, a vital production input. The economic interests of the company are linked to the environmental interests of the nonprofit. A McKinsey & Company survey of 721 top executives around the world found that only about 20 percent considered their philanthropic programs highly effective. The main difference between the more and less effective firms, as the executives described them, was that the philanthropic programs in the more effective firms were addressing the social and political trends most relevant to their businesses.[22] This alignment creates the value conduit.

The World Economic Forum study cited earlier[23] also found that over 80 percent of the executives who responded to the survey cited "committing to the company's own values, principles, policies and traditions" as a reason for partnering. This is often expressed as "giving back" or "doing good" that is based more on altruism than on specific utility to the company.[24] But even such values-based giving should not be satisfied with good intentions. Random acts of kindness are nice precisely because they are unexpected, but more value can be created when a collaboration's resources and capacities are focused on and aligned with an important social problem. Doing better at doing good is the preferred value-creation mindset. The global pharmaceutical company Merck developed the drug Mectizan, which can effectively treat river blindness, a serious disease in many African countries, but those afflicted did not have the resources to pay for it. In effect, there was market failure. Therefore, Merck's CEO, Roy Vagelos, created a drug-donation program, citing the basic values of George W. Merck Jr., the son of the company's founder: "Medicine is for the people, it is not for the profits." Merck then identified and partnered with the nonprofits and government agencies needed to deliver the drug to over 25 million people annually.[25] Former President Jimmy Carter observed, "Merck showed that the corporate world can, indeed, be committed to the alleviation of suffering. Obviously, Merck doesn't get anything for these tablets—they give them away free. What they get is the recognition by their own employees and potential customers that Merck has a heart."[26] The rest of what George W. Merck Jr. said reveals an alignment between social and economic value: "The profits follow, and if we have remembered that, they have never failed to appear . . . we cannot rest until the way has been found, with our help, to bring our finest achievements to everyone."[27]

Engagement at Stage 1 (Philanthropic Relationships)

One key focal point for engagement is with the social or environmental problem being pursued. One should seek both intellectual and emotional engagement. This requires learning about the problem, its causes, its consequences, and its cures. Thinking of philanthropy with an investment mindset leads to a focus on producing ever-greater returns. Intelligent investing requires being knowledgeable about the investment area and the benefits to be generated. In addition, creating emotional connections with the cause intensifies commitment to the partnership and can stimulate bigger and more durable philanthropic relations.[28]

Another focal point is the engagement of the organizations' personnel in the partnership. This can begin by involving them in the identification of the causes to be supported and in the selection of partners. Corporations' matching-grants programs are one vehicle for such engagement. One survey of 213 major U.S. companies revealed that matching gifts were 11.7 percent of total cash giving, which averaged $695 per employee.[29] Through matching gifts, the company is aligning its philanthropy with the social preferences of its employees, thereby creating associational value. Nevertheless, such alignment with diverse individual employees' preferences will probably not create a coherent action agenda. Therefore, grants matching employees' donations are useful engagement vehicles but are not a substitute for a strategic focus at the corporate level.

One should strive to move the interactions of company and nonprofit personnel beyond the processes of applying for grants and making donations. Transcending the procedural relationship and moving to a more substantive interactive engagement can deepen mutual understanding. This in turn can lead to more productive use of the donated resources. Corporate employees' voluntarism is an important vehicle for fostering interactive engagement.[30] Almost all major U.S. companies have some form of employee volunteer service,[31] with around 500,000 volunteers giving over 9 million service hours.[32] Volunteer programs that are relatively informal and marginal to the company's strategy fall into the category of traditional philanthropy. When these engagements become more highly structured and strategic, however, they progress along the Collaboration Continuum to the transactional stage (discussed more fully in a later section of this chapter).

Consumers are another key stakeholder group, and advertising is the traditional vehicle that companies use to reach them. But who needs the Superbowl? Pepsi decided to abandon that high-visibility advertising venue, with its 100 million viewers, and the company used the $20 million it saved to engage consumers and other community groups through populist philanthropy that leveraged social media.[33] Pepsi created an online contest for nonprofits and community groups to nominate their donation candidates, with monthly winners selected by online voting.

According to Pepsi's digital director, "When you use these brand dollars to have consumers share ideas to change the world, the consumers will win, the brand will win, and the community will win. That was a big bet. No one has done it on this scale before." Respondents used their social networks to garner support for their projects, with almost a quarter of the 77 million votes coming via Facebook. Pepsi saw this not as a way to stimulate short-term sales but rather to cultivate a long-term relationship and brand awareness with consumers and community organizations through this high-engagement philanthropic activity with its ripple-effect dynamic.

The underlying thrust of greater engagement is to begin to create interaction value and to assemble a collaborative constellation that combines the needed complementary resources. Fostering greater engagement requires partners to become more proactive. Rather than waiting for proposals to cross the threshold, one should take the initiative and seek out opportunities. According to a director of the General Mills Foundation, "After so many years of being reactive, we [saw] problems getting worse."[34] Consequently, the foundation began to actively identify specific nonprofits with shared interests and appropriate competencies to address identified problems. As another example, let us turn to the nonprofit social enterprise Goodwill Industries of North Central Wisconsin, which approached the regional newspaper to discuss how the paper might help with Goodwill's upcoming capital campaign.[35] This dialogue revealed that the nonprofit was having problems obtaining enough donated goods during the winter months. The newspaper's editor offered to help publicize that need, which led to the assembly of a multidonor undertaking. The newspaper printed an insert, created by Goodwill, that described the process for donating merchandise, and a folded plastic bag was attached to the insert. Readers filled the bags and took them to the deposit location, where Boy Scouts, members of the National Guard, and high school volunteers picked them up. This increased and evened out the flow of donated goods to be recycled in the Goodwill workshop, thus avoiding layoffs of the special-needs workers whose employment is the social mission of Goodwill.

Leverage at Stage 1 (Philanthropic Relationships)

Leverage is focused on the nature of the resources as the source of value. As Bob Thust, head of corporate responsibility at Deloitte, has commented, "The underlying trend is very much [that] corporates want to get more involved through the provision of skills and expertise as well as through traditional forms of philanthropy."[36] Traditional philanthropy largely uses cash as its medium, which is essential to nonprofits' operations and has the advantage of being applicable to a wide range of uses. Many companies, however, donate their products or services. This moves the philanthropy from generic resource use to organization-specific resource use, which creates greater differentiation for the donor and provides a more specialized asset to the recipient. In one survey, three out of four Americans preferred that companies accompany their cash donations with expertise.[37] The regional newspaper mentioned earlier in connection with Goodwill Industries of North Central Wisconsin donated its capacity to publicize Goodwill's collection campaign. Avon's Breast Cancer Crusade, a cause highly aligned with the company's consumer base and developed in collaboration with the National Alliance of Breast Cancer Organizations, used Avon's sales force to raise donations by selling a range of products, pins, candles, pens, and pink ribbons, and the company organized other fund-raising events as well, generating donations of $740 million over a period of twenty years to cancer programs around the world.[38]

In the mid-1990s, Microsoft sought to move its philanthropy to a more strategic and higher-value platform.[39] While preserving its generous matching-grant program with employees, it decided to create a focused approach that was more aligned with its strategy and that would leverage its specialized assets. The result was a partnership with the American Library Association (ALA) through which Microsoft would donate computers and software to public libraries throughout the country. ALA and Microsoft shared the vision of making knowledge widely available to the public. The donation in kind, combined with the ALA's technical expertise, provided a technology package that enabled a transformation of services in the libraries that was far greater than would have been possible through a simpler cash contribution. The Libraries Online project garnered Microsoft an award as the most philanthropic company in the country. Furthermore, it stimulated greater use of the Internet by the public, thereby expanding the software market, an example of philanthropy focused on and aligned with demand factors; according to Porter and Kramer, "Philanthropy can often be the most cost-effective way to improve [the] competitive context, enabling companies to leverage the efforts and infrastructure of nonprofits and other institutions."[40]

Another avenue for multiplying philanthropic value creation is to leverage partners' connections, a form of organization-specific intangible asset, so as to engage multiple businesses or nonprofits in a philanthropic project. In 1997, the Beta San Miguel Group, Mexico's largest private producer of sugar, entered into a partnership with the nonprofit school Colegio de San Ignacio de Loyola Vizcaínas to create the Programa Emalur, with a focus on education and community development in the sugar-producing zones.[41] Over the years, success in one initiative led to creation of another as additional community needs and communities were addressed. To support this geographical and programmatic expansion, the partners used their connections to enlist more donors, who often provided in-kind contributions, and additional nonprofits with the needed new capacities. This broadened and leveraged engagement increased the scale and social value of the philanthropic undertaking. The business partner fulfilled its corporate values and also created a healthier and stronger operating environment.

Stage 2: Transactional Relationships

The nature of the relationship at the transactional stage is quite different from that at the philanthropic stage; many of the kinds of benefits generated at the philanthropic stage continue, but they are magnified. The collaborative arrangements are more focused, with explicit objectives and programmed activities, responsibilities, and timetables. There is mutual access to each party's resources, which, when incorporated synergistically with their nonshared resources, enhance performance capabilities.[42] In terms of the *sources* of value, we see the following shifts:

- *Resource directionality* becomes bilateral, with explicit reciprocal exchange.
- *Resource complementarity* is greater, and organizational compatibility is more significant.
- *Resource nature* is shifted to more specialized assets.
- *Linked interests* are clear in that creating value for one's partner is essential to creating value for oneself.

Regarding the *types* of value, associational value is the predominant benefit for businesses, through its effects on key stakeholders. The magnitude of transferred-asset value increases for nonprofits, and one goes beyond the monetary donation that dominates the philanthropic stage. In the words of Alex Gourlay, CEO of the Health & Beauty Division of Alliance Boots, a U.K. company, "In a world of complex sustainability issues it is our fundamental belief that we can achieve more by working together and sharing our respective knowledge and best practice."[43] New opportunities for interaction value and synergistic value arise for both partners. The benefits to the partnering organizations tend to be clearer and more quantifiable in some ways, although the attainment of greater societal welfare is often less clear.

Types of Transactional Relationships

Transactional relationships can take many forms, but the more common ones include highly structured employee volunteer programs, cause-related marketing (CRM), sponsorships and licensing, certification arrangements, and problem-focused projects.

Employee Volunteer Programs

This form of transactional collaboration is perceived as highly valuable to companies and nonprofits. According to Lim, 92 percent of 131 major U.S. corporations that were surveyed had formal employee volunteer programs.[44] A survey of employees found that 75 percent of the respondents wanted to be involved in company-sponsored volunteer days.[45] Volunteer engagement is found throughout the world; for example, the Brazilian Volunteer Partners

Network works with 2,522 companies.[46] Greater value is generated when the volunteer program is integrated into a clearly structured strategic collaboration. According to the Global Corporate Volunteering Research Project, "Planning, setting goals, managing for results, accountability—ultimately these must become routine if volunteering, indeed all forms of community involvement, is to become a core activity."[47] For example, General Electric (GE) focused collaborative efforts on strengthening low-performing school districts near several of its major facilities over a five-year period.[48] In addition to GE's sizable cash donations, the company's personnel tutored and mentored students, advised administrators, and provided technology, helping 100,000 students improve their math scores by 30 percent. The company was able to leverage its generic cash donation by combining it with the more specialized skills of the company volunteers. That package of transferred assets was aligned with the needs of the partnering schools.

Meaningful and well-managed engagement of employees in community service does not simply produce social value through this transfer of economic resources to the partnering nonprofit. It also reverberates back to the company, with several economic benefits. It is a reciprocal value exchange. There is associational value in the form of greater affinity with the company on the part of actual and potential employees. A survey by the Conference Board showed that 90 percent of 454 companies judged their volunteer programs as helping to attract better employees.[49] In a 2010 survey of employees, 57 percent agreed with the statement "My company's commitment to addressing social/environmental issues is one of the reasons I chose to work there," and 79 percent felt "a strong sense of loyalty" to their companies.[50] Morale in companies with high community involvement has been shown to be three times as high as morale in other companies, and morale can positively affect loyalty and retention.[51] Job performance can be enhanced by these attitudinal influences and skill development.[52] In a survey of one group of companies with award-winning volunteer programs, 97 percent of the respondents said that volunteering built teamwork, and 74 percent reported improved productivity.[53] A survey of multinational companies with international volunteer programs cited skill development and corporate affinity as the biggest benefits.[54] One senior executive of a financial services firm said, "It's important to keep the people within my ranks involved and happy in the community, to avoid being attracted to move elsewhere. If they have ties with a charity, it's going to be a lot harder for them to uproot."[55] IBM's Corporate Service Corps places top rising talent as volunteers with nonprofits and government entities in emerging markets, and this practice results in strengthening of their leadership skills, expanded cultural intelligence, and global awareness; almost all Corporate Service Corps members stated that the experience had increased their loyalty to the company.[56]

Researchers' observation that greater social value can be created through deployment of the specialized skills of employees is consistent with our concept of leverage as a value driver; for example, if employees have financial expertise, then it may be more productive to let them use it instead of having them engage in manual labor, such as painting a school, if they don't have much skill in that area.[57] Nevertheless, it is important to recognize that significant skill development, attitudinal enrichment, and relational capital are generated through partner interactions in whatever form they take. If employees' underlying motivations and desire for benefits are satisfied by volunteer experience, and if volunteering is reinforced by strong support from the company and the nonprofit, then there is a greater likelihood that employees will become long-term repeat volunteers, an outcome representing higher transferred-asset value for the nonprofit as well as for the company.[58] This is an example of the interaction value arising from mutual engagement. One of the joint benefits of this type of interaction is greater donor "stickiness" and a higher degree of commitment between the partners than would have occurred with only a monetary contribution.

One frequently used form of business executives' engagement with nonprofits is through their service as board members, usually with support from their companies. This is a form of microlevel-to-mesolevel collaboration, whereby an individual's resources are transferred to the nonprofit organization. In one survey, 81 percent of Harvard M.B.A. graduates reported being involved with nonprofits, and 57 percent reported service as board members.[59] This is a bilateral value exchange. Executives and nonprofits alike state that the greatest benefit comes from the application of their business expertise to strengthening nonprofit governance, with accompanying personal and company donations being of secondary importance. Of course, overcoming the organizational differences between businesses and nonprofits is a significant challenge to leveraging this expertise successfully.[60] One CEO board member told the nonprofit's executive director, "If all I need to do is write checks, I'll go somewhere else. I want to go where I am needed. You have to involve me, because involvement leads to understanding. Understanding leads to commitment. Unless I'm involved, I can't be committed, and if I'm not committed, I'm never going to give you any money."[61] The most important benefits perceived by the business board members are satisfaction from making a meaningful contribution, but they also expand their networks, develop their collaborative skills for leading peers, and broaden and enrich their perspectives from the interaction with more diverse colleagues. Greater breadth of view and empathy enhance leadership capability.

Employee Volunteer Programs as Transactional Relationships: Case Examples

Timberland and City Year

Timberland's quarter-century partnership with City Year began with a small donation of boots for the nonprofit's youth members engaged in community service projects. The relationship began to flourish when City Year organized a community service project for Timberland employees, including top management: fixing up a local addiction-recovery home for adolescents. Jeff Swartz, then Timberland's CEO, recalls the impact of that original experience: "I came back to my desk and I said, 'Service. Wow! That was so spectacular. We have got to find a way to make that part of our business day.' I felt purposeful and powerful and that was cool. I saw that we should do this at Timberland now."[62] This led to the creation of the company's Path of Service program, aimed at engaging the energy and talents of employees to create long-term

(continued)

Employee Volunteer Programs as Transactional Relationships: Case Examples (*continued*)

solutions for critical community needs. Swartz saw this as a vehicle for incorporating values-based management into the corporate strategy, expressed by the slogan *boots, brand, belief.*

In partnership with City Year, Timberland evolved this into a highly developed community service program, one that included giving employees forty hours of paid release time per year to work with nonprofits of their choosing, and annual companywide service days. Employees have given 350,000 paid-time hours since the inception of the program. City Year has provided team-building training and project management. The deep alignment of values between the company and the nonprofit has created the basis for an enduring relationship. The continuing interaction value that has been harvested from ever-broadening engagement activities has further strengthened the alignment. (More generally, a nationwide survey found that 79 percent of employees involved with companies' cause-related activities felt proud of their companies' values.[63]) Service engagement is a very tangible way of creating credibility in organizational values. One of the tests of the durability of values is whether they can survive the sale of the company and the transition to a new CEO. In 2011, Timberland was acquired by VF Corporation. According to Jeff Swartz's successor, Patrik Frisk, "Our commitment to sustainability dates back nearly 40 years and continues today, a core belief that business can create positive impact in the world. Timberland's corporate responsibility leadership was one of the drivers in the company's acquisition by VF Corporation."[64]

Standard Charter Bank and Sightsavers International

In 2003, in celebration of its 150th anniversary, Standard Charter Bank launched a collaboration with Sightsavers International. Seeing Is Believing was an employee-based volunteer fund-raising initiative aimed at generating resources for treating cataracts in various developing countries where the bank operated. This undertaking grew in scale, organizational complexity, and impact. By 2012 it had raised $40 million and reached 20 million people through a multitude of NGOs, implementing partnerships with a broadened focus, from curative surgery to comprehensive eye care. It evolved into an increasingly formalized transactional partnership with well-developed co-governance structures, procedures, and targets. It became integrated into the bank's business model, as recounted by Gil James, the bank's head of sustainability: "Seeing Is Believing is like a business within a business. We put as much acumen and expertise into this project as we do into any of our businesses. Our aim is to deliver maximum return—in this case by reaching as many people as possible."[65] In effect, the mindset is one of integrated social and economic value.

Nordson

Nordson's former CEO, William Madar, emphasizing how community service has helped to reinforce the company's culture, states that the values that make an organization responsive to its customers, to its suppliers, and other organizations "are the very same values of caring that lead to concern for our neighbors and participation in the community. Community involvement is part of the whole. It is integral to the success of the business."[66]

Helene Curtis

Helene Curtis, Inc., created the Development Through Service program to provide "an opportunity for experiential learning [to] assist employees' personal and professional development." The company assessed twenty-eight business-skill areas (such as project management, planning, organization, team building, and presentation), identified opportunities for employees to practice these skills through engagement with nonprofits, and tracked the process to help employees meet developmental expectations.[67]

Cause-Related Marketing

This form of collaboration enjoys widespread public support. According to Cone Communications, 88 percent of American consumers who were surveyed in 2010 reported that they deemed it acceptable for companies to involve a cause or an issue in their marketing, a figure that was 33 percent higher than the figure reported in 1993.[68] Furthermore, 85 percent of the surveyed consumers reported having a more positive image of a product or a company when the company supported a cause they cared about, and 83 percent reported wishing that more of the companies, services, and retailers they used would support causes. For products equal in quality and price, 80 percent of the surveyed consumers reported being likely to switch to a company that supported a cause, 61 percent described themselves as willing to try a new product, 46 percent said they were willing to use a generic brand, and 19 percent said they were willing to use a more expensive brand.[69] Another survey, this one targeting 8,000 adults in sixteen countries, found that about 72 percent of the respondents were willing to recommend and promote a product associated with a social cause.[70]

Companies' experiences confirm the effectiveness of CRM. American Express's pioneering 1983 affinity marketing campaign to support the restoration of the Statue of Liberty donated one cent for every transaction and one dollar for every new American Express card application. The company's similar, smaller effort in 1982 had revealed this potential by raising $100,000 for the San Francisco Arts Festival.[71] In the first month of the Statue of Liberty campaign, American Express card usage increased 28 percent, and applications rose 45 percent, generating $1.7 million in donations.[72] Coca-Cola's six-week promotion to support Mothers Against Drunk Driving (MADD) boosted the company's sales by 490 percent in 400 Walmart outlets and provided the nonprofit with fifteen cents for each case sold.[73] To address the additional question of whether consumers would pay more for a product related to a social cause, Hiscox and Smyth conducted experiments in a major retail store in New York City and not only discovered an increase in sales of 12 to 26 percent for products labeled as having been manufactured under good labor standards but also found that when prices for such products rose by 10 percent, demand also rose, and sales increased by 21 to 31 percent.[74]

Sponsorships and Licensing

A variant of cause-related marketing is a company's financial sponsorship of a nonprofit's cause or event, or the company's licensing the use of the nonprofit's name or logo. Much of the preceding value analysis of CRM partnerships is applicable to sponsorships and licensing, and so we will highlight only some of the key differences. The financial transfer is not a function of the sales generated but is instead a previously negotiated fee. There are no established standards for such fees, and the preceding discussion of nonprofits' brand valuation is therefore relevant to the determination. Analogously, the nonprofit needs to enter into its calculations the added value it will receive from the greater visibility accruing to it through the company's promotion. In one CRM partnership, the Nature Conservancy considered that exposure even more valuable than the accompanying cash payment from its corporate partner, Canon.[75]

Although alignment is equally important, the engagement mechanisms are different. There is no direct triggering mechanism from consumers making purchases. Nevertheless, event sponsorships provide direct engagement of individuals involved in the activity. Sometimes this involvement can be quite powerful. The Susan G. Komen Race for the Cure began as a 5-kilometer race in Dallas with 800 participants. By 2011 there were 140 races organized by 100,000 volunteers for more than 1.5 million entrants, with 18 races scheduled for 2012 in thirteen countries. These events serve to educate and motivate as well as to fundraise. Survivors, families, and friends participate with intense emotional engagement to celebrate the struggle, commemorate lost loved ones, and support the cause. The collective engagement creates social capital and valuable support networks. In addition to funds raised from the participants, contributions flowed from the corporate sponsors of the 2012–2013 Race for the Cure Series. These sponsors included American Airlines, Ford, New Balance, RE/MAX, *Self* magazine, Stanley Steamer, Walgreens, Bank of America, Yoplait, ZTA, and Georgia-Pacific.[76]

Because there is a wide range of sponsorships, one useful distinction is based on the difference in primary motivation between commercial and social sponsorships.[77] Whereas commercial sponsorships place dominant emphasis on generating greater corporate revenue, social sponsorships give priority to meeting social needs. In commercial sponsorships, actions are considered more narrowly as tactics to be evaluated, like other marketing tactics,[78] and they carry legal implications for nonprofits.[79] Examples of commercial sponsorships would be the sporting events that captured 70 percent of sponsorship dollars in 2012.[80] In a social sponsorship, the partners' interaction has an explicit focus on how the collaboration can most effectively address a social problem. Economic value will be derived through the synergistic links to the social or environmental value produced, but economic value is not the primary concern or the dominant motivating factor.

Certification Arrangements

As pointed out in Chapter Three, one of the more recent forms of transactional collaboration is development of social and environmental standards for various products and practices, with accompanying certification systems to corroborate compliance. These systems have often emerged from confrontations over business practices that were deemed socially or environmentally harmful, but experience shows that conflict can pave the path to collaboration. For two years, the Rainforest Action Network mounted over 700 demonstrations at Home Depot stores and annual meetings, to protest the company's purchasing of wood products from old-growth forests. Home Depot announced in 1999 that it would cease that practice and give preference to lumber from sustainably managed forests, as certified by the Forest Stewardship Council. The Rainforest Action Network then took out a full-page ad in the *New York Times* that urged consumers to shop at Home Depot.[81] Similar conversions have also occurred, with a wide array of companies agreeing to purchase fair trade products, financial institutions adopting the Equator Principles (see Chapter Three) for socially and environmentally improved lending, mining firms agreeing to the Initiative for Responsible Mining Assurance, and many other examples. These are distinct from other transactional relationships because they are rooted in changing business practices. Seen through our value lens, these relationships have three distinct but interrelated components: standards, certification, and marketing.

Standards of business practice are created and aimed at changing existing ways of operating, to remove deleterious effects and generate positive ones. The development of the standards involves, in varying forms and degrees, the interaction of businesses and nonprofits and sometimes governmental entities. Engagement of the companies has often proceeded more by the stick than by the carrot. Actual or threatened demonstrations, negative advertising, and boycotts have been relatively effective in dragging the affected companies into dialogue. The processes have varied, but the underlying source of value has been linked interests, sometimes by way of forced linkages. On the side of positive incentives was the prospect of capitalizing on consumers' growing interest in social and environmental causes, or of ensuring a sustainable supply of an endangered raw material, such as depleted stocks of fish. The process of creating the standards leveraged the complementary competencies and knowledge of the companies and the advocacy organizations. The participation of many companies and NGOs multiplied this leverage. Unilaterally set standards would have been either irrelevant or unacceptable. Intensive interaction was essential, and it represents another type of value emerging from the process. Mutual and substantive understanding was broadened and deepened, as was the ability to work with adversaries until they were converted into allies with shared interests.[82]

Once standards are set (although refinement continues), the certification process occurs. Beyond the value of final approval of practices that meet the standards, the certifying process generates interaction value because it enables the company to identify weaknesses and make corrections in its practices, often with the assistance of an NGO's proprietary or specialized knowledge.[83] It is the change in internal business practices that creates the social and environmental value. Often the new methods produce direct economic value by achieving cost efficiencies, productivity improvements, or product enhancements.

The final value emerges from the market value of the certification label. The company and its branded products bearing the certification label communicate externally to consumers and other stakeholders an enriched value proposition represented by the social and/or environmental benefits produced by compliance with the standards. There is associational value with the certifying nonprofit, which transfers credibility to the company through its logo. The transaction usually also involves a licensing fee to the certifying agency, often a nonprofit. As with the other types of cause-related marketing configurations, the company needs to surround the logo with the appropriate communication efforts to make the worth of the certification visible. As ecolabels proliferate, with more than 400 now in the marketplace, their power to differentiate a brand is reduced.[84] In effect, certification standards and labels raise the minimum-performance bar. Partnering must move to higher levels of collaborative value creation.

Problem-Focused Projects

Undertakings sharply focused on addressing a particular problem constitute a somewhat distinctive form of transactional collaboration, one that merits mention here. There are specific goals and project completions, and there is often no cash transfer involved, but core competencies are mobilized.

Problem-Focused Projects as Transactional Relationships: Case Examples

DHL and Red Cross/Red Crescent

The global logistics company DHL entered into a partnership with the International Federation of Red Cross and Red Crescent Societies (IFRC) to assist in disaster response.[85] The company uses its logistics expertise and global network for the shipment of relief materials mobilized by the IFRC.

TNT and the World Food Program

The logistics giant TNT provided training and IT support to the World Food Program to strengthen its supply chain and fleet management systems, with over half of the company's 128,000 employees participating.[86]

A Doll Shop and a Museum

Collaboration is not size-dependent; projects also occur between smaller organizations. In Appleton, Wisconsin, a small museum received a donation of a large collection of dolls but had neither expertise in dolls nor a staff curator, and so it asked the owner of a local doll shop to curate the collection.[87] And sometimes transactional projects lead to deeper engagement. In this case, the store owner subsequently helped the museum revitalize its gift shop and assumed ongoing management of it, moving the relationship into the integrative stage.

McDonald's and the Environmental Defense Fund

In 1989, McDonald's faced increasing pressure from environmentalists and consumers to reduce the waste-disposal burden caused by its iconic Styrofoam clamshell hamburger containers. Some cities were even proposing a total ban on polystyrene packaging. At this time, the Environmental Defense Fund (EDF) approached McDonald's to discuss environmental issues surrounding solid waste. They agreed to collaborate and formed a joint task force composed of an EDF scientist, an EDF economist, an EDF chemical engineer, and McDonald's managerial team. EDF took no money from the company, to ensure objectivity and to enable the nonprofit to make the data publicly available. The team members jointly immersed themselves in the many dimensions of the operations relevant to the problem, and they generated a framework, a policy, and an operating plan for solid-waste reduction. During the ensuing decade, this eliminated over 300 million pounds of packaging, recycled 1 million tons of corrugated boxes, and reduced waste by 30 percent, with no additional cost to the company.[88] The collaboration produced direct economic

(*continued*)

Problem-Focused Projects as Transactional Relationships: Case Examples (*continued*)

and environmental benefits, but in addition there were ripple-value effects. McDonald's vice president of corporate social responsibility, Bob Langert, observed, "We believe this positive relationship created not only an environmental benefit but a model for us on how we've addressed substantive issues with NGOs going forward. We're proud of all of the significant results achieved and business benefits attained over the years." EDF's president, Fred Krupp, stated, "Our work with McDonald's sends a strong message about the potential and profitability of sustainability. This partnership showed that collaboration can effectively spur innovation and lead to powerful results that make sense for both business and the environment."[89] The collaboration between the Environmental Defense Fund and McDonald's continued for the next twenty years, discovering dozens of additional opportunities for collaborative problem-focused projects. For EDF, the success with McDonald's led to the formation, with the Pew Charitable Trusts, of the Alliance for Environmental Innovation, which institutionalized this collaboration model and encouraged other leading U.S. businesses to undertake similar initiatives. Research has shown that success is fostered by cross-sector R&D projects characterized by strong relational trust and competence in project management.[90] Good collaboration produces more collaboration.[91]

Alignment at Stage 2 (Transactional Relationships)

There are multiple paths of alignment between a company and a cause. Because consumers' purchases are the trigger that releases the cash flow, aligning the cause with consumers' interests is critical.

Alignment as a Value Driver in Cause-Related Marketing: Case Examples

TUMS and the First Responder Institute

In 2003, TUMS launched a CRM program with the First Responder Institute. At first glance, there is no obvious link between the company's business and firefighting, but the firm came up with a clever conception with its "TUMS Helps Put Out More Fires Than You Think" campaign. TUMS donated ten cents for every bottle of TUMS sold, which generated $238,000 channeled through the institute to sixty fire departments throughout the United States. TUMS experienced a 30 percent increase in store displays and a 16 percent jump in sales.[92] More than the clever campaign slogan, the likely connection was the fact that the company's broad base of consumers felt an easy identification and empathy with firefighters, who work for everybody's security.

American Express and Share Our Strength

American Express entered into a robust cause-related marketing partnership with Share Our Strength (SOS), an antihunger and antipoverty nonprofit.[93] The alignment was multifaceted. The cause elicited widespread empathy among the public and American Express cardholders, and the campaign was called Charge Against Hunger. While the mechanism was standard—a three-cent donation for each dollar charged during November and December, up to $5 million—the campaign was wrapped in a broader strategy aimed at aligning the effort with three stakeholder groups. First, to reach actual and potential cardholders, the company launched a $15 million television advertising effort, including inspirational messages from the SOS founder and leader, Bill Shore. Second, the company provided a new and direct way to energize and involve merchants, a group critically important to American Express. Third, the company aligned with its own employees by seeking

(*continued*)

Alignment as a Value Driver in Cause-Related Marketing: Case Examples (*continued*)

out service opportunities related to fighting hunger. American Express charges increased 12 percent, and affinity with card-holders, merchants, and employees strengthened. The resulting donation equaled half of the nonprofit's budget. What was perhaps even more significant, the public exposure of Bill Shore and SOS greatly strengthened the company's brand and opened the door to the development of many additional innovative cause-related partnerships with other companies. In addition, the advertising served to heighten public awareness of a significant but underrecognized social problem.

Kraft Foods and Feeding America

Kraft Foods has a three-decade-long partnership with Feeding America. Through this leading food-relief charity, Kraft has provided one billion meals to the needy. In September 2012, in partnership with the 1,000-store Five Guys hamburger restaurant chain, the company launched a two-week CRM promotion aimed at generating another 100,000 meals, to celebrate National Cheeseburger Day and support Hunger Action Month.[94] The restaurant chain uses Kraft cheese slices in its hamburgers, and so there was a producer–client alignment as well as a business–cause alignment. For every Five Guys customer who used a mobile device to check in at a designated page on the company's website, Kraft donated one meal to Feeding America. This CRM activity was part of Kraft's long-term social value strategy aimed at fulfilling its corporate values and enhancing its reputation with key stakeholders. This resonates with a survey finding that when consumers face a choice between two products of equal price and quality, and when the producers of both products support social causes, 61 percent of consumers prefer the product from the company that makes a commitment on its own to a focused issue that it will support over the long term.[95]

Walmart's Good Works

In 2012, Walmart and the Walmart Foundation donated over $1 billion in cash and in-kind contributions around the world, and Walmart's Good Works and Community Grants Program channels millions of dollars every year to local groups serving community needs. The program's activities include allowing nonprofits to hold fund-raisers outside Walmart stores and then giving matching grants to them.[96] These efforts align the company's interests with citizen groups and public officials and have helped overcome public opposition to Walmart's entry into communities. According to Gourville and Rangan, "In the same way that cause-related marketing can be viewed as a more effective vehicle for selling a product, so can it be viewed as a more effective vehicle for 'selling the corporation' to the public—serving to improve relations with the general public, with local interest groups, and with government regulators."[97]

The American Medical Association and Sunbeam

Because associational value is at the heart of CRM relationships, misalignment can carry dire consequences; as Warren Buffet is reputed to have said, "It takes twenty years to build a reputation and five minutes to ruin it." One of the most publicized examples of such misalignment was the 1997 arrangement whereby the American Medical Association (AMA) agreed to give its "seal of approval" to Sunbeam home health care products in return for "royalties" in the form of millions of dollars that would enable the AMA to significantly expand its public health educational efforts. When the deal became known, it caused an uproar from consumer groups and AMA members, who saw the alignment as inappropriate to the AMA and its mission. The AMA board cancelled the agreement, and then the AMA paid almost $10 million in damages (and fired several staff members) after Sunbeam filed a breach-of-contract suit against the organization.[98]

(*continued*)

Alignment as a Value Driver in Cause-Related Marketing: Case Examples (*continued*)

The lure of big money short-circuited the advisable process of consultation with key constituencies. The resulting costs represented negative value creation.

KFC and Komen

A more recent controversial CRM deal was Buckets for the Cure, the 2010 Susan G. Komen for the Cure's partnership with Kentucky Fried Chicken (KFC). In this CRM arrangement, 5,000 KFC restaurant operators donated fifty cents for every specially designed pink bucket of chicken that customers purchased during the promotion. The campaign raised $4.2 million, the largest single donation in the nonprofit's history. According to Komen's CFO, Mark Nadolny, "Buckets for the Cure helped to reach hundreds of thousands of people with breast cancer information while raising funds for the research and community outreach programs that support women and men with breast cancer." Upon handing over the donation check, KFC's president, Roger Eaton, remarked, "This was a campaign that allowed our customers to fill up their stomachs and their hearts at the same time. On behalf of the extended KFC family of franchisees and restaurant employees, we are so proud of having worked on this campaign with Susan G. Komen for the Cure."[99] So everybody was happy. Or not.

Criticism erupted from health professionals, Komen donors, and CRM and nonprofit specialists.[100] At the heart of the controversy was a perceived misalignment between a health-related cause and what critics considered an unhealthy food. The problem was further exacerbated by the campaign's having been launched just after KFC introduced what one critic called its "mammoth-scale, heart-stopping Double Down sandwich." The perceived failure on Komen's part to recognize an incompatibility with its mission eroded the organization's credibility in the eyes of some observers and was seen in certain quarters as having betrayed the trust of its constituents, some of whom asserted that they would abandon the nonprofit and shift their support elsewhere. Such controversy generates negative associational value. Good intentions went awry, but possibly they had been awry from the inception. Misalignment can be a very costly partnering malfunction. In contrast, Komen's alliance with Yoplait yogurt, through its Save a Lid, Save a Life campaign, was very well aligned, given the healthy image of yogurt, and has generated $34 million since its inception in 1997.[101]

Engagement at Stage 2 (Transactional Relationships)

CRM has an advantage over traditional corporate philanthropic donations to a cause because it provides consumers with a direct engagement opportunity. One survey found that when respondents chose between two companies that had similar products and supported similar causes, 53 percent preferred the one that allowed them to have an impact by tying a purchase to a donation.[102] Buying is a form of active engagement, and the social cause enables emotional connection and satisfaction. It expands the value proposition to the consumer and cultivates a richer relationship with the company. Experiments show that local donations and positive framing of messages increase consumer engagement.[103]

Danone de Mexico, a subsidiary of the French yogurt producer, discovered through market research that although consumers regarded the company's products highly, the company was perceived as rather detached from consumers, a quite disturbing finding. A company spokesperson stated, "Danone's social policy consists of what we call the 'double project': our social and economic objectives cannot be separated."[104] Consequently, Danone saw supporting a social cause through a CRM partnership as a potentially effective way to build emotional connection with consumers. After considering many potential partners, the company selected La Casa de Amistad, which provided housing and medical care for children who had cancer and were from low-income families.

As part of the mutual familiarization process, Danone's president visited the facility and met the children. He was deeply moved, and this emotional engagement strengthened the commitment to the partnership. The partners' "Let's Build Their Dreams" campaign was launched with promotional material explaining to consumers that each yogurt product they bought would benefit the children. The company's product was seen as nutritious and therefore as aligned with the cause of better health.

The cause had high evocative power for consumers' emotions and influenced their purchasing behavior and perceptions of the company. Danone's marketing director commented, "During the campaigns, our prices remain the same. The competition lowered theirs in response, and though we didn't, we still kept our [market] share."[105] In effect, consumers were willing to pay a premium to support the cause. The marketing director went on to say, "We detect a brand-image evolution in some key attributes related to proximity, as a company that cares about children. We have turned from a cold top-quality brand into a partnering and social-citizen brand."[106]

CRM campaigns that are one-shot promotions cannot create a durable relationship; Danone's partnership went on for six years. One action by Danone's nonprofit partner, an action of which the company knew nothing in advance, reinforced the relationship by using a huge donated billboard on one of Mexico City's major commuting arteries to publicly thank Danone for its support. The company's public relations manager exclaimed, "People remember the campaign every time they see it. No other institution advertises like that."[107] Beyond direct consumers, the public was engaged, and the company reported that new-employee recruits often mentioned the campaign as one of their motivations for being attracted to the company. Cone Communications reports that 90 percent of consumers who were surveyed said they wanted companies to tell them the ways in which they were supporting causes, and that 34 percent of the respondents said they would choose another brand if a company did not offer enough information about how a purchase would affect the cause.[108]

Communication is critical for engagement, and social media have opened up powerful opportunities for CRM, as revealed by the "Mean Stinks" campaign to combat bullying that was launched on Facebook in January 2011 by Secret, a brand of deodorant from Procter & Gamble. The alignment of the cause with the company and the product was explained by Laura Brinker, a spokesperson for the company: "We're more than just products and brands . . . we're actually doing something meaningful for our consumers. Secret as a brand inspires women to be more fearless . . . Bullying is one area that we know is of great concern to our target consumer, both young women and mothers, so understanding how to identify these behaviors and stand up for yourself and your friends is one way to express your fearlessness. On a more simple articulation, Secret stands against things that stink, whether it's body odor or mean behavior like girl-on-girl bullying."[109] The Secret brand's Facebook page had more than 1 million fans, and the "Mean Stinks" launch increased their engagement exponentially. In addition, the campaign motivated 10,000 women to trigger $1 donations to the National Bullying Prevention Center run by the Parent Advocacy Coalition for Educational Rights (PACER) in connection with coupon requests and downloads. This kind of engagement is a form of co-creation that taps consumers' knowledge, passion, and networks.[110] Since the campaign, there has been a noticeable upward bump in sales of Secret.

Leverage at Stage 2 (Transactional Relationships)

The associational value central to CRM transactions emerges significantly from the leveraging of partners' brands. How consumers react to a brand depends on different elements of the marketing mix, including the social dimension.[111] Brand valuation is common for businesses but uncommon for nonprofits. This complicates the value exchange and can lead to undervaluation. Brand-valuation methodology for nonprofits has been developed;[112] when applied to Habitat for Humanity International, it revealed a brand value of $1.8 billion, equivalent at the time to the brand value of Starbucks Coffee Company.[113] Brand value is tightly related to the trust that constituencies have in institutions, and great care should be taken by partners in considering how the cause-related marketing relationship will affect brand identity.[114] Leveraging this asset can be a powerful value driver, but protecting it from harm is equally important. In one survey of

30,000 people in twenty-five countries, 58 percent of the informed public considered NGOs, for the fifth year in a row, to be the most trustworthy institutions, a response rate that was even higher in China (76 percent) and India (68 percent); trust in business was lower, but not all businesses were perceived as being the same, with technology companies seen as trustworthy by 79 percent of respondents and financial services companies trusted by only 45 percent.[115]

A second form of leverage is the use of partners' special capabilities. The standard CRM arrangement uses the company's whole set of business operations to promote and sell the cause-related product. An executive from the Nature Conservancy commented as follows on the benefit deriving from company capabilities in a cause-related marketing relationship with Canon USA: "As long as we have some control over how our trademarks appear and how our image is used, we're very interested in having them take advantage of that right, because it's garnered us millions and millions of exposures in media that we could never hope to purchase for ourselves."[116] The higher visibility arising from the firm's media-management skills as it promoted the nonprofit's brand and mission was of even greater value than the cash transfer to the nonprofit. This was also true of the partnership, described earlier, between American Express and Share Our Strength. There was mutual leveraging of complementary resources.

A third form of leverage is expansion of the CRM configuration into a multiparty undertaking. Kraft Foods' incorporation of the Five Guys restaurants into its food-donation campaign broadened the set of specialized assets deployed in the endeavor so as to generate more donated meals.

A much more expansive multiparty CRM effort is the (Product)[RED] campaign launched in 2006 at the World Economic Forum by the musician and activist Bono and Bobby Shriver of Debt, AIDS, Trade, Africa (DATA) and the ONE Campaign. The aim is to leverage private-sector capabilities in raising awareness and funds to help eliminate AIDS in Africa. Over twenty-five leading companies have created a product using the (Product)[RED] logo, with a portion of the proceeds flowing through the (Product)[RED] company to the Global Fund to Fight AIDS, Tuberculosis and Malaria.[117] For example, Nike sold red shoelaces and donated

100 percent of the revenue. Apple offered a red iPod Nano and donated 50 percent of the profits. Armani sold red sunglasses and a watch and donated 40 percent of the gross profit margin. American Express issued a red card in the United Kingdom and contributed 1 percent of card charges. Starbucks offered holiday beverages served in red cups and donated about 3 percent of the price. The Global Fund reported that by 2012 the (Product)[RED] campaign had contributed over $195 million. Before then, corporate contributions to the Global Fund had been only $5 million, and the difference shows the leverage of the multiparty CRM configuration. Neither the Global Fund nor the (Product)[RED] campaign charges overhead, and the funds raised have helped provide life-saving antiretroviral therapy for 220,000 HIV-positive people, placed over 130,000 HIV-positive pregnant women on preventive antiretroviral therapy to reduce the risk of mother-to-child transmission, and provided 13 million people with HIV testing and counseling.[118] There have been critics of (Product)[RED], however, especially in the campaign's early days, when the amount that companies had spent on promoting the campaign far exceeded the amount raised for the cause.[119] While the advertising expenditures generate economic value for the companies in terms of value derived from association with the cause, most consumers clearly want companies to tell them what causes they support. Furthermore, the advertising serves to raise the visibility of the problem, which is particularly important with respect to social problems in distant countries. Helping overcome the "out of sight, out of mind" problem has societal value.

Stage 3: Integrative Relationships

All the types of transactional relationships examined in the previous section of this chapter are now broadly accepted by the public and widely practiced among businesses and nonprofits. This is highly positive in that it indicates significant progress along the Collaboration Continuum. But the omnipresence of transactional relationships also makes it more difficult for collaborations to differentiate their efforts from those of other collaborations. This is what led Diane Knoepke, vice president for client leadership at IEG Consulting Group, to make the following observation in a 2011 report published by the Association of Fundraising Professionals: "The right transactional cause campaign can make sense if it is part of a well-planned nonprofit partnership strategy. Without a bigger-game approach, however, that campaign becomes background chatter that consumers are quick to avoid or deride."[120] And this points us in the direction of integrative relationships.

A nonprofit and a business can evolve together toward an integrative relationship, building on their interactions at the philanthropic and/or transactional stages. A collaboration has arrived at the integrative stage when "the partners' missions, people, and activities begin to experience more collective action and organizational integration" and when "the relationship begins to look like a highly integrated joint venture that is central to both organizations' strategies."[121]

Alignment at Stage 3 (Integrative Relationships)

At the integrative stage there is much richer and closer alignment. The connections are deeper and broader. The collaboration is central to the missions and core strategies of both partners. It is no longer a nice thing to do but rather a necessary part of everyday operations, essential to institutional success. The collaboration has become a key success factor for both partners. The partners' cultures and values are not just compatible but intermingled. There is a reconciliation of their different value-creation logics so as to achieve a viable value-frame fit;[122] in effect, they get on the same "value page." The partners' collaborative value mindset conceives of value broadly, with different types of value seen as not only compatible but also synergistic. One's primary role as partner is seen as that of a value adder rather than that of an extractor. Timberland's former CEO, Jeffrey Swartz, refers to the company's nearly twenty-five-year integrative relationship with City Year as characterized by a state of "boundarylessness," saying, "It's not them and us . . . Our organization and their organization, while not completely commingled, are much more linked. It's not simply personal; it's also collective. While we remain separate organizations, when we come together to do things, we become one organization."[123]

Engagement at Stage 3 (Integrative Relationships)

Engagement intensifies, and the scope expands. Internally, the participation is top to bottom and spans all areas and departments. Externally, engagement is throughout the value chain. For example, as Kanter notes in connection with one welfare-to-work collaboration, "While Marriott provides uniforms, lunches, training sites, program management, on the-job training, and mentoring, its partners help locate and screen candidates and assist them with housing, child care, and transportation."[124] Each partner's full range of stakeholders is engaged, either directly or through communication. The mindset is one of inclusiveness and interdependence. The intensified process of working together creates even greater interaction value. The repeated discovery of linked interests and of synergistic value creation motivates still closer collaboration to co-create even more value.

It is at the integrative stage that interaction value emerges as an even more significant benefit derived from the closer and richer interrelations between partners. Bowen, Newenham-Kahindi, and Herremans assert that "value is more likely to be created through engagement which is relational rather than transactional."[125] The intangible assets that are produced—for example, trust, learning, knowledge, communication, transparency, conflict management, social capital, sensitivity to social issues—have intrinsic value to the partnering organizations, to individuals, and to the larger society but are also enablers of integrative collaboration.

John Garrison, former CEO of Easter Seals, said that his organization's ability to develop deep relationships with several companies was greatly enabled by the establishment of an emotional connection between the Easter Seals children and the CEOs and their employees.[126]

Psychological bonds foster cohesivenessin a partnership. The deeper mutual trust and commitment also mean that when your partner encounters difficulties, including attacks by others, you try to assist rather than flee. During the Timberland–City Year integrative alliance, there have been two distinct instances of each partner coming under external fire. In both instances, the other partner offered solidarity and assistance in dealing effectively with the problems. As one manager of a health care company puts it,

"You weather those storms, and I think that's a sign of a good partnership, that unforeseen things happen but you respectfully and mutually work through them with a sense of urgency."[127]

Responsiveness to a partner's needs is an essential element of an integrative relationship. The executive director of United Way of Seattle, which had a long-standing and deep relationship with the retailer Nordstrom, recounted such a situation when Blake Nordstrom called him and said, " 'We're looking at our community programs nationally. Can you help us?' We put a lot of work in on this and gave them some good recommendations. You have to be prepared to give that level of effort, because when you're in a close relationship, they will always be coming to you for advice."[128]

Leverage at Stage 3 (Integrative Relationships)

The partners deploy and combine their specialized and key success-related resources. This intermingling of high-powered complementary assets creates an entirely new constellation of productive resources. This holds potential for co-creating greater value for the partners and for society through synergistic innovative solutions. Synergies are often emergent rather than immediately apparent. The harnessing of synergism emerges from close and continual interaction of the collaborators. In a collaboration that IBM undertook with schools, the company's employees had their offices in the schools, and they interacted constantly with the teachers in a continuous co-creation process of learning, feedback, and development. Whereas collaborations at the transactional stage tend to be clearly defined and to last for a specified period, innovative co-creation has a different dynamic at the integrative stage. Kanter notes, "Like any R&D project, new-paradigm partnerships require sustained commitment. The inherent uncertainty of innovation—trying something that has never been done before in that particular setting—means that initial project plans are best guesses, not firm forecasts."[129] The integrative mindset sees collaborative innovation as an investment process with a long time frame.

The nonprofit Alliance for Environmental Innovation worked with companies in collaborations in which the partners integrated their respective expertise to co-create innovative solutions aimed at environmental improvement of the companies' products and processes. These collaborations' larger aspiration was to create best practices that would be emulated throughout a sector, thus multiplying the creation of social value. The alliance collaborated with UPS and its suppliers in integrated, cross-functional teams that combined their respective technical expertise in material-usage life cycles to form a collective discovery process that "created new designs and technologies, resulting in an almost 50 percent reduction in air pollution, a 15 percent decline in wastewater discharge, and 12 percent less in energy usage."[130]

In connection with the evolution of Base of the Pyramid (BoP) undertakings, Brugmann and Prahalad highlight co-creation that "entails the development of business models in which [a company] become[s] a key part of [an] NGO's capacity to deliver value, and vice versa."[131] Aravind Eye Hospital's nonprofit Aurolab, in India, manufactures low-cost intraocular lenses to restore cataract patients' vision, sells to 109 countries, and holds 8 percent of the global market. It partnered with the social entrepreneurship nonprofit Ashoka, the International Agency for the Prevention of Blindness, and Deutsche Bank to set up a $15 million loan fund to enable eye-care groups to expand their services through this new "hybrid value chain."[132] Collaborative entrepreneurship is a central strategy and tool used by what Ashoka's Bill Drayton labels "changemakers," who aim to create powerful social innovation.[133] According to Drayton and Budinich, who see the alliance of business with nonprofits as imperative, "If you're not thinking about such collaboration, you'll soon be guilty of strategy malpractice."[134]

Although partner benefits are a priority at the integrative stage, producing societal value also takes on greater importance. Until social value has become an integral part of a company's value system and operating strategy, the company cannot undertake an integrative collaboration. As discussed in Chapter Two, the collaborative value mindset synergistically integrates economic, social, and environmental value. According to Googins, Mirvis, and Rochelin, one of IBM's values is innovation that matters for the world, with the corollary that collaboration matters; the company takes the approach that in its "socio-commercial efforts, the community comes first," these researchers say, and that "only when the company proves its efforts in society . . . does it . . . leverage marketing or build commercial extensions," and they cite Sam Palmisano, then the company's CEO: "It's who we are; it's how we do business; it's part of our values; it's in the DNA of our culture."[135] The more institutionally embedded CSR is, the more powerful the value co-creation process will be.

Starbucks and Conservation International: Case Study of an Integrative Relationship

To scrutinize further the value-creation dynamics at the integrative stage, let us examine the long-standing partnership between Starbucks and Conservation International. Starbucks Coffee Company and Conservation International (CI), both leaders in their fields, came together in 1998 to create a collaboration that evolved over the ensuing fifteen years into a highly integrative relationship. Starting with a pilot project aimed at helping small coffee growers in Chiapas, Mexico, adopt production practices that conserve biodiversity, the collaboration led to the development of a dramatically different set of coffee-purchasing guidelines with environmental, social, economic, and quality standards; to the introduction of a new line of shade-grown coffee; and, in parallel, to a major increase in purchases of fair trade coffee. The collaboration expanded geographically and broadened its co-creation activities. The relationship leapt over the philanthropic stage and started out as a small project-focused transactional collaboration that developed into a large, multicountry, multifaceted integrative partnership.

Tight Alignment

Both partners see the collaboration as closely aligned with their strategies and missions. Ben Packard, vice president of global responsibility for Starbucks, reflects as follows on the relationship: "Our partnership with CI is a critical component of our commitment to continuously improve our coffee-sourcing practices. We are working together to mitigate the impact of climate change on coffee-growing communities globally, and to ensure the long-term stability of coffee farms and coffee quality. As a result of our past and future work with CI, farmers are ultimately better positioned to protect their livelihoods while we are able to ensure a long-term supply of high-quality coffee for our customers through our responsible coffee-purchasing practices."[136] Jen Morris, executive vice president of corporate relations for Conservation International, confirms this perspective: "Our partnership with Starbucks remains innovative and ambitious: from developing sustainable coffee-farming practices in key coffee-growing countries to raising awareness of priority environmental issues among Starbucks customers and the general public in Starbucks stores here and abroad."[137]

There were clearly linked interests. Conservation International focused on preserving the world's biodiversity hot spots, and most of these were in coffee-growing countries. Most Starbucks suppliers were small farmers, and so their economic and environmental sustainability was essential to the long-term viability of the company's strategy of rapid expansion of its retail outlets globally. Orin Smith, president and CEO of Starbucks at the time when the collaboration was formed, offers this comment on the partnership's initiation: "This was a partnership that I got comfortable with really early. There is an overlapping interest, and that's a good starting point for working together. Furthermore, they were really pragmatic and trying to get something done. And getting it done was what mattered most."[138] More broadly, as Smith observes, "aligning self-interest to social responsibility is the most powerful way to sustaining a company's success."[139]

For this to become a strong strategic collaboration, the company's approach to corporate social responsibility had to be deeply embedded in its strategy and values, and those

(*continued*)

Starbucks and Conservation International: Case Study of an Integrative Relationship (*continued*)

values had to be in alignment with those of its partner. Orin Smith comments, "We want to create an important difference in the lives of our stakeholders, and shareholders are not our only stakeholders. They include our partners, customers, coffee growers, and the larger community. I think a really important part is that we are proud of the company we work for. It's more than a paycheck. You're proud to tell your peers, or your parents, or whomever, where you work. That's a pretty powerful factor in your loyalty, how long you're going to stay with us, what kind of job you're going to try to do for us. So it's an integral part of the whole business strategy."[140] Howard Schultz, founder and chairman of Starbucks, asserts, "I would, with absolute conviction, say to you that the success of the company, not in large part but in totality, is directly linked to the culture, the values, the guiding principles, and this balance that we try to achieve every day between profitability and benevolence . . . The intimacy with our people is based on what we stand for, and our strongest critics and watchful eyes are our people. This, in many ways, creates tension but is the absolute reason why we're able to succeed."[141]

An integrative relationship requires alignment of the partners' value-creation mindsets. A basic premise of Conservation International's philosophy is that the organization gains opportunities to realize its mission, and to transform global markets as well as industry standards, when it establishes win-win partnerships with influential corporations that encourage use of the best practices.[142] This resonates with Howard Schultz's conception of value creation: "You can't create long-term value for the shareholders if you don't create long-term value for your people who do the work and for the communities that you serve."[143] Both Starbucks and Conservation International view value broadly, as multifaceted and synergistic.

Strong Engagement

This partnership was built through an incremental process of interaction that was fueled by ongoing mutual learning and continual progress. Both organizations operated with a collaborative mindset, but trust building early on was critical. Central to the project in Chiapas was the concept of using the small farmers' land as a protective ecological buffer zone for the adjacent El Triunfo biosphere reserve, a highly valuable conservation area of more than 60,000 acres that had been experiencing encroachment from the 14,000 surrounding small farmers. Shortly after the partners' memorandum of understanding was signed, in February 1998, those on both sides who were responsible for implementing the collaboration traveled to Chiapas, met with farmers, and also trekked the twenty kilometers to the top of the biosphere reserve. Ben Packard of Starbucks commented as follows on this early interaction: "The trip enabled us to see each other's dirty laundry. We were able to build trust by sharing that intense experience."[144] The CI team discovered that Starbucks was genuinely committed to conservation as well as to quality and had clearly defined corporate social principles. According to CI's senior director of business development and marketing, Amy Skoczlas, "We realized during the time we spent together that we were not that different from one another. We both share the same sense of integrity with our marketing messages, and we are both dedicated to talking about results, not intentions."[145] Trust building, a form of interaction value, also enabled the development of further initiatives.

After successfully exporting larger and larger quantities of shade-grown coffee, which was well received by consumers, the partners took on the more significant task of formulating new purchasing guidelines. This process began with the development of *Conservation Principles for Coffee Production*, published in 2001 by a group of environmental

(*continued*)

Starbucks and Conservation International: Case Study of an Integrative Relationship (*continued*)

nonprofits that included Conservation International, the Rainforest Alliance, the Smithsonian Migratory Bird Center, the Consumers Choice Council, other nonprofits, and actors from the coffee industry. Starbucks worked with this group and endorsed the principles outlined in the joint publication. This broadened engagement revealed that the company was operating with an inclusiveness mindset, which it had developed over time, as explained by Starbucks founder Howard Schultz:

> The world at large has changed, where these groups have great influence. And the power of the Starbucks brand and the size of the business has changed, where we are both a revered company as well as a target for things that are unpleasant. So it's very important that we view those groups, good and bad, as important constituents that we have to communicate with, and take a proactive stance. And we're consistently doing that. So we take the level of surprise out of the marketplace and provide an opportunity for dialogue if we're doing things that are in any way controversial or are going to be misunderstood. Organizationally, we've brought people into the company who had a skill base and experience beyond our own, not only with these particular nonprofit groups but also with the size and scale of the issues and complexities that we're dealing with. And they have provided us with a competency in our leadership in areas that we did not understand.[146]

It was from these principles that the Starbucks C.A.F.E. Practices ultimately emerged. The C.A.F.E. Practices are essentially an incentive system that provides price premiums for suppliers who adhere to the environmental, social, economic, and quality standards stipulated in the purchasing guidelines.[147] This step involved the engagement not only of even more local actors in the coffee system but also of certification agencies, academics, and even critics of the company. Sue Meckenburg, senior advisor to Starbucks, offers this reaction to the guidelines: "While the Chiapas project is totally amazing and beyond what any of us could have imagined, it pales in comparison to what we've done with the sourcing guidelines. What we wanted to do with these is really define what sustainable coffee production is."[148] In effect, the partners broadened the engagement, intensified their relationship, and ratcheted up their co-creation by moving beyond the production project to address a fundamental mechanism in the value chain. They then increased the geographical scope by replicating the system, in stages, in other countries in Central and South America, Asia, and Africa, which involved the engagement of additional partners. Throughout this process, the CI–Starbucks relationship became increasingly integrative, with Orin Smith, then CEO and president of Starbucks, becoming a member of the CI board of directors.

Complementary Leverage

A key driver of the partnership's value creation was the continual leveraging of the partners' resources. From the beginning, they leveraged their aligned complementarity. As Sue Mecklenberg notes, "We're good at opening four stores a day, but that is different from ensuring transparency in coffee farms in the Latin American highlands. We needed help to do that."[149] CI had the set of skills and field-level personnel to provide environmental, production, and technical organizational assistance to the individual small farmers and their cooperatives. But CI lacked knowledge of and access to the specialty coffee market, which is what Starbucks offered. The company provided partial and increasing funding to CI, and that generic resource was a helpful enabler, but the leveraging of the company's organization-specific and

(*continued*)

Starbucks and Conservation International: Case Study of an Integrative Relationship (*continued*)

key success-related resources was much more valuable. The Starbucks brand and the company's retail infrastructure provided unparalleled market access. Initially, the two partners were engaged in a bilateral exchange of resources, each one handling its side of the arrangement. Soon, however, they began to integrate their efforts and work side by side, directly providing producers with feedback and assistance on market quality and other requirements. That effort included teaching them about taste testing so as to achieve improvements in production.

Additional leverage came from incorporating other organizations into the undertaking, starting with the coffee producers and their cooperatives, which were simultaneously the primary beneficiaries and key economic actors. In essence, this was a BoP collaboration, one that took place before that term was popularized.[150] A key to strengthening the entire value chain is understanding producers' needs and identifying key bottlenecks. One of these was the lack of access to credit. To address this, CI and Starbucks brought the Verde Ventures Fund into the multiparty collaboration. This was a newly launched firm dedicated to making loans to small farmers and promoting environmental sustainability. Starbucks assisted the start-up with a $2.5 million direct loan. As of 2012, Verde Ventures had provided financing benefiting over 14,000 farmers and helping to conserve nearly 50,000 acres. In each new country where the C.A.F.E. Practices were introduced, additional partners were incorporated, and their core competencies were leveraged.

Toward Transformation

The vibrancy of this long relationship is fueled by continuous innovation that renews the value proposition. In 2012, the partners launched a new effort aimed at mitigating the effects of climate change through forest-conservation incentive programs that link coffee farmers to carbon markets. Furthermore, the partners systematically evaluate their efforts in order to assess their impact. As Peter Seligmann, Conservation International's CEO, noted in a 2000 press release, "Starbucks is making a real difference in the quality of the natural environment while helping farmers that live in sensitive ecosystems. Our project in Chiapas has resulted in a 40% average increase in coffee farmers' earnings, a 100% growth in the cooperatives' international coffee sales."[151] In the aggregate, in 2012, Starbucks bought 93 percent of its total coffee—509 million pounds—under its sustainability purchasing guidelines, with the 2015 goal of having 100 percent of Starbucks coffee third-party verified or certified through the company's Coffee and Farmer Equity (C.A.F.E.) Practices, fair trade, or another externally audited system.[152] The integrative relationship with Conservation International continues to evolve, with some elements moving toward the transformational stage of the Collaboration Continuum.

Stage 4: Transformational Relationships

The new stage that we have added to Austin's original Collaboration Continuum (Austin, 2000) represents the most advanced and still-emerging type of partnering relationship. While generally building on and carrying with it the characteristics of a highly developed integrative collaboration, the transformational stage sees alignment focusing primarily on societal problems, engagement broadening to more complex collaboration configurations, and leverage arising from system-changing innovations. This stage represents collaborative social entrepreneurship that, in the words of Martin and Osberg, "aims for value in the form of large-scale, transformational benefit that accrues either to a significant segment of society or to society at large."[153] In this connection, another good source is the work of Nelson and Jenkins on corporate investment in social investment.[154] While the locus of the transformation is external, internal transformation is a prerequisite. The degree of difficulty at this stage increases significantly. As McKinsey & Company's experts put it, however, "The rewards of success can be large and lasting. Companies that can meet difficult environmental, social and governance (ESG) challenges will be positioned to succeed in the years ahead, especially in markets that require new business models and untraditional partnerships."[155]

Alignment at Stage 4 (Transformational Relationships)

The partners direct their collaboration toward having an impact on significant social or environmental problems. Co-creating societal betterment is the partnership's principal orientation. This requires reaching agreement on what Selsky and Parker refer to as a "social issues platform" for the collaboration.[156] There is joint learning about the problem and its relevance to the partners.[157] The linked interests are focused more on the connections between the partners and on the societal problem than on the partners themselves. Similarly, the alignment has to do with how the conjoined efforts of the partners can effectively address the selected problem. This focus graduates from narrower organizational interests to ever-higher levels of system change.

Kanter observes that in highly successful enduring companies, "articulating a purpose broader than making money can guide strategies and actions, open new sources for innovation, and help people express corporate and personal values in their everyday work," and she notes that these companies "undertake actions that produce societal value—whether or not those actions are tied to the core functions of making and selling goods and services. Whereas the aim of financial logic is to maximize the returns on capital, be it shareholder or owner value, the thrust of institutional logic is to balance public interest with financial returns."[158] Institutional logics also shape cross-sector social partnerships.[159] This entwining of public and private interests will require organizational science to use more interdisciplinary approaches to understanding the value creation generated by collaborative structures.[160]

A further alignment involves creating one's self-identity as an agent for transformational change. Guilherme Peirão Leal, CEO of the leading Brazilian cosmetics company Natura, states, "We need to stop thinking of our firms as business enterprises and begin thinking of them as social transformation agencies."[161] The multinational pharmaceutical company GSK spearheaded a multisector global alliance aimed at eliminating lymphatic filariasis; the company's CEO later made the even more socially transformative decision to put all the company's patents for neglected tropical diseases into the public domain.[162] Societal betterment was deemed a higher priority than intellectual property rights. Howard Schultz of Starbucks also reflects on this new phase: "The conversations we're now having about the impact that we could have in the world, around our responsibility that goes beyond making a profit, have us all pretty excited. And maybe Starbucks could be a role model for others. We need to selectively speak out, as we have been, on these issues and take these issues on and not hide behind them. One issue is how we can leverage the brand not only to sell things but leverage the brand to create an ongoing message about what we stand for and ask others to help us, partner with us."[163]

Alignment on Social Issues as a Value Driver at the Transformational Stage: Case Examples

Starbucks and Conservation International

The changed aspirations of Starbucks moved first from the company level to the industry level. According to Mary Williams, senior vice president of coffee, and Marc Schonland, vice president of coffee, "We hope to create a network of industry leaders who will join us in finding a way to create positive changes within our global coffee community."[164] Glenn Prickett, executive director of Conservation International's Center for Environmental Leadership in Business, affirms this orientation: "From the beginning both sides saw the partnership not as an exclusive initiative, but more as a leadership initiative which we hoped to extend throughout the industry."[165] In 2011, the partners moved their efforts

(continued)

Alignment on Social Issues as a Value Driver at the Transformational Stage: Case Examples (*continued*)

to the even larger problem of global climate change. As CI explained, "Our partnership with Starbucks moves beyond the coffee farm to surrounding landscapes, including private and government lands, to promote mutually beneficial forest conservation and the sequestration of carbon."[166] According to Howard Schultz of Starbucks, "If we thought there was an initiative that was transformational in nature and we could build a case, define it quantitatively, and connect the dots for everybody, I'm sure we would strongly consider it, absolutely. Even if it meant taking a short-term hit on the bottom line."[167] At the transformational stage, the partners' mindsets about value and value creation become even more resolutely fused with societal betterment. Schultz observes:

> Making money as a primary or singular goal is a very shallow quality as it relates to achieving anything in business. People want to be part of something bigger than themselves. So if you can establish an anomaly in the marketplace around an aspirational goal, and a relationship of trust and confidence with your people and the customer, [one that is] based not on advertising or a sales promotion or some sexy spokesperson but on authenticity and truth and exceeding expectations, then you have a real sea change in your ability to transform the marketplace. And at the end of the day, these aspirational components of the business will add more value to the equity of the brand and more value to the shareholders.[168]

Timberland and City Year

Another integrative collaboration that raised its aspirations to the system-transformation level is the twenty-five-year relationship between Timberland and City Year.[169] Its early years focused on engaging employees in community projects and developing company values rooted in serving the community. This evolved into the partners' championing a national service ethic and enabling legislation. Timberland hired Carolyn Casey, who had been City Year's director of national affairs, to work closely with Jeffrey Swartz, then Timberland's CEO, to realize Timberland's "potential of being an incubator for the ethic of service."[170] Cikaliuk observes that even when it comes to seemingly unattainable goals, "those with a collaborative-oriented mindset and corresponding behaviors are able to generate compelling and enticing images of the future."[171]

Engagement at Stage 4 (Transformational Relationships)

At the transformational stage, because the change agenda and aspirations are much more ambitious, collaborations need to be correspondingly broader and more complicated. Larger-scale change dictates expanded engagement. Consequently, the partnering-dyad format often morphs into a multiparty configuration, within sectors as well as across business, nonprofit, and government sectors.[172] Dealing with climate change, for example, requires engagement with local, national, and international government organizations, companies, and NGOs.[173] Kania and Kramer, on the basis of their examination of several successful multiparty collaborations, assert that "substantially greater progress could be made in alleviating many of our most serious and complex social problems if nonprofits, governments, businesses, and the public were brought together around a common agenda to create collective impact."[174] Eggers and Macmillan refer to these collaboration constellations as "solution ecosystems," whereby organizations from all sectors form close relationships and combine their complementary capabilities to effectively address such complex global problems as affordable housing, access to electricity and potable water, prevention of fatal diarrhea and other diseases, and human trafficking.[175]

Central to attaining significant transformation is having a collaborative mindset that places higher priority on what can be achieved collectively than on the narrower interests of individual institutions' interests. In transformational collaborations, the end beneficiaries also take a more active role in the transformation process.[176]

The *GE Global Innovation Barometer* 2011 found that 86 percent of the respondents agree that "21st Century innovation is about partnerships between several players more than the success of an organization alone."[177]

Engagement as a Value Driver at the Transformational Stage: Case Examples

Starbucks and Beyond

To achieve industry-level transformation, companies need to join together. Thus we see Starbucks becoming a founding member of the Business for Innovative Climate and Energy Policy Coalition to work with other companies to advocate for stronger policies on clean energy and climate change. For over a decade, the company has been working with the U.S. Green Building Council to create scalable green building solutions for the retail sector. To further recycling, it works with the Paper Recovery Alliance. This led Peter Senge, director of the Center for Organizational Learning at the MIT Sloan School of Management, to observe, "All companies operate within larger systems. Starbucks understands that by joining with others in their materials value chain, even competitors, they can find recycling solutions that can make a much greater impact than they can possibly achieve alone."[178] Orin Smith, former CEO of Starbucks, notes one of the manifestations of the interaction value from expanded collaborations: "I often think that one of the core competencies that we're developing is partnering."[179]

Unilever, WWF, and Beyond

As mentioned in Chapter Two, Unilever and the World Wildlife Fund launched a project in 1996 to understand and address problems of overfishing, a relationship that began as a transactional project-focused collaboration and progressed to the integrative and transformational stages. The effort led to the creation of the Marine Stewardship Council and to a consultative process involving industry participants and concerned nonprofit and governmental entities, and it later resulted in a sustainable-fisheries certification system with transformational implications for the industry and global fisheries.[180] Similarly, the collaboration of a wide range of forest stakeholders, including environmentalists, timber and wood-products companies, and foresters, gave birth to the Forest Stewardship Council and its sustainable-forest certification system, which has had transformational effects on the global forest-products industry.[181] The Fair Labor Association (FLA) is composed of over twenty apparel manufacturers and dozens of NGOs that provide oversight for the application of the FLA's Workplace Code of Conduct, encompassing such issues as forced and child labor, workplace safety and harassment, and compensation in a multitude of countries, collaborating for what Peloza and Falkenberg call "communal contribution."[182] Analogously, Social Accountability (SA) International has collaborated with businesses, trade unions, and NGOs to create workplace standards.[183] Various social- and environmental-standards organizations have joined together in the ISEAL Alliance to pool their knowledge as best practices to ensure that existing certification systems continue to improve and lead to significant marketplace transformation.[184]

Nordstrom and Organic Exchange

The nonprofit Organic Exchange was created to link organic fiber producers and buyers. It began by engaging the Nordstrom department store chain, showing Nordstrom how this would create a competitive advantage through product differentiation. Organic Exchange was later able to add dozens of additional corporate sponsors to create a network of buyers

(continued)

Engagement as a Value Driver at the Transformational Stage: Case Examples (*continued*)

and sellers. Many of these companies were competitors, and so they had to balance competition with collaboration. As Patagonia's environmental analysis director, Jill Dumain, explains, "We realized that if we wanted true environmental change, we had to get companies bigger than us to embrace organic cotton,"[185] and so the company helped connect others to its organic farmers and spinners. There was a collaborative mindset oriented toward system transformation.

Cleveland Business Coalition and Others

In many major cities throughout the United States, business leaders have joined together to create coalitions focused on mobilizing their capabilities to collaborate with government and nonprofits and address pressing problems.[186] One such leadership coalition was formed in Cleveland to begin an effort to rescue the city from the effects of its 1978 near-bankruptcy as well as from urban decay, economic deterioration, and social unrest. This involved rethinking business's leadership role and engaging in new and strategic ways with civil society, government, and the population at large. This multiparty, multisector alliance combined its resources in a multitude of major initiatives that by 1996 had transformed Cleveland from being a national joke to having accumulated an unprecedented five coveted All-American City Awards from the National Civic League.[187] To tackle major weaknesses in the public transportation system, the Toronto Transit Commission directly involved the ultimate beneficiaries—the transit riders and activists—in a collaborative quest for creative solutions, which resulted in a major overhaul of transit operations and led to a larger ongoing collaboration with nonprofits, public agencies, and beneficiaries to improve all forms of transport in the greater Toronto and Hamilton areas.[188] The importance of "integrative leadership"[189] increases as one moves across the Collaboration Continuum.

Transformational Collaborations Around the Globe

Merck and Mectizan

Merck's program for donating Mectizan to combat river blindness illustrates philanthropic motivation, but the intent and effect of the program were transformational with respect to a disease that afflicted 125 million people in Africa. The program's execution required the engagement of over thirty NGOs, dozens of ministries of health, the World Health Organization, UNICEF, and a multitude of village-level health workers. According to Raymond Gilmartin, former chairman of Merck, "This public/private partnership has helped produce great success, reaching an estimated 25 million people annually."[190]

The U.S. State Department

The U.S. State Department created the Global Partnership Initiative to engage businesses, government, and civil society organizations in addressing significant development problems by coordinating and combining their respective competencies so as to stimulate innovative undertakings that otherwise would not have been possible.[191]

Kraft

Kraft participated in the Global Partnership Initiative and undertook a major effort to revitalize the cocoa industry in Ghana, a major source for Kraft and a vital sector for Ghana. Kraft's Perry Yeatman points to the importance of having a long-term mindset: "Recognize that multipartner collaborations take longer and are more complicated. Set your internal stakeholder expectations for the longer term—five years minimum. That's a long time in corporate life these days, but it's also the only way to ensure broad, lasting change. So be sure to make the business case compelling enough that even management changes won't derail your efforts."[192]

(*continued*)

Transformational Collaborations Around the Globe (*continued*)

Hewlett-Packard

Hewlett-Packard, in collaboration with public and social service health services, deployed its technology in Kenya to dramatically accelerate the early diagnosis of infants with AIDS, thereby enabling quicker life-saving treatment.[193]

Leverage at Stage 4 (Transformational Relationships)

Transformational innovation is the fulcrum of leverage at this stage. Although innovation is also central to the integrative stage, at the transformational stage the aim is to create what Christensen and colleagues call "catalytic social innovations" that disrupt existing systems.[194] Phills, Deiglmeier, and Miller define social innovation as "a novel solution to a social problem that is more effective, efficient, sustainable, or just than existing solutions."[195] The Centre for Social Innovation defines social innovation as "new ideas that resolve existing social, cultural, economic and environmental challenges for the benefit of people and planet. A true social innovation is system-changing—it permanently alters the perceptions, behaviours and structures that previously gave rise to these challenges."[196] The *GE Global Innovation Barometer 2011* revealed that 86 percent of 1,000 executives who were surveyed in twelve countries strongly or somewhat agreed that innovation in the twenty-first century will be about partnerships among multiple players rather than about the success of single organizations, and 77 percent expressed the belief that the greatest innovations will be those that help meet human needs rather than those that bring the greatest profits.[197]

The essential and ever-present question that each of the groups in the following case examples must ask themselves and each other in designing their collaborations is this: *What is the distinctive and significant value that each organization can contribute toward the attainment of the collective transformational goal?*

Leverage as a Value Driver at the Transformational Stage: Case Examples

Sustainable Conservation and Toxic Copper Dust

Collaborative innovation leverages key competencies of the collaborators by intermingling them in a unique pool of combined resources, enabling the creation of new and superior approaches to social or environmental problems. Knowledge assets and joint learning are central to this stage.[198] The California nonprofit Sustainable Conservation partners with businesses and other stakeholders to find environmental solutions that also have economic benefits and are therefore feasible and lasting. To address the problem of toxic copper dust polluting waterways, the nonprofit assembled brake-pad manufacturers, environmental organizations, and city agencies and enabled groundbreaking scientific research that identified brake pads as the principal source of the pollution, which led all parties, including the manufacturers, to push for legislation requiring every manufacturer to phase out copper in brake pads.[199] Research suggests that when a collaboration has a narrow scope, innovation is likely to be incremental, whereas a more open-ended search would potentially produce more radical and even unexpected results.[200] Bojer, pointing to the need for systems thinking that shifts existing logic, states that "systemic solutions aim at problem-*dissolving*, as opposed to problem-*solving*."[201]

IBM and the World Community Grid

IBM's values-based strategy, focused on "innovation that matters" for the company and the world, is rooted in asking transformational questions. As the company's chairman, Samuel J. Palmisano, has observed, "There is much serious work ahead of us, as leaders and as citizens. Together, we

(continued)

Leverage as a Value Driver at the Transformational Stage: Case Examples (*continued*)

have to consciously infuse intelligence into our decision-making and management systems . . . not just infuse our processes with more speed and capacity. We are moving into the age of the globally integrated and intelligent economy, society and planet. The question is, what will we do with that?"[202] One of the company's responses, in 2004, was to launch the World Community Grid by bringing people together from across the globe to create the largest nonprofit computing grid, voluntarily pooling surplus computer-processing power that is then made freely available for high-priority science research. IBM notes, "We believe that innovation combined with visionary scientific research and large-scale volunteerism can help make the planet smarter."[203]

As of 2012, the World Community Grid had over 600,000 members from 227 countries, with 2 million computers providing 654,000 years of run time. Over 450 partnering nonprofits, foundations, corporations, and governments are involved. IBM provided the hardware, software, technical services, and expertise to build the grid's infrastructure and provides free hosting, maintenance, and support, and the Berkeley Open Infrastructure for Network Computing developed the software for the grid at the University of California, Berkeley, with funding from the National Science Foundation. An observation on the transformational impact of this innovation, typical of the scientists using the grid, comes from Arthur J. Olson of the Scripps Research Institute: "World Community Grid has enabled my lab to engage in research projects that we would not have attempted in the absence of this powerful public computing grid. It's allowed us to complete complex work in six months that would have taken five years."[204] All supported research enters the domain of public knowledge.

Merck and ACHAP

In 1996, Merck introduced Crixivan, a revolutionary prote-ase inhibitor that decreases the amount of virus in a person suffering from HIV/AIDS. Selling this medication in the United States and Europe was a clear goal for the company, but Merck was unsure of what to do about developing coun-tries. When Merck sought the advice of William Foege of the Carter Center, who had helped earlier with the company's Mectizan donation program, Foege said, "One of the unique things that you can do is to act as a catalyst—you can be a leader and do things others can't do because you are willing to take risks."[205] This transformational opportunity led the company to create a collaboration with the Bill & Melinda Gates Foundation to mount a five-year, $100 million pro-gram in partnership with the government of Botswana. The goal was not only to have a significant impact on HIV/AIDS in Botswana, where the virus had reached crisis proportions, but also to let this collaboration serve as a demonstration and source of lessons to be replicated in other countries.

To implement the program, Merck created a new, jointly governed organization, the African Comprehensive HIV/AIDS Partnerships (ACHAP). In effect, organizational inno-vation was needed for such a transformational undertaking. The evolution of this new organization, like its operating partnership with the government and other local and inter-national public and private HIV/AIDS organizations, con-fronted many of the common interaction-process challenges of new collaborations.[206] By 2004, ACHAP had developed into a more independent and mature organization, with progress sufficient to earn renewed support from Merck and the Gates Foundation for another five years. An analogous organiza-tional innovation was the collaboration between Pfizer and the Edna McConnell Clark Foundation to create a new orga-nization, the International Trachoma Institute, as the most effective way of achieving the goal of eliminating trachoma.[207]

(*continued*)

Leverage as a Value Driver at the Transformational Stage: Case Examples (*continued*)

Rockefeller Foundation and Solar Light

Transformational innovation often requires a collaborative network.[208] When the Rockefeller Foundation wanted to find a way to convert a solar-powered flashlight into a more powerful room light, it partnered with the firm InnoCentive, which specializes in linking problems with solutions.[209] The company approached 160,000 independent inventors who belonged to its Web-based network of solvers, and one of them came up with the sought-for innovative solution. In effect, the network expanded the scale and scope of expertise that could be mobilized to address the problem. Nambisan points to networked "collaboration platforms" as effective in exploring problems, experimenting with solutions, or executing them.[210]

Honeywell and "Murderopolis"

In 1996, Minneapolis, with a homicide rate exceeding New York City's, was labeled "Murderopolis." The governor of Minnesota asked Minneapolis-based Honeywell to fund a consultant to figure out what to do. Instead of engaging in this token variety of philanthropy, the company confronted the systemic problem by creating a coalition of businesses, judges, law enforcement officials, nonprofits, and community leaders. They collectively focused on the immediate problems of guns, gangs, and drugs through a coordinated community-based prevention approach, and they simultaneously began addressing the structural problems of jobs, housing, and neighborhood revitalization. Management practices for interorganizational communication, coordination, and resource integration enabled the previously unlinked organizations to combine their distinctive and complementary competencies into highly innovative approaches. The murder rate dropped in one year, to an impressively low seven homicides. As Honeywell Foundation president Patricia Hoven explains, "It's not about money or Honeywell getting credit. It's about leveraging the unbelievable perceived leadership ability to bring multiple groups together."[211] Multisector collaboration continues among business, governmental, and nonprofit organizations in the Minneapolis–St. Paul region, where innovative approaches to boosting the economic and social health of communities are actively sought out.[212]

Logistics Emergency Teams and Disaster Relief

As a final example of leveraging the complementary competencies of organizations from different sectors to create an innovative and superior approach to a major global problem, logistics emergency teams have been mobilized to provide disaster relief.[213] Several leading logistics companies have joined together with humanitarian agencies led by the World Food Program. The companies provide their logistics expertise, infrastructure, and operating capabilities in coordination with the local knowledge, delivery capacities, and organization of NGOs and governments. Company volunteers are given special training in advance, operating procedures and contingency plans are specified, and coordination agreements (including those that involve media management) are established. This transformational collaboration has created a new response-ready system that can deliver needed supplies within forty-eight hours to any location anywhere in the world where an emergency has been declared.

Reviewing the Collaboration Continuum

The third component of the CVC Framework enables us to understand how value creation changes as partner relationships evolve through the philanthropic, transactional, integrative, and transformational collaborative stages. In different ways and degrees, each stage taps into the four sources of value (resource directionality, resource complementarity, resource nature, and linked interests) and generates the four types of value (associational value, transferred-asset value, interaction value, and synergistic value), creating economic, social, and environmental value for partners, individuals, and society.

The three interrelated value drivers—alignment, engagement, and leverage—propel the collaboration to greater and greater value co-creation across the Collaboration Continuum. We have demonstrated how each value driver encompasses a constellation of value contributors that change in their nature and significance from one relationship stage to another. Each of these value contributors serves as a useful descriptor of the different stages, but, what is more important, each one also represents variables for analysis and managerial action. Let us summarize the three value drivers and how their respective value contributors evolve across the stages from philanthropic to transformational, as depicted in Figure 4.2:

1. *Alignment.* The relevance of the collaboration to the partners' *missions* moves from being peripheral to being central. *Strategic importance* rises from weak to vital. The connection between the partners' *values* shifts from shallow to profound. The partners' respective *knowledge* of the social or environmental problem is often unbalanced initially but becomes synchronous as they get deeper into addressing it. Their *value-creation frames* evolve from being disparate to becoming fused. The *benefits focus* in the beginning is on the partners but shifts to society.

2. *Engagement.* The shared *emotional connection* with the cause and with each other is shallow in the beginning but becomes profound. The *focus of the interaction* at the start is procedural but becomes substantive. *Involvement* grows from encompassing a few people to encompassing personnel throughout the organizations as well as their stakeholders. The *frequency* of their interaction moves from occasional to very frequent. *Trust* grows deeper as engagement intensifies and results are produced. The *scope of activities* broadens as the partners discover new value-creating opportunities. The dyadic partnership's *structure* may expand to encompass the multiple parties

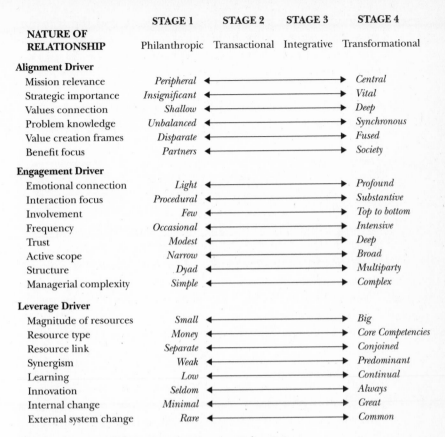

Figure 4.2.   Collaboration Continuum Value Drivers

needed to address more complex and larger undertakings. Correspondingly, *managerial complexity* magnifies.

3. *Leverage.* The *magnitude of the resources* required by the collaboration moves to higher levels and later stages; larger investments are required to produce higher returns. The *resource type* deployed is generic at the philanthropic stage, but higher stages mobilize the partners' more powerful specialized assets and core competencies. The leverage of these assets is magnified when they are more closely *linked* at each successive stage. As linkages grow, *synergism* multiplies. Mutual *learning* is limited in traditional philanthropic relationships but becomes an increasingly powerful value contributor, especially with respect to fueling *innovation*,

which becomes predominant and systemic at the transformational stage. Very little *internal organizational change* is required initially, but it becomes critical later on, to support high-value transformation focused on *external system change*.

In Chapter Five, to convey a still deeper understanding of value creation, we scrutinize the key underlying partnering processes.

Questions for Reflection

1. Using the Collaboration Continuum, identify the relationship stage of two of your cross-sector collaborations. What are the differences between the two collaborations in terms of (a) the sources of value deployed and (b) the types of value created?

2. *Alignment-engagement-leverage* is a value-enhancing framework for all collaborations, irrespective of their positions on the Collaboration Continuum. Select a cross-sector collaboration case study and apply the framework. In what ways can you increase the value for the collaboration through enhanced alignment, deeper engagement, and greater leverage?

3. Has your organization developed an integrative relationship with an organization from a different sector? Has the relationship passed through previous stages along the Collaboration Continuum (for example, the philanthropic and transactional stages)? What were the main reasons for moving the relationship forward?

4. How would you define *synergy* in cross-sector collaborations? Do the determinants of synergy vary according to the stage on the Collaboration Continuum?

5. The fourth stage on the Collaboration Continuum is the transformational stage. Using the individual, organizational, and societal levels of analysis (that is, the micro-level, the meso-level, and the macro-level), can you provide examples of what would constitute transformational economic, social, and environmental value for a collaboration that has reached this stage?

Chapter Five

Collaborative Value Creation Processes

According to results published in 2010, respondents representing an overwhelming 83 percent of surveyed businesses and 89 percent of surveyed nonprofits believe that partnerships will play a more important role in corporate and NGO agendas in the future.[1] Processes are the motors for value creation in partnerships. They are the means by which partners structure, develop, and sustain relationships in ways that multiply resources and create actual value. Processes range from informal to formal, from internal to external, and from implicit to explicit. Developing efficient, effective, and inclusive processes contributes to value creation not only for the organizations directly involved in a collaboration but also for society.[2]

This chapter discusses partnership processes as the fourth component of our Collaborative Value Creation framework, showing how processes can deliver maximal value. Partnership development involves four interrelated phases, which constitute value creation process pathways: *formation, selection, implementation,* and *institutionalization.* For each value creation process pathway, we identify the corresponding subprocesses that enable different sources of value to produce various types and amounts of value. We will again point to the CVC Framework's four sources of value (resource directionality, resource complementarity, resource nature, and linked interests) and to its four types of value (associational value, transferred-asset value, interaction value, and synergistic value). Value accumulates as a collaboration moves through each of the four phases. In the formation and selection phases, the subprocesses are shaping the potential value of the partnership, value that may then be realized as a function of the subprocesses belonging to implementation and institutionalization, the next two phases of partnership development. In effect, the pathways constitute the Collaboration Process Value Chain, which generates environmental, economic, and social value for individuals, organizations, and society, as depicted in Figure 5.1. This chapter describes how managers can improve collaboration by adding or changing key subprocesses in each of the four value creation process pathways. Although rich process is a source of value in a collaboration, this chapter also recognizes that a combination of complex processes and social issues can be a source of failure if not managed effectively.[3]

Collaborative value creation can be planned, or it can simply emerge in the course of interactions across organizations. In either case, using processes to maximize the potential for value creation means incorporating two key elements:

1. *Intention* leads to *planned* collaborative value creation, associated with an intended strategy[4] and requiring clear direction, knowledge, and experience in collaboration. Making intention a priority in the design of processes corresponds with what is called an *outcome orientation* approach.[5]
2. *Flexibility* leads to *emergent* collaborative value creation, associated with emergent strategy[6] as well as with adaptability and requiring endurance, learning ability, and systems thinking. Prioritizing flexibility is associated with the *process orientation* approach.[7]

The combination of intention and flexibility in the design of processes can maximize the value potential of partnerships, allowing for intention to guide and for flexibility to adjust the processes as the collaboration evolves.

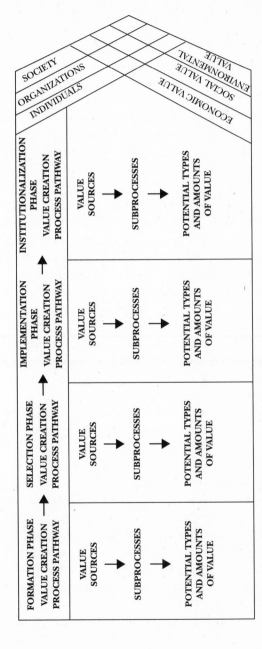

Figure 5.1.   The Collaboration Process Value Chain

Four Phases of Partnership Development

The first two phases, *formation* and *selection*, are closely interrelated partnership phases in which processes can maximize the potential creation of collaborative value through early identification of the sources of value before a final decision is made to proceed with the next two phases—*implementation* and *institutionalization* of the partnership. In this section of the chapter, we describe the value creation process pathways in each phase and show the different value-adding effects of their associated subprocesses.

Phase 1: Formation

We use the term *formation* to group processes that lead to the emergence of a partnership. Partnership formation refers to the pre-partnership period. This is not just for a start-up collaboration but can also include situations in which an existing partnership moves to a higher and distinct stage on the Collaboration Continuum (see Chapter Four), as from a philanthropic to a transactional relationship, or from a transactional to an integrative relationship. Comparable terms often used in the literature[8] are *initial partnership conditions,*[9] *problem-setting processes,*[10] *coalition building,*[11] and *partnership preconditions.*[12]

There are two traditions in examining partnership formation. One commingles it with the implementation process[13] so that the processes of formation and implementation "overlap and interact."[14] The other examines formation as a distinct phase that takes place prior to partnership selection and implementation.[15] In order to analyze more systematically the determinants of collaborative value creation potential, we examine partnership formation and selection as distinct although interrelated phases. Employing a process-based view,[16] we also move from examining the static characteristics of partnerships[17] to examining "the variety of managerial challenges and conditions affecting collaborations as they progress through stages."[18] In effect, each phase has corresponding processes that shape the cumulative potential and realized value as the partnership develops.

Decision makers commonly underestimate the costs and potential negative effects of poor organizational pairing. The problem may be insufficient experience in the co-creation of value, planning, and preparation.[19] For example, 85 percent of businesses and 89 percent of nonprofits are aligned with the view that effective planning at the beginning leads to successful partnerships,[20] but managers often "think about it" without investing "a huge amount of time in that process."[21] In fact, neglect of planning during formation can lead to inappropriate partner matching and poor value creation potential, resulting in time delays and unnecessary costs. For effective intentional planning and, ultimately, large value potential, formation processes must be robust.

The formation phase for start-up collaborations and for shifts to higher stages can last from a few months to several years. In other words, the interval is variable, as illustrated by the collaborations between Rio Tinto and Earthwatch and between the Royal Bank of Scotland Group and the Prince's Trust.

Formation Phase: Case Examples

Rio Tinto and Earthwatch

In the partnership between the environmental nonprofit organization Earthwatch, specializing in biodiversity, and the mining company Rio Tinto, the formation phase started in 1990 and only in 1995 shifted from the philanthropic stage (delivering predominantly associational value) to the transactional stage. Then, also in 1995, a series of events led Earthwatch–Rio Tinto to want to shift quickly again from the transactional to the integrative stage. Negotiations for an integrative partnership started only in 1997, however; two years later, in 1999, the two organizations co-signed their first memorandum of understanding, which marked the beginning of their first global partnership. Thus the formation phase lasted five years, but it took a total of nine years from the partners' first interactions for the creation of their first global partnership.[22] Because neither organization at the time had significant experience in developing integrative relationships, the predominant strategy in operation was process-based, delivering *emergent collaborative value.*

(*continued*)

Formation Phase: Case Examples (*continued*)

Royal Bank of Scotland Group and Prince's Trust

The partnership between the Prince's Trust (the leading youth charity in the United Kingdom) and the Royal Bank of Scotland Group (RBSG, one of the leading financial service providers in the world at the time the partnership was formed) started in the 1980s as a philanthropic relationship between the Scottish branches of both organizations. In 2000, RBSG took over Natwest Bank, which also had an employee volunteer program in place with the Prince's Trust. The integration that followed the takeover led to a review of corporate social responsibility programs, and this review in turn resulted in the decision to develop a structured relationship between the newly formed RBSG Group and the Prince's Trust. The formation stage lasted only from 2000 to 2001, given the level of previous familiarity. The twenty-year relationship between the organizations allowed a speedy shift in stages, from philanthropic to transactional and then to integrative. In addition, because both organizations had previous partnership experience, both had knowledge about and experience in collaboration, which enabled the development of a well-structured partnership with clear direction and strong potential to deliver *planned collaborative value*.

A formation process can be either formal or informal, depending on organizational aims and the amount of resources allocated to developing collaborative value potential. By considering systematically the subprocesses in the formation value creation process pathway, managers can improve their ability to anticipate and capture the full potential of collaborative value.

The value creation process pathway in the formation phase includes the following six subprocesses, as depicted in Figure 5.2:

1. Articulating the social problem
2. Determining the partner's intentions

3. Charting the value creation experience
4. Assessing compatibility on the question of visibility
5. Mapping the potential collaborative value portfolio
6. Detecting prepartnership champions.

The six subprocesses that we discuss here provide early indications[23] of the benefits that are likely to be produced by the partnering organizations as they assess value creation potential, usually referred to in the literature as partnership fit.[24] Our conceptualization[25] of *value creation potential* in the formation value creation pathway reveals how subprocesses have different value-adding effects. As an early assessment mechanism, formation allows the partners to evaluate the likelihood of the collaboration's evolution

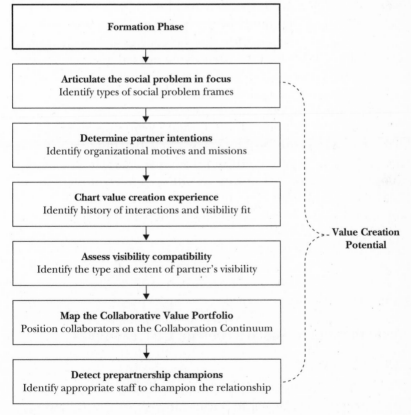

Figure 5.2.   The Collaboration Process Value Chain: The Formation Phase

to the *integrative* or the *transformational* relationship stage,[26] where the value creation potential for the partners and society is higher.[27] Deciding which partner holds the higher potential for the production of *synergistic* value[28] is time-consuming and challenging but should begin with an understanding of the social problem that the collaboration intends to address.

1. Articulating the Social Problem

Articulating the social problem is the first subprocess in the formation value creation pathway (see Figure 5.2). How two organizations articulate a social issue reveals their perspectives on it, including commonalities or differences in how they perceive its dimensions.[29] This important discussion reveals to what extent partners are aligned in how they frame the social issue and the dimensions of it that affect each of them.[30] It is often hard to develop a shared definition of the problem,[31] but that is a key subprocess in identifying different perspectives that can signal incompatibilities or lead to identifying linked interests.[32] This subprocess commences in the formation phase, but it continues during partnership selection, resurfacing as one of the linked interests of the partners.

Assessing the position of a potential partner on a social issue can be tricky because positions are often dynamic rather than static and often require continuous surveillance. Do not assume homogeneity across organizations within an economic sector. Likewise, time is a crucial parameter because the strategies, frames, and positions of a company or a nonprofit organization can shift dramatically.

Articulating the Social Problem: Case Examples

Rio Tinto and NGOs

In 1998, the British mining company Rio Tinto organized two forums with NGOs to invite answers to the following questions aimed at informing its code of business practice:

"What social and environmental standards do you expect a company like Rio Tinto to meet? What measures might it take to meet these goals? And how should Rio Tinto report on its activities?"[33] One might assume that many nonprofit groups would have been interested in participating or would have been invited. This, however, was not the case. Only environmental NGOs that accepted discussion as a means of engaging in debate with companies on environmental issues participated in the meeting. Participants included the Green Alliance (a London-based think tank), Earthwatch, Oxfam, Amnesty International, and Save the Children. More critical groups, such as Friends of the Earth, the World Development Movement, and Minewatch, refused to participate. But Rio Tinto also excluded its leading nonprofit critics (Partizans, People against RTZ, and Subsidiaries) from the forums. Partizans boycotted the second forum, suggesting that the absence of affected stakeholders from the table of discussions was unacceptable.[34]

Should Rio Tinto wish to develop a partnership with any of the excluded or boycotting nonprofits, it would need to conduct an in-depth investigation to uncover each organization's environmental frame of reference. Only such an investigation would allow it to assess the possibility of articulating a shared definition of environmental issues. The ideology of Earthwatch, for example, is based on the belief that the conservation of natural resources should take place through the mobilization of the private sector's resources, implying a clear acceptance of the private sector's role.[35]

BP and the Global Climate Coalition

On May 19, 1997, after exiting the Global Climate Coalition (GCC), a consortium of fifty companies that rejected proof of global warming,[36] Lord John Browne, then CEO of BP, shocked the oil and gas industry by making the following announcement in a speech delivered at Stanford University: "The time to consider the policy dimensions of climate change

(*continued*)

Articulating the Social Problem: Case Examples
(*continued*)

is not when the link between greenhouse gases and climate change is conclusively proven, but when the possibility cannot be discounted and is taken seriously by the society of which we are part. We in BP have reached that point."[37] Lord Browne's statement pleasantly surprised the environmental movement and shifted perceptions of BP's intentions.

2. *Determining the Partner's Intentions*

This second subprocess involves assessing the partner's motivations and missions as an early indication of the partner's intentions, and hence of the expected outcomes,[38] including those that are transformational. For example, integrative and transformational relationships require a long time horizon,[39] and instances of previous value creation—such as transferred-asset value, through the transfer of resources like cash, or associational value, through improvement in employees' morale, productivity, and motivation[40]—can be clues to the expectations of the partners. There is a tendency to assume that an NGO has inherent moral legitimacy because of its mission, but one should scrutinize its actions, just as one should examine a company's track record.[41] This assessment subprocess can safeguard the appropriateness of fit between the organizations and enable the generation of synergistic value, which is likely to lead to greater value creation. Mission fit—a key indicator of linked interests—is a particularly important element to be assessed in measuring organizational compatibility. When the partners' missions align strongly with the partnership,[42] the relationship has more potential to be important to both organizations for a long time, a requirement of generating substantial value. Therefore, when the social issue is strategically important to the business, the potential goes up for a long, valuable partnership.

Many nonprofit organizations now include cross-sector collaborations in their missions or strategies, whereas other, more traditional nonprofits collaborate with business only as a tactic for generating income. Collaborative nonprofits often have extensive experience in partnering with business, and so fewer barriers to collaboration are likely to exist, but such organizations are equally likely to provide a less exclusive relationship with a company, since they probably have many partners.[43] The articulation of the organization's mission in printed or electronic literature, and in previous and current collaborative projects, will provide the first indicators of the organization's intentions and thus will serve as a window into the potential for value creation.

Determining a Partner's Intentions: Case Example

Earthwatch Institute

Since the inception of the Earthwatch Institute, the organization's mission, according to its website, has been to "engage people worldwide in scientific field research and education to promote the understanding and action necessary for a sustainable environment."[44] Earthwatch later added a clarification to reassure its business partners, describing itself as an organization that is "non-political, non-confrontational, [and] non-campaigning." Such reassurances are important signals of a nonthreatening value creation process, in particular with respect to attitudes toward what are considered controversial or high-risk industries, such as tobacco, mining, oil and gas, and pharmaceuticals.[45]

---

3. *Charting the Value Creation Experience*

This charting subprocess is also important for estimating potential collaborative value. Each partner's experience in creating value,[46] including each partner's unique history[47] in developing value relations, identifies existing capabilities[48] while uncovering novel ones.[49] Charting this experience will indicate the degree of "structural embeddedness,"[50] that is, the extent to which the partners have interacted positively and consistently in the past to produce value.[51]

The history of the interactions between two organizations, or with previous partners, will also reveal aptitude for moving toward an integrative or transformational relationship.[52] The more the partners deploy their distinctive organization-specific resources, the greater the potential for value creation. Similarly, the value potential is also dependent on the direction and use of resources across the partners, that is, the extent to which the exchange of resources has been unilateral, bilateral and reciprocal, or characterized by a conjoined intermingling of organization-specific and complementary resources. Unilateral flows or parallel exchanges can create value, but combining resources can co-create greater value, and so it is important to examine previous mutual interactions[53] or interactions with other partners[54] in order to assess the availability of resources and the likely direction of resource flows.

Often it is difficult to develop high-quality insights very early in the formation stage, especially if an organization has little previous experience. Online company reports—specifically, those pertaining to corporate social responsibility, sustainability, citizenship, and shared values—can be a source of real but limited help.

Developing High-Quality Insights into a Partner Organization: Case Examples

Rio Tinto and Earthwatch

Today, Earthwatch is a highly acclaimed, award-winning organization. In 1991, however, when Earthwatch began its relationship with Rio Tinto, the nonprofit was small and relatively unknown. Also in 1991, Earthwatch developed the Corporate Environmental Responsibility Group (CERG), allowing the organization to develop experience in interacting with its forty corporate members, including Rio Tinto.[55] The relationship between Earthwatch and Rio Tinto progressed along the stages of the Collaboration Continuum,[56] from the philanthropic stage to the transactional stage and, in 1999, on to the integrative stage. Thus, for Rio Tinto, partnering with the nonprofit was a *planned decision*, part of testing the partnership concept by developing a range of partnerships with environmental organizations. The company considered that the best way of assessing the collaborative value creation experience was the development of a step-by-step planned strategy with each partner organization, through the escalation of associational relations. In the case of this particular partnership, that was the only way for the company to proceed, since the nonprofit organization did not have previous experience in developing integrative collaborations. Therefore, it would have been impossible to gather interaction intelligence regarding previous integrative relations. By contrast, if a business requires an integrative or transformational relationship for its partnership portfolio, it will be necessary to select an experienced nonprofit organization in order to demonstrate leadership and facilitate the process.

Nestlé and IFRC

In the *Nestlé Creating Shared Value Summary Report: Meeting the Global Water Challenge*,[57] the company refers several times to its partnerships, implying that they are with nonprofit or community organizations. Only in some cases does it explicitly mention previous collaborations with such organizations as the International Federation of Red Cross and Red Crescent Societies (IFRC) and the Red Cross Society of Côte d' Ivoire, although the company has developed a global partnership with IFRC around water, sanitation, and food security (the priority social issues of Nestlé). Unfortunately, company reports do not always provide much detail. Hence, prospective nonprofits interested in forming relationships will find it difficult unpacking, learning, and understanding the level of integration between the two partners and learning how the organization developed transformational outcomes. Businesses can also delve deeper into a nonprofit partner by accessing information on its website. In this way,

(*continued*)

Developing High-Quality Insights into a Partner Organization: Case Examples (*continued*)

you can develop assumptions of the type of nonprofit a business is interested in and compare that with your own business, although online reports of nonprofits can also be insufficient.

HP and Partners

The Hewlett-Packard (HP) Company's *Global Citizenship Report* for 2011[58] refers to one of its partners, the ILA Trust, a social enterprise in India developed in 1994 and making healthcare available to the poor. Thanks to the collaboration with HP, the ILA Trust has sophisticated access to data while diagnosing in the Delhi streets. The information available on the ILA Trust website paints a clear picture of the organization's focus, type of work, target groups, and programs. Similarly, in Africa, HP collaborates with mPedigree, an organization that aims to fight counterfeit drugs. Searching for information on the nonprofit partner allows for deeper understanding of why it is a transformational outcome for the region if a potentially life-saving service is introduced to target counterfeit pharmaceuticals and enable people in Nigeria and Ghana to easily check on the authenticity of their malaria medication. HP's press releases also describe the collaboration. Developing an indirect initial understanding of your prospective partner can improve the process of formation and inform your decision to move forward.

4. Assessing Compatibility on the Question of Visibility

One frequent central motive for forming partnerships is to gain visibility[59] so as to generate associational value that may enhance reputation,[60] public image,[61] and public relations.[62] Visibility contributes to social license to operate, access to local communities[63] for high-risk industries, credibility,[64] and increased potential for funding from the for-profit sector.[65] In effect, positive visibility can be a highly desired outcome for business and nonprofit partners; we consider it one measure for value creation potential that should be used either explicitly or implicitly during the process of formation. The heart of this essential subprocess is for each partner to determine its comfort level with the potential quality (negative or positive) and type (low or high) of the potential partner's visibility. This determination will depend on the previous organizational history, the level of risk associated with the sector, and organizational reputation.

The corporate responsibility index FTSE4Good refers to high-, medium-, and low-impact sectors (FTSE Group, n.d.), particularly in relation to its inclusion of environmental criteria demonstrating the existence of a correlation between sectors and levels of risk. This suggests greater risk of negative reputation being associated with certain industries. Partnerships have been deemed to be risk-management instruments, particularly for controversial industries.[66] Partnering with a high-profile company may bring undesired visibility and criticism to a nonprofit organization. Therefore, the potential cost of negative visibility should be taken into account during the process of assessing the value creation potential in the formation phase. For example, Nestlé, McDonalds, Nike, and Coca-Cola are high-visibility global brands that could be prestigious partners for nonprofits, but these companies also have been among the most boycotted companies around the world.[67] As a result, close association with these companies could also bring criticism and scrutiny. If the nonprofit organization is not prepared, or lacks the capacity, to deal with such high-visibility issues, it should think carefully before developing a long-term partnership with a high-risk industry or a high-profile company, since incompatibility on the issue of visibility could result in negative value creation.

5. Mapping the Potential Collaborative Value Portfolio

This fifth subprocess involves mapping the potential collaborative value portfolio, which is significant because each type of value (associational value, transferred-asset value, interaction value, and synergistic value) serves a distinct function, and their combination will lead to the optimal mix for each organization. Analyzing the collaborative value portfolio is a good way to develop a deeper understanding of the sets of key assets the organization is missing before embarking on the selection phase. Several steps are important:

- Each partner organization needs to determine the relative strategic importance of each of the four types of value. Emphasizing associational value might make sense for a particular organization in a controversial industry.
- Each partner should position its relationships with existing collaborating organizations on the Collaboration Continuum[68] to assist in identifying organizations that have the potential to co-create the four different types of value.[69] The compatibilities and differences across the partners allow for diverse sets of generic resources, organization-specific resources, and key success-related resources[70] to become unique combinations of resources that not only can benefit the partners in new ways but also can externalize the socioeconomic value to society.
- From that follows the step of recognizing the nature of the resources that each partner brings to the relationship, including tangible resources (money, land, facilities, machinery, supplies, structures, natural resources) and intangible resources (knowledge, capabilities, management practices, and skills). This step is needed in order to assess the complementarity of the resources and their value creation potential and, in particular, the types of value created.

By showing how a potential collaboration might fit into one's existing collaborative value portfolio, this mapping subprocess can reveal the potential value-added factor of the collaboration under consideration. Will the collaboration under consideration fill a gap in the current partnering mix? The optimum portfolio mix allows organizations to increase their impact strategically by focusing their collaborations according to social issues and geographical regions while spreading the risk across different partners.[71]

Most organizations have a range of stakeholder organizations to interact with in order to deliver value, depending on the issues in focus and the resources available. One strategy for developing a collaborative value portfolio is to focus on the central social issue for the potential partnering organization. A recent survey of Australian partnerships around poverty issues in developing countries showed that companies within a given industry tend to focus on the same social issues and the same measures for alleviating poverty; as a result, the companies' collaborative value portfolios[72] appear to be intentionally focused and to be directed by the way in which the industry's core business and its poverty-focused activities seem to align. For example, the banking industry contributes to poverty alleviation through new-product offerings and education, the health and life sciences industry focuses on health programs, and the consumer goods and services industry concentrates on supply-chain practices, whereas in the mining and energy industry and in the professional and legal services industry, 47 percent and 38 percent of the respondents, respectively, expressed the belief that infrastructure development is the most important business activity contributing to poverty alleviation.[73] By employing and evolving their core competences and core skills, businesses can co-create value at the local level. It is crucial for nonprofit organizations to understand these important underlying patterns in order to identify the companies and types of collaborations that will have both strategic priority for a business and the potential to deliver the high impact being sought by the nonprofit.

Many companies choose to concentrate their community social investments[74] on one issue in order to maximize the impact of their collaborations. For example, IBM focuses on public education, Citibank concentrates on the promotion of microcredit lending in Latin America,[75] and HP focuses on education, entrepreneurship, and health globally. Nestlé, the company that employs the term *shared value*,[76] prioritizes rural development, water conservation, and nutrition;[77] the first two areas are relevant to the company's supply chain, and the latter is relevant to its consumers. In other cases, however, partnerships have been developed to reduce a community's dependence on company-funded infrastructure. For example, in the Maasai region of Kenya, the Magadi Soda Company, a soda-ash extracting firm, facilitated the design of a community development plan for teaching local communities how to plan, design, and implement development initiatives.[78] Magadi's aim was to reduce the load of multidimensional welfare it was providing. Clearly, collaborative value portfolios can vary widely in order to meet the specific needs of each organization.

6. Detecting Prepartnership Champions

The final strategically important subprocess along the formation value creation process pathway is detecting prepartnership champions,[79] particularly among senior executives. When senior executives show long-term commitment to a potential relationship, cross-functional teams are likely to develop within, across, and beyond the organizations. Experts suggest that "the correct partnership is everything,"[80] but also essential is having the correct people on board from the formation stage onward. One study, which dealt with sixty-six health partnerships comprising multiple partners promoting health and well-being in communities in twenty-eight U.S. states across urban, suburban, and rural areas, reported high levels of synergy associated with leadership that effectively facilitated "productive interactions among partners by bridging diverse cultures, sharing power, facilitating open dialogue, and revealing and challenging assumptions that limit thinking and action."[81] Other, previous research has shown the importance of identifying leaders in partnerships in different phases (formation, selection, and implementation) and at different levels (corporate, strategic, and operational). Partnerships need leaders to champion the social issue, the relationship, and the partnership vision and to identify people for the partnership team who are able to understand the different perspectives of the organizations and people involved.

Detecting Prepartnership Champions: Case Example

Prince's Trust and a Management Consultancy

The Prince's Trust recently extended its collaboration with one of the world's leading management consultancy firms in order to develop a bid on new funding worth hundreds of thousands of pounds. This goal required the trust to form a new relationship with a different part of the consultancy firm. At first the effort appeared to founder on the consultancy's high expectations and its rigorous process of due diligence. But previous experience in partnerships and familiarity with the particular firm allowed the trust's fundraising team to persist and resolve the issues. An important aspect of this resolution had to do with the commitment and favorable judgment of two partnership champions, one from each organization, whose attitude and assistance enabled the parties to identify the right project and secure support from within each organization in the process of co-creating the bid. The bid was successfully submitted, and the Prince's Trust gained a completely new perspective on the development of skills for the young people it serves.[82]

Phase 2: Selection

Academic and practitioner communities agree that selecting the most appropriate partner is fundamental to a partnership's success. The selection subprocesses[83] take place mainly at the organizational level of each partner. In addition, interactions across external multiple stakeholder groups are encouraged as a way of managing power distribution and thus demonstrating that collaboration can be a different model of political behavior rather than being devoid of political dynamics.[84]

The selection process builds on and extends the assessment of value creation potential that was introduced in the formation phase. Avoiding poor collaboration pairing[85] and loss of valuable resources, such as critical time,[86] will require a systematic process that combines formal/informal, internal/external, and explicit/implicit subprocesses. In searching and negotiating, the process requires "collaborative know-how,"[87] encompassing specific "knowledge, skills and competences."[88] It also requires the freedom to terminate, early on,[89] relationships that do not portend substantial co-created value. The selection process can be brief or prolonged,[90] depending on whether the partners have shared a previous relationship. Parties without prior collaborative experience are more likely to pay inadequate attention to selection.[91] The result can be a short-lived collaboration. Long-term collaborations[92] usually hold the highest value creation potential, allowing for integrative and transformational collaboration to emerge.[93] During the formation phase, some subprocesses take place separately within each organization, and interactions may be sparing and occasional. During the selection phase, however, the relationship moves into active, frequent interactions, providing a first deep understanding of a potential partner's people, processes, and structures. The value creation process pathway in the selection phase encompasses the following five subprocesses:

1. Mapping linked interests
2. Determining the value of resources
3. Recognizing organizational capabilities
4. Developing partnership-specific criteria
5. Assessing risks

Figure 5.3 adds feedback loops[94] and other details to the basic partnership-selection process. Feedback loops are particularly important in informing the risk-assessment subprocesses and allowing the partners to make their final selections before moving forward to the implementation stage.

1. Mapping Linked Interests

Successful mutual selection requires knowing the breadth and depth of shared linked interests. Steps include determining what constitutes value for each potential partner and identifying the unique amalgamations of value co-creation that the linked interests will allow. When the social problem is linked to the interests of both organizations, the potential rises for institutionalizing the partnership. This will lead to better value capture at the meso-level and the micro-level, for the organizations and for the intended or unintended beneficiaries.[95] Assessing external linkages moves "beyond how the benefit pie is divided among the collaborators . . . to the potential of cross-sector partnerships to be a significant transformative force in society."[96] If the partners are

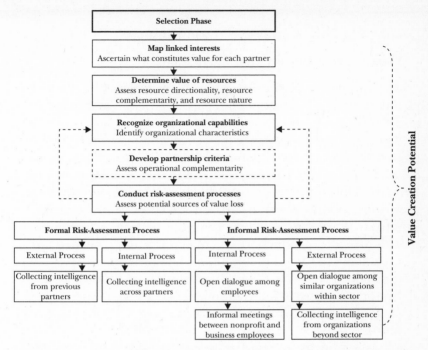

Figure 5.3. The Collaboration Process Value Chain: The Selection Phase

Source: Adapted from M. M. Seitanidi and A. Crane, "Implementing CSR through Partnerships: Understanding the Selection, Design, and Institutionalisation of Nonprofit–Business Partnerships," *Journal of Business Ethics* 85 (2009).

encouraged to look at the potential partnership's "broader political implications"[97]—that is, if they are encouraged to examine the partnership's implications at the macrolevel—the partnership can serve as a global governance mechanism,[98] and the chances of spreading transformational outcomes to an entire industry or region will increase. In effect, if organizations are able both to link their interests and to draw on links with broader societal betterment through articulation of the social issue, this can be an early indication of high potential for co-creation of value for the social good (that is, synergistic value capture at the societal level). This central subprocess requires in-depth discussions to identify current and potential common interests that can lead to innovation.

Mapping Linked Interests: Case Example

Starbucks and Conservation International

The formation period for this partnership was brief—only four months—because of both partners' previous experience with other organizations. As a result, the partnership was based on clear direction, experience, and knowledge aimed at delivering planned collaborative value. It was developed on the two mutual and thus linked interests of the partners: conservation and coffee production. The perfect overlap of their central interests allowed selection to proceed very quickly. Each organization wanted environmental conservation in the production of coffee, and each needed the capabilities of the other organization in order to achieve that outcome. Therefore, the partners very clearly saw the potential for synergistic value creation, not only for themselves but also with respect to long-term, broad societal benefits, that would result from amalgamating their linked interests.

The priority of Starbucks was to obtain high-quality coffee but also to minimize the adverse impacts of coffee production on the environment in terms of habitat destruction and pollution related to waste disposal.[99] By retaining a stable and high-quality source of raw material, Starbucks would add environmental and social value to its supply chain while safeguarding economic value.

Conservation International's aim was to continue with its conservation and field-level project management, helping farmers shift to shade-grown, organic cultivation techniques that would protect environmental value while providing the farmers with the greater market knowledge and access in order to enhance and sustain economic value.

2. Determining the Value of Resources

In this second subprocess along the selection value creation process pathway, partners formally assess overall the four sources of potential value (resource directionality, resource complementarity, resource nature, and linked interests) by collecting and analyzing information about previous interactions of the potential partner. Partners can exchange organizational documents and analyze notes from meetings with different levels of executives across departments. Informal discussions, in which partners share their expectations and perceptions of each other, are equally important in assessing both the partner's potential and one's own resources. Gradually the partners develop a clear picture of the nature of the resources available, the potential for bilateral and conjoined resources, the extent of resource compatibility, and the linked interests that draw on these resources and determine the potential for economic, social, and environmental value creation. These interactions begin to build mutual understanding and a platform for creating trust.

The next step in this subprocess is to relate the possible sources to their projected value. The Value Configuration Matrix (Figure 5.4) can help partners think systematically about which mix of the four sources of value might produce the desired mix of the four types of value (associational value, transferred-asset value, interaction value, and synergistic value).

3. Recognizing Organizational Capabilities

The third selection subprocess is to assess the organizational capabilities of a potential partner. The potential partner's structural and nonstructural organizational characteristics[100] should also be identified.

	Value Type			
	Associational Value	Transferred-Asset Value	Interaction Value	Synergistic Value
Source of Value				
Resource directionality				
Resource complementarity				
Resource nature				
Linked interests				

Figure 5.4. The Value Configuration Matrix

The following structural characteristics should be determined for the nonprofit partner:

- Whether the nonprofit is a programmatic organization or a grant-making organization
- Whether the organization is independent or controlled by a central headquarters
- Whether the organization is big and well established or small and entrepreneurial
- Whether the development of cross-sector social partnerships is inherent in its mission or just one of its options

The followng structural characteristics should be determined for the business partner:

- Organizational structure (flat versus hierarchical)
- Target market or markets (a broad consumer market versus specific target markets)
- Branding (preeminent versus less eminent brands[101]

The following nonstructural characteristics can determine the potential compatibility of the partners:

- Ideology and point of view regarding collaboration with the other sector
- Reputation
- Level of confidence (which is linked to size, reputation, and years of experience)[102]

Combining both partners' structural and non-structural characteristics with their intentions (determined during the formation phase) yields the organizational capabilities.

Recognizing the organizational capabilities of a potential partner presupposes an understanding of the type of value and key assets the organization requires. Therefore, in order to recognize the complementarities across the organizations, it will be essential to identify their generic resources, their organization-specific resources, and their key success-related resources.

Complementarity: Case Examples

Starbucks and Conservation International

These partners assessed their complementarity. Conservation International's mission is to conserve the planet's living natural heritage and global biodiversity while advocating harmonious living between human societies and nature. The combination of that mission and the nonprofit's organization-specific expertise in conservation and biodiversity (including in-depth knowledge of the production of shade-grown coffee) made Conservation International a strong potential partner for Starbucks in terms of the nonprofit's capabilities. In structural and nonstructural characteristics,[103] Conservation International also matched Starbucks with respect to size, scale, reputation, and confidence levels. This symmetry allowed the complementary organizational capabilities to surface quickly, and so the partnership was set on developing planned collaborative value creation from a very early point.

Rio Tinto and Earthwatch

In the case of these two partners, there were problematic asymmetries that prolonged the selection process to two years, despite Earthwatch's expertise in biodiversity, its keen interest in mobilizing the resources of the private sector to conserve the environment, and its mission alignment with Rio Tinto. It was of particular importance that Rio Tinto is a large multinational in mining (a high-impact sector, according to FTSE4Good), and that Earthwatch at the time was a small and relatively unknown nonprofit. In addition, the particular organizational capability that the company was eventually interested in did not play a part in the key organizational assets of Earthwatch, whose concern was development of biodiversity policy. Moreover, during the selection process, the company's lack of clarity regarding the key organizational asset did not allow for clarity and planning.[104] Given this lack of focus, the partnership could only develop emergent collaborative value.

4. Developing Partnership-Specific Criteria

Intentionally or unintentionally, partners usually have been exploring partnership simultaneously with more than one organization. The fourth selection subprocess builds on the knowledge the partners have accumulated to date during the formation and selection phases. The literature includes the following suggested examples of selection criteria:

- Industry of interest
- Scope of operations
- Cost-effectiveness (investment required versus generation of potential value)
- Time scales of operation
- Personal affiliations
- Availability and type of resources[105]

Creating specific criteria can reveal how well the potential partnership could tap into each of the four sources of value (resource directionality, resource complementarity, resource nature, and linked interests) and what that configuration might yield in terms of the four types of value (associational value, transferred-asset value, interaction value, and synergistic value). In order for partners to realize value, they must also be (or become) organizationally compatible. The difficulties entailed in developing high-value integrative and transformational collaborations are extensively documented in the literature.[106] Differences may exist in goals and characteristics,[107] values, motives and types of constituents,[108] objectives,[109] missions,[110] and organizational characteristics and structures.[111] Such differences require early measurement of fit, to gauge the potential for co-creation of value. The following problems may be discovered:[112]

- Misunderstandings
- Misallocation of costs and benefits
- Mismatches of power
- Lack of complementarity in skills, resources, and decision-making styles
- Mismatching of time scales
- Mistrust

Many such partnership problems, but not all, are predictable and may eventually be resolved.[113] Early measurement of partnership fit[114] and compatibility can help the partners assess existing and potential value creation.

When selecting partners, many organizations forgo formal, explicit criteria. But the need for systematic criteria grows as collaboration becomes imperative, and as legislation proliferates in connection with the co-creation of environmental, economic, and social value. An example of such legislation is Chapter 3 of the United Kingdom's Public Services (Social Value) Act of 2012.[115]

Developing Partnership-Specific Criteria: Case Examples

Rio Tinto and Earthwatch

Once their partnership was formed, the following criteria emerged as significant for these two organizations:[116]

- Previous experience working across sectors, with coverage of similar geographical areas (both organizations had offices in Melbourne and London)
- A cost-effective relationship
- A platform deemed safe for the partners' experimentation
- Similar time frames for the operations
- A mutual focus on biodiversity
- Personal chemistry that allowed the champions from both sides to develop a good working relationship

Prince's Trust and Royal Bank of Scotland

For this partnership, the criteria[117] were almost identical to those for Rio Tinto and Earthwatch (indeed, these criteria can be used for many partnerships):

- Previous cross-sector experience
- Coverage of similar geographical areas

(continued)

Developing Partnership-Specific Criteria: Case Examples (*continued*)

- Cost-effectiveness
- Provision of a safe profiling platform
- Good personal chemistry
- A royal affiliation for both organizations
- Mutual core interests (in this case, social exclusion and business start-ups)

5. Assessing Risks

Despite the need for risk management in partnerships,[118] models of partnership selection do not usually include a risk-assessment process.[119] But it can be inspirational and mutually comforting to start a partnership by focusing on clear synergies between the partners, and systematic due diligence on both sides can save costs and unnecessary delays at the implementation phase. Risk assessment is particularly necessary in cases of potentially high adverse visibility (that is, negative associational value), or where there is significant uncertainty about compatibility.[120]

In a formal internal risk-assessment subprocess, one collects information about a potential partner's previous interactions. Sources can include internal reports, process and output reports, and external assessment of previous collaborative projects. In a formal external assessment, one gathers assessments from previous partners of the potential partner, to uncover formal incidents or serious concerns.

An informal internal risk-assessment subprocess[121] consists of an open dialogue among the constituents of each partner organization (including a nonprofit's employees, trustees, members of the board, and beneficiaries) and informal meetings between the partners and particularly the potential members of the partnership teams. An informal external risk-assessment subprocess consists of open dialogue of each partner with its peer organizations within their own sector and across other sectors in order to collect anecdotal and other evidence regarding the potential partner's accountability and decision-making mechanisms.[122] The informal gathering of information begins during partnership formation, but its assessment is conducted during the selection process.

At the integrative and transformational stages of value creation, one type of risk appears when value creation reaches the stage of product or process innovation. Developing rigorous criteria is usually one way to protect the likelihood of high-quality outcomes, which are assessed only after the implementation phase. Beyond developing rigorous product or process criteria, the next two elements of most importance for mitigating risk are vigilance and patience.

Assessing Risks: Case Example

Starbucks and Conservation International

For Starbucks and Conservation International, the central product risk was the quality of the shade-grown coffee, which would determine the coffee's marketability, in keeping with Starbucks' high standards.[123] In the organizations' memorandum of understanding, it was stated that Starbucks was not obligated to buy coffee not meeting its standards. As experienced collaborators, these partners conducted two-way due diligence, each organization assessing the other. The standard due-diligence subprocess of Conservation International comprised fifteen questions as well as talks with senior executives at Starbucks. One aim of the talks was to identify partnership champions within Starbucks.[124]

Phase 3: Implementation

In the implementation value creation process pathway, collaboration actually begins to pay off. This phase encompasses design and operations, and its four main subprocesses lead to a decision to continue or exit the relationship, as depicted in Figure 5.5.

During the formation and selection phases, partners will have discussed a few decisions about the development of partnership

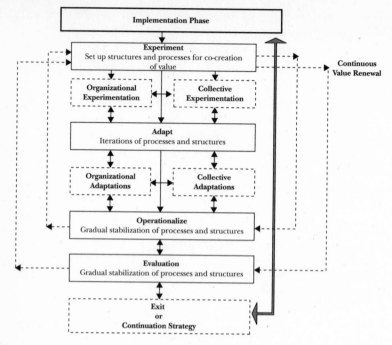

Figure 5.5.   The Collaboration Process Value Chain: The Implementation Phase

policies and programs, but most decision-making needs will emerge only at implementation. A survey in the United Kingdom revealed that businesses as well as nonprofits see implementation as necessarily including steps that ensure "clear processes for reviewing and measuring performance" and steps to get "internal colleagues to understand and value cross-sector partnering."[125] Successful implementation for collaborative value creation also requires having established what the linked interests are. Linked interests guide interactions internally, both at the collaborative (partnership) level[126] and at the intraorganizational level (between the partnership team and the rest of the organization). A broad set of deeply linked interests can produce the highest degree of value potential for both partner organizations. When the partners' interests are well linked, connected to the social problem, and clearly articulated, stakeholders will find it easier to anchor their perceptions of value to the partnership during the implementation.

Participation in implementation activities by local communities of beneficiaries brings inclusivity and embeds the partnership in the community, a feature of cross-sector partnerships that over 90 percent of CEOs seek.[127] Mark Moody-Stuart, former chairman of Anglo American PLC, comments that if there is no local benefit of a corporation's activities, then the corporation's activities "are called into question and [its] business becomes untenable . . . As businesses, we cannot and should not try to address this issue on our own."[128] Therefore, efforts must be made to safeguard the internal and external mandate for inclusive implementation. An inclusive mindset will facilitate the production of value and its later capture and diffusion at different levels.

In the theoretical analysis of partnerships, there are two traditions. The first, which we term the *process school* of partnership analysis, views processes as distinctive elements to be analyzed. In response to calls[129] for more complex[130] studies on the processes of interactions, it develops microstage models.[131] For example, this approach conceives of implementation as a distinct system of subprocesses[132] and therefore does not incorporate examination of outcomes into its implementation processes. The second tradition, which we term the *governance school* of partnership analysis, incorporates outcomes[133] into implementation. Its aim is to inform the governance of organizations by demonstrating connections between partnerships' broad chronological stages and their outcomes.

Nevertheless, such models often do not examine subprocesses in sufficient detail and thus do not provide adequate guidance for practitioners. For the implementation phase, we move beyond broad-stage chronological models.[134] Instead, we follow the process school of partnership analysis. We provide a process-based dynamic view[135] while introducing subprocesses as a way of addressing implementation difficulties[136] and of demonstrating the steps toward high-quality collaboration processes. We extend the model of Seitanidi and Crane[137] by discussing how the dynamics between the partners can facilitate the co-creation of social, environmental, and economic value. We further indicate the two levels of implementation: organizational and collaborative.[138]

The design and operations phase of partnership implementation aims to develop the structures and processes that will facilitate the collaboration's creation of value. As shown in Figure 5.5, this process pathway includes feedback mechanisms between experimentation and operationalization, allowing for adaptations at every circle of experimentation. Similar feedback travels between experimentation and evaluation, allowing for continuous value renewal, that is, for the formulation of new value-creating propositions that fuel collaborative continuance. The subprocesses range from formal to informal influence and from explicit to implicit influence over the quality of implementation and, eventually, outcomes. In the interest of effective partnering, design parameters and operating actions need to be spelled out. For example, one should be explicit about the participation[139] of parties that have a direct stake in the social issue, since this will increase the likelihood of inclusive solutions.

The following new sets of competencies are among those that will be required by many processes for design and operations:

- Managing interdependent generic resources, organization-specific resources, and key success-related resources
- Coordinating laterally (that is, without hierarchical authority)
- Responding to heightened requirements for adaptation of bilateral, reciprocal, or conjoined resources[140]

We now examine each of the four subprocesses of the implementation phase:

1. Experimenting
2. Adapting
3. Operationalizing
4. Evaluating

1. Experimenting

The first group of subprocesses in the implementation phase includes setting up structures and processes for the co-generation of value that will allow both partners to experiment with the procedural and substantive partnership issues:[141]

- Setting objectives and structural specifications[142]
- Formulating rules and regulations[143]

- Drafting a memorandum of understanding[144]
- Establishing leadership positions[145]
- Deciding organizational structures[146]
- Agreeing on the partnership's management[147]

These subprocesses take place both within and across the two organizations,[148] adding congruency of structure and purpose[149] and contributing to organizational compatibility and to the generation of interaction value. Co-designing coordination mechanisms collectively adds value to the partnership,[150] allowing key employees from different functions within each organization to become familiar with the partnership and buy into the co-creation of value.

Experimenting: Case Example
Prince's Trust and Royal Bank of Scotland

A virtual team emerged for this collaboration—that is, participants in the partnership rarely met physically, but some members were working more with people across the two organizations than with people from their own organizations. The partners referred to this team as the "partnership team," and there were central "partnership managers" who oversaw all other partnership-management roles and aimed to keep both partners informed of the latest evolutions within each partner's operations. Over time, the team evolved in such a way that there were counterparts with similar functions across the two organizations (for example, the communications manager for the trust had a direct relationship with the bank's manager of media relations). This partnership team developed its own collaborative subculture and served as the vehicle for cultural cross-pollination (Seitanidi, 2010).

Throughout this initial period, and continuing thereafter, another fundamental and critical subprocess is to build trust. Trust is developed through personal interactions. A vital role is played by those individuals primarily responsible for managing the partnership's interface. These "boundary spanners" have several essential qualities: perceived competence, goodwill toward the partner, commitment to making the extra effort to help the collaboration, and sufficient decision-making authority to ensure that promises will be kept.[151] Trust can also be built when the partners undertake initially small initiatives, which enable each to interact with the other and gain the experience and mutual confidence that will then provide the basis of trust for larger undertakings.[152] Ben Peachley, director of communications for the International Council on Mining and Metals, observes, "You have to have process integrity and you must understand the power of taking the time to build trust. In the long term, you will [realize] the value of the time invested."[153] Trust is perhaps the most valuable form of interaction value.

Partnerships are resource-intensive relationships that require comprehensive teams on both sides. Discovering how best to interact is often the result of experimentation. As part of this process, drafting a memorandum of understanding is an important task that can vary in complexity.

Drafting a Memorandum of Understanding: Case Examples

Starbucks and Conservation International

After four months, this partnership developed its first memorandum of understanding, based on the linked interests of the partners. It indicated the planned outcomes and their timelines, thereby also indicating the types of value to be created. One reason for the quick development of the memorandum of understanding was the previous experience of both partners and their explicit decision to develop a leadership initiative that they both aimed to scale up, instead of confining it to an exclusive relationship. This is an indication of potential for an advanced relationship, with high and planned creation of synergistic value. It was an up-front arrangement allowing for the generation of shared economic, environmental, and social value for stakeholders beyond the two partners. Potential was further highlighted by several key elements in the second memorandum of understanding, such as "developing coffee-sourcing guidelines [to incorporate] sound environmental management practices and [provide] for [the] livelihoods [of] farmers."[154]

Rio Tinto and Earthwatch

Given lack of experience, high levels of risk associated with mining (a high-impact sector), and the fact that the company was listed on the stock exchange (and thus had high visibility), this partnership took twenty-four months to develop its first memorandum of understanding. Furthermore, the initial aim of Rio Tinto UK and Rio Tinto Australia was to partner both with Earthwatch Europe in the United Kingdom and with Earthwatch Australia under a unified memorandum of understanding. Differences between the respective legal systems made it impossible to develop a global memorandum of understanding, but it was possible to develop a global partnership regulated by two national memoranda of understanding.[155]

2. *Adapting*

Gradually, through experiments at the organizational and collaborative levels, internal and external partnership subprocesses and structures adapt. Policies, programs, and actions develop and change. Through these adaptations, new frames of creation lead to interactive and synergistic value. In this sense, value creation both requires and produces valuable intangibles. A collective learning subprocess propels the adaptation.

To solve problems that require social change, partners must embrace their adaptive responsibilities[156] and take a collaborative value approach to co-designing new approaches. A prerequisite to such co-creation is recognizing the value of a partner's knowledge, which is more difficult in cross-sector partnering because of the multitude of organizational differences. Partner relations that promote greater communication enable understanding and appreciation of the partner's knowledge and its value.[157] One study of intense collaborations[158] revealed that deliberate and continuous adaptation of the role of each partner organization, as a response to the other partner's changing needs, drives successful social innovations. This research stresses the need for change within the partnership (facilitated by the partners' linked interests) in order for the partnership to contribute to the potential for change outside the relationship—in other words, to reach the transformational level.

Despite the positive connotations of the word *adaptation* (agreeable learning and positive outcomes), adaptations may be, in reality, among the most difficult but doable steps in value creation. For example, in a partnership between a Canadian hospital and a digital imaging company, the partners detected signs of failure, but instead of abandoning the collaboration, they engaged in deep reflection and intensive interaction to redesign their roles in order to reverse the process.[159] Thus, despite the challenges of the implementation phase, gradual adaptations and role recalibrations at the organizational or collective level allow for rebalancing the course of a relationship.

Through adaptation, it is possible for the collaboration to escalate to higher value creation. The key subprocesses for driving value creation during experimentation and adaptation are joint discovery and learning.

Adapting: Case Examples

CTA–Toyota and an NGO

In this collaboration in Jordan, the company, the NGO, the ministry of education, and school stakeholders reached a formal agreement, with specific objectives and responsibilities. Still, as one company manager noted, "Flexibility is one reason why we stick to that initiative. We can adapt it to our own schedule . . . So this doesn't take us out of breath, out of time, or out of ideas."[160]

Marks & Spencer and Oxfam

The collaboration between this British retailer and Oxfam began as an effort to help the company with recycling but evolved into a dramatically different social business model involving customer engagement and a clothes-for-vouchers exchange mechanism. As Mike Barry, head of sustainable business for Marks & Spencer, put it, "You don't get all the opportunities from day one in a partnership, you have to work with your partner to create the ideas and solutions together."[161]

3. Operationalizing

Decisions gradually reach operationalization, passing through several adaptations because of internal or external factors,[162] and lead to stabilization of the partnership's content, processes, and structures[163] until the next cycle of iteration. In each cycle, the value drivers of alignment, engagement, and leverage intensify (see Chapter Four). As interactions intensify in quantity and quality, trust increases, managerial complexity intensifies, and processes become increasingly intertwined, leading to sophisticated amalgamations of resources. Resource complementarity increases because of the partners' familiarity with the content, structures, and processes of the partnership.

Operational measures can be formal or informal. Formal measures, including control mechanisms,[164] are likely to be introduced at the early stages and play an important role in developing familiarity across the organizations. Informal measures, however, are more likely to be effective in dealing with tensions around indeterminacy, vagueness, balancing interpretations between the partners,[165] and uncertainty.[166] Sometimes this involves exerting symbolic power that can influence individual organizations and industry macroculture.[167] Informal measures of control, such as trust-based governance, can play an important role in nonprofit–business partnerships,[168] in determination of a partnership's viability,[169] and in co-creation of value. The following factors are relevant here:

- Management of the partnership's culture so as to blend and harmonize two different organizational cultures[170]
- Charismatic leadership, to inspire employees' participation[171]
- Types of communication that enable the formation of trust (indeed, communication subprocesses are at the heart of interactions)[172]
- Mutual respect, openness, and constructive criticism with external as well as internal audiences[173]
- Continual learning[174]
- Management of conflict[175]
- Encouragement of open dialogue[176]

These factors produce interaction value and also enable and preserve collaborative value creation. Among the intangible resources they produce are trust, relational capital, learning, knowledge, and joint problem solving, all of which contribute to the co-creation of value and thus generate benefits for partners, individuals, and society.

4. Evaluating

The fourth implementation subprocess focuses on operational evaluation. Part of operationalization is establishing routines and setting performance expectations. Against these standards, evaluation identifies which aspects of the operations are working well and which are marked by problems. Assessment information flows continuously from operations, often informally, and periodically and more formally from evaluation procedures. Hunter refers to this element of performance management as "formative evaluation," which monitors, on an ongoing basis, what is being done, and how, in order to inform "tactical decision making" aimed at making adjustments to strengthen operations.[177] To be effective, these evaluation efforts need to be accompanied by subprocesses that hold staff and managers accountable for performance.

Evaluating: Case Example
Starbucks and Conservation International

The partners' engagement in collaborative discovery and learning led to adaptation and redesign. Each partner's understanding of the other's organizational culture deepened as they experimented with the processes, allowing for gradual adaptation that led to operationalization. The partners continually monitored and evaluated operations. As problems were encountered, they were addressed, sometimes by the individual partners and other times jointly. There were formal evaluation studies of operating results, some conducted internally and some conducted by external evaluators. These assessments led to the scaling up of the partnership program as the number of assisted coffee farmers increased, as production loans were given, as quality standards were refined, and as the quantity of coffee purchased at premium prices grew. As evidence of the successful progression to operationalization, the project became integrated into the standard procurement operations of Starbucks.

Phase 4: Institutionalization

Institutionalization, the fourth value creation process pathway, includes three subprocesses (see Figure 5.6):

1. Embedding collaboration
2. Converging the value frames
3. Governing collaboratively

1. Embedding Collaboration
Collaboration processes evolve into operational routines. Gradual stabilization of structures and processes (partnership operationalization) leads to the institutionalization of the partnership. A partnership has reached institutionalization when its structures,

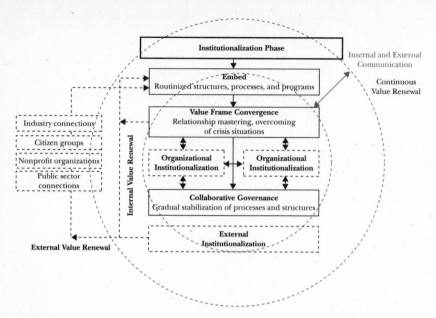

Figure 5.6.   The Collaboration Process Value Chain: The Institutionalization Phase

processes, and programs are accepted by the partner organizations and their constituents and are embedded within the organizations' existing strategies, values, structures, and administrative systems.[178] One way to test the level of the collaboration's embeddedness is to assess how the partners refer to the relationship. If the partnership team members use *we* instead of *us and them*, this demonstrates that the relationship has been successfully ingrained within each organization. A second way is to examine the impact of crises. If the impact is low, it indicates high embeddedness. In the partnership between the Prince's Trust and the Royal Bank of Scotland, there were several crises, but both organizations dealt with these situations in a mature way, which testified to the level of institutionalization. A final acid test of institutionalization is whether the collaboration is able to survive the exit of key leaders on both sides.

One subprocess of embedding collaboration within organizations could be called *mastering relationships*, that is, accepting and managing both the strengths and the weaknesses of the partner organization.[179] This is part of the subprocess of institutionalizing trust, in which the trust-building work of individual boundary spanners and others gets translated into organizational routines, practices, and matching expectations.[180] "Competency trust"[181] rests on the belief that the partner can deliver on its promises.

Another important embedding subprocess is the accumulation of interaction value. Information interactively turns into knowledge, and knowledge turns into capabilities. This important subprocess progresses through the following stages:

- *Information is collected.* During the formation, selection, and early design of the partnership, the partners have only the information they have gathered about each other.
- *Information becomes knowledge.* This basic information about the key product/service value proposition gradually increases, first among the members of the partnership team and later among other departments of the organization. As interactions intensify, they gradually transform information into knowledge.
- *Knowledge grows into capabilities.* As explicit knowledge grows, and as the partners become more and more familiar in their interactions, their tacit knowledge of each other also expands. Together with positive interpersonal chemistry, this tacit knowledge locks the partners together emotionally. A higher level of knowledge is integrated with enthusiasm and pride, and with the explicit aim of sharing the unique resources of the organizations. As the partnership progresses, knowledge about the partner organization, its resources, and its use of resources becomes deeper and turns into capability. At this stage, the partner is able to apply the knowledge in the contexts of both organizations. The partners are able to speak the same language and embark on co-creation that may produce innovative products, services, and skills.

This subprocess is a manifestation of the iterative and accumulating generation of interaction value, which can also progress to synergistic value.

2. Converging the Value Frames

Diagnostic frames encode individuals' experiences and assist in the assessment of a problem; prognostic frames use those experiences to assess a possible solution.[182] In order to co-generate social, environmental, and economic value, partners must adjust their perspectives on value so that the frames converge[183] or fuse.[184] Frame fusion is defined as "the construction of a new prognostic frame that motivates and disciplines partners' cross-sector interactions while preserving their distinct contribution to value creation"[185] by retaining the identity and differences of each partner. In effect, the partners get their ways of thinking about value in sync. Value-frame fusion assists in overcoming the partners' disagreements and allows for transformation of the "current means into co-created goals with others who commit to building a possible future."[186] To bring this about, each partner needs to do the following things:

- Perceive the strategic direction of the other's decisions[187]
- Observe organizational change processes[188]
- Participate in multiplayer interactions[189]
- Monitor and interpret the other partner's frames[190]

When partners align their perceptions of value, they create a shared language by developing a vocabulary of meaning.[191] Stafford, Polonsky, and Hartman[192] provide evidence for how the partners align their socioeconomic value frames in order to co-create "entrepreneurial innovations that address environmental problems and result in operational efficiencies, new technologies and marketable 'green' products." Stafford and Hartman[193] demonstrate that partners may consciously decide to embark on a transformational collaboration. In many cases, however, the potential for social change or social innovation emerges from within the process.[194] Partners can have quite different and even conflicting value perspectives.[195] These differences can adversely affect outcomes,[196] but they may also lead to creative reconciliation that generates even greater value.

Converging the Value Frames: Case Example

The Cape Town Partnership

The CEO involved in this multisector partnership, which was focused on developing Cape Town's inner city, stated, "Tensions do emerge. We need to communicate and to work through them. We need forums for these issues to surface. Differences and tensions are fun. They give rise to a dynamic. We try not to shy away from them."[197]

Particularly novel tasks[198] allow for balancing the potential tension associated with power dynamics;[199] collaborators may face unprecedented undertakings that make the partners equally important for the creation of a distinctive solution. Adaptations are essential to survival[200] and present opportunities at the individual, organizational, and sectoral levels[201] to unlearn and (re)learn how to frame and act collectively in order to develop a synergistic framework, which in turn is essential to providing solutions for social problems. The value capture will depend on the linked interests of the partners, which will influence the level of institutionalization of the co-creation of value.[202]

A subprocess that fosters value-frame convergence is the development of personal familiarization at the individual level across the members of the two organizations, as illustrated by the following example.

Personal Familiarization: Case Examples

Prince's Trust and Royal Bank of Scotland

In this collaboration, the partnership teams enjoyed a number of benefits that were due to the personal familiarization of the relationship. First, they were in a position to ask each other for advice. Second, they encouraged each other

(continued)

Personal Familiarization: Case Examples (*continued*)

when new ideas were put on the table. Third, the partners increased their contacts by capitalizing on each other's networks. The familiarization process was even institutionalized and actively encouraged when, for example, the partners embarked on a partnership "away day" to get to know each other better.[203] Thus it is clear that one of the levels at which the partnership makes sense is the individual level, where people develop personal relationships that are beneficial at the organizational level.

Starbucks and Conservation International

From both sides, individuals created interpersonal bonds, mutual trust, and shared commitment to the project. These intangibles represented interaction value and became enabling capabilities as well as informal mechanisms of control and coordination, which further advanced the collaboration.

Rio Tinto and Earthwatch

This relationship was tested through internal crises, and it survived. But the partnership teams developed reservations about the level of institutionalization, since they believed that the relationship was dependent on the personalities of key partnership members, a factor that affected the dynamism and creativity of the relationship after those members' departure.

3. Governing Collaboratively

The final subprocess of the institutionalization value creation pathway deals with achieving collaborative governance. Partnerships are faced with issues of accountability,[204] appropriateness of the standards developed, effectiveness and enforceability of mechanisms, decision making by for-profits and NGOs, and control.[205] Therefore, there have been calls for shared decision making,[206] consensus decision making,[207] and co-regulation[208] in order to balance the power dynamics across the partners.[209] But power does not have to be shared equally in order to be workable. A weaker power position may actually be a preferable path that fits an organization's culture or strategy.[210] Subprocesses for creating enduring collaborative governance include the following:

- Allowing multiple stakeholders to voice concerns
- Incorporating feedback loops[211]
- Decentralizing social-accountability checkpoints
- Inviting suggestions from the grassroots to facilitate answerability, enforceability, and universality[212]

The partners' respective managerial incentive systems need to explicitly incorporate accountability for the collaboration's performance.

In effect, to co-generate social, environmental, and economic value, particularly as one moves into the transformational stage, there needs to be a highly engaged, decentralized community network.[213] This expands participation from a few stakeholders to a broader constituency. Such broadening could even include engagement with fringe stakeholders as a means to achieve creative destruction and innovation for the partners and society.[214] Incorporating as many voices as possible allows not only internal value renewal but also external value renewal and eventually institutionalization of the collaboration externally. In effect, many voices increase a collaboration's opportunities to deliver impact. When the collaboration achieves scale, it gains the potential not only to be successful for the partners and organizations directly involved but also to externalize the value creation to the macro-level.

In the integrative and transformational stages of collaboration, social betterment takes center stage, and so multiple stakeholders become a key component in the co-creation process and in the reshaping of the dialogue,[215] which allows for value capture at multiple levels. Embedding the partnership across interested communities introduces a new layer of partnership institutionalization outside the original business–nonprofit partners (see Figure 5.6). This can take the form of a network with distinct governance processes. According to Wei-Skillern, Silver, and Heitz, "In the network mindset, trust and shared values are far more important than formal control mechanisms such as contracts or accountability systems."[216]

A look back at Figure 5.6 will reveal the reiterating phase of institutionalization. Although partnerships may end unexpectedly, they have the potential to deliver continuing cycles of value creation, depending on the quality of the processes, the evolution of the partners' interests and capabilities, and changes in the environment and the level of internal and external communication.

Reviewing the Collaboration Value Creation Processes

The following example is a good illustration of how the value creation process pathways can create value in practice.

Alcoa and Greening Australia: Summary Case Example

As a final illustration of the four partnering-process pathways discussed in this chapter, we turn to the thirty-year partnership between Alcoa and the environmental nonprofit Greening Australia (GA), a collaboration that began in the early 1980s.[217] In the formation and selection stages, with their particular value creation process pathways, several subprocesses stood out. The social problem—namely, the restoration of natural areas—was clearly articulated by both. Alcoa's mining operations were criticized for decades by communities and environmentalists, and so for years the company had responded by rehabilitating mined areas. Greening Australia was a new NGO with the mission of creating an environment that was healthy, diverse, and productive.

The organizations had linked interests in the form of congruence around a social mission. In addition, they both sought legitimacy, a form of associational value that could be derived from their partnering. Alcoa could gain credibility from the status of the environmental NGO, and Greening Australia, as a new nonprofit, needed the recognition that could come from being selected as a partner by one of the country's major companies. Both sought significant external visibility. There was some risk to both: GA could be criticized for presumably having been co-opted, and Alcoa was betting on an inexperienced organization. Nevertheless, the complementarity of their respective resources offset the risks. Alcoa brought experience with land restoration and access to sites needing rehabilitation; GA provided superior access to communities and government. Each partner needed what the other had.

In the implementation phase, the collaboration did go through a continual iterative process of experimentation, learning, and adaptation, both individually and collectively. Driving and restraining forces, both internal and external, create a dynamic of ongoing adjustment.[218] The partners pointed to open, frank, and honest communication about what was working and not working as a critical subprocess enabling continual operational modification. Understanding the partner's needs and seeking to meet them ensured bilateral value exchange and continual innovation, which led each partner to find new ways to add value to the other. In effect, there was ongoing value renewal to sustain the collaboration.

Over time, new capabilities were developed, particularly GA's environmental expertise and governmental influence, which enabled it to transfer these more valuable resources to Alcoa, thereby opening up new collaboration opportunities. The use of "partnership managers" enabled more effective

(*continued*)

Alcoa and Greening Australia: Summary Case Example (*continued*)

interaction between leadership and operating levels, both within and across the organizations. Employee engagement became central to the collaboration activities, and this in turn generated greater employee support. In this way, there were improvements in employee motivation, retention, and recruitment as well as in the credibility of the company's involvement in and support from the community. The collaboration became institutionalized internally and externally. The value creation process pathways have become embedded, the partners' value frames have converged, and governance is collaborative.

The partners' relationship migrated along the Collaboration Continuum from the philanthropic stage to the transactional and integrative stages and even to the transformational stage. New opportunities were discovered, and actions were expanded. The partners have participated in a multitude of collaborative initiatives, many of them simultaneous, and with characteristics of each of the stages; in effect, they have created a collaborative value portfolio. Their most advanced actions have been transformational in character. They have moved from having a regional focus to operating nationally and addressing broader and more systemic problem areas, such as river recovery, carbon mitigation, and agricultural sustainability. The search for innovative solutions in these complex problem areas has led to engagement of many other organizations with additional complementary resources from the public, private, and social sectors, with a goal orientation toward generating value at the macro-level. Underlying this evolution have been close alignment, deep engagement, and innovative leveraging of distinctive competencies.

Each of the four phases of partnership development—formation, selection, implementation, and institutionalization—constitutes a value creation process pathway consisting of a multitude of subprocesses. In the formation and selection phases, the first two value creation process pathways in the Collaboration Process Value Chain, the subprocesses are identifying and shaping the potential collaborative value. Then, in the implementation and institutionalization phases, potential value can be converted to actual value.

Along each of these four sequential pathways, value is created by the multitude of subprocesses that tap into the different sources of value and convert them into various types and amounts of value. To reiterate, the four *sources* of value are resource directionality, resource complementarity, resource nature, and linked interests; the four *types* of value are associational value, transferred-asset value, interaction value, and synergistic value, with their respective value subsets, as previously discussed. Value accumulates across the Collaboration Process Value Chain, ultimately manifesting as economic, social, and environmental value accruing to individuals, organizations, and society.

For each value creation process pathway, or phase, this chapter has identified a set of distinct subprocesses that enable value creation to occur. In the *formation* phase, there are six main subprocess areas. Each of the potential partners (1) examines how the other articulates the social problem to be addressed in the collaboration, in order to judge whether common ground exists regarding the basic focus. Each potential partner also needs to (2) determine what the other's intentions are regarding the kind of collaborative relationship that is sought. To provide empirical evidence, each (3) looks at the other's actual collaboration experience. Each also tries to (4) assess compatibility on the issue of desire for visibility. To make a judgment regarding the additional value that this partnership would add, both partners need to (5) assess how it would fit into their existing portfolios of collaborations. There is also an effort to (6) identify individuals in both organizations who would champion the potential collaboration. Each of these six subprocesses is made up of other, more specific microprocesses.

In the *selection* phase, the five subprocess areas are aimed at consummating the collaboration. There is (1) a more detailed mapping of the potential partners' linked interests, a fundamental fountain of value. Each partner also examines the complementarity of (2) the other's resources and (3) distinctive organizational capabilities. Moving beyond these critical and always present elements, the partners (4) develop selection criteria tailored to their specific organizational situations and context. Before proceeding, they should also (5) carry out a systematic assessment of the risks accompanying the collaboration.

Having chosen each other, the partners enter the *implementation* phase. The initial subprocess area involves (1) experimenting with the design of the collaboration. The resultant learning about what works and what does not leads to (2) the adaptation subprocesses. Gradually, (3) the operations develop routines, and the collaboration stabilizes. Nevertheless, there are (4) informal and formal operational evaluations. Although the partners may conclude that the collaboration is not feasible, the evaluation subprocesses primarily provide feedback aimed at adjustments that will strengthen implementation.

In the *institutionalization* phase, the collaboration is (1) embedded into each partner's mission, strategy, values, structures, and operating systems. The partners have a deep sense of joint ownership. The collaboration is able to survive crises and leadership changes. Information becomes knowledge, and knowledge becomes capabilities. At this point, (2) the value frames converge. Each of the partners is sensitive to the other's changing needs, and each is able to make adjustments that keep the partners' views on value creation synchronous. As a result, (3) the partnership is governed collaboratively and inclusively, and power imbalances are addressed constructively. The web of personal interrelationships across the partnering organizations expands and provides collaborative cohesion.

Through the value-creating power of the formation, selection, implementation, and institutionalization phases, the Collaboration Process Value Chain produces cumulative economic, social, and environmental value for individuals, organizations, and society. In Chapter Six, we take a closer look at these value outcomes.

Figure 5.7 presents a more fully elaborated picture of the Collaboration Process Value Chain.

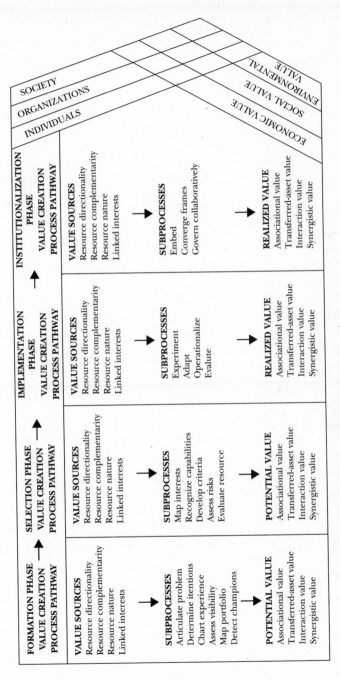

Figure 5.7. The Elaborated Collaboration Process Value Chain

Questions for Reflection

1. The first subprocess in the formation phase is that of *articulating the social problem.* Focus on one of your organization's significant cross-sector collaborations. What is the social issue on which the relationship focuses? Find written examples (annual reports, CSR and sustainability reports, internal reports, organizational websites) of how your organization and your potential partner organization have articulated a social problem. Can you uncover articulations that signify different assumptions, understandings, and strategies?

2. The fourth subprocess in the selection phase is that of *developing partnership-specific criteria.* Does your organization have specific selection criteria? Are some more important than others?

3. The second subprocess in the implementation phase is that of *adapting.* What adaptations have you made in your most important collaboration, and to what extent have you co-designed new approaches with your partner?

4. What is the difference between *emergent* and *planned* collaborative value? How have these two types of value manifested in collaborations?

5. The accumulation of interaction value involves three steps: collection of *information,* conversion of information to *knowledge,* and conversion of knowledge to *capabilities.* These three steps capture the generation of interaction value, which can lead to synergistic value. How and to what extent do collaborations move through these three steps?

Chapter Six

Assessing the Value of Collaboration Outcomes

Assessing the outcomes of collaborations between nonprofits and businesses is difficult but critical to their effective management. In practice, such assessment is generally fraught with complications. This chapter presents the final component of the CVC Framework: a systematic, multilevel approach to assessing collaboration value outcomes aimed at advancing the complicated task of evaluation.

Why Evaluate?

One is not collaborating for the sake of collaboration. Partners are investing scarce resources to generate value, and this investment, like all others, should be assessed to ascertain its productivity and to provide guidance for further enhancing the collaboration's value generation. A recent empirical study notes the extent to which the corporate philanthropy of 500 firms listed in the Dow Jones Sustainability Index is strategic by measuring its impact on society, business, and reputation/stakeholder satisfaction; despite the lack of common practice in how impact is measured, 76 percent of the firms assessed some sort of impact.[1] Corporate social responsibility (CSR) reports are now common practice, although Porter and Kramer assert that, instead of offering a coherent or strategic framework, "they aggregate anecdotes about uncoordinated initiatives to demonstrate a company's social sensitivity," and that "philanthropic initiatives are typically described in terms of dollars or volunteer hours spent but almost never in terms of impact."[2] Peloza suggests three key reasons for businesses to strengthen their metrics regarding social performance: to facilitate cost-effective decision making, to avoid interference in the allocation of resources due to lack of hard data, and to enable inclusion of social-performance budgets in the mainstream budgeting of companies.[3]

Similarly, demands for nonprofit organizations to measure impact have emerged because of the need to demonstrate the effectiveness of programs to all stakeholders, including funders, in an increasingly competitive philanthropic marketplace. In the United Kingdom, for example, the Charity Commission requires NGOs to report in terms of their core strategic objectives. The Innovation Network's "state of evaluation" study of U.S. nonprofits found that 90 percent measure their performance, but that less than half use this information to adjust their operations annually, evaluation being considered among their lowest priorities.[4] Mario Morino, founder of Venture Philanthropy Partners, contends that managing to outcomes is "a way for leaders and nonprofits to learn and grow" and is "essential for achieving lasting impact."[5] Nevertheless, a survey of nonprofit evaluation in Brazil revealed that, although assessment efforts did focus on results, they "were not concerned with creating spaces for self-reflection and learning."[6] Our CVC Framework creates an even sharper focus: on managing for the co-creation of value. Geoff Mulgan, director of policy under British Prime Minister Tony Blair, contends that value metrics should be used for three key functions—"external accountability, internal decision making and assessment of broader social impact"—but notes that rigor in such assessments is often lacking.[7]

It is not uncommon for collaborations to state performance in terms of the *inputs* provided (for example, the number of books supplied in a literacy program) or the *outputs* (for example, number of students reading the books). While these indicators describe programmatic activities, value assessment requires a focus on the *outcomes* (for example, the increased level of reading capability and comprehension, and the resultant benefits in terms of both social and economic value). An even further refinement in assessment is to utilize rigorous *impact* evaluation methodologies to determine the extent to which the outcomes are attributable directly to the collaboration rather than to other possibly intervening factors.

Collaborators recognize the need for evaluation. Its execution, however, is often deficient. If it were easy, everyone would be doing it. Outcomes assessment is fraught with complexities embedded in the very nature of value creation in social-purpose collaborations. As we have pointed out elsewhere, collaborative value is "the transitory and enduring multidimensional benefits relative to the costs that are generated due to the interaction of the collaborators and that accrue to organizations, individuals, and society."[8] While Porter and Kramer assert that such "shared value" is a superior kind of value,[9] these multiple forms of value and beneficiaries and their interactive dynamics create assessment complexities for both collaborative and individual social-purpose undertakings. Porter, Hills, Pfitzer, and Hawkins acknowledge that "the tools to put this concept into practice are still in their infancy."[10]

The Outcomes Assessment Framework

While there is no simple solution to evaluation complexities, one can focus the assessment process more systematically on outcomes by concentrating specifically on who benefits, and how. Too often the actual value generated by collaborations is undercounted because the focus of assessment is conceived too narrowly. Consequently, a critical step in ensuring a more comprehensive value assessment is to examine who has benefited and how far those benefits have spread in terms of three interrelated levels: that of individuals, that of organizations, and that of society (these are also referred to as the *micro-level*, the *meso-level*, and the *macro-level* of analysis). Collaborative value is created at each level, either sequentially or simultaneously.

A further distinction is between those benefits that accrue internally to the organizations and the individuals within the partnership and those benefits that are external to the partnership, including benefits to the larger society. Although evaluations tend to focus on how collaboration enhances the performance of the partnering organizations, it is important to recognize that the internal benefits derive fundamentally from the creation of value for external beneficiaries. For every category of beneficiary, one can specify the value generated. This locational multilevel mapping of outcomes enables a more comprehensive and systematic assessment. It is beyond the scope of this chapter to provide a comprehensive and detailed treatise on outcomes assessment, but the chapter does present a systematic approach to the task, and the works cited in the chapter point the way to the more detailed information that supports the chapter's conclusions.

Because value, like beauty, is in the eyes of the beholder, some outcomes may not be perceived in the same way by both partners. There may be ambiguity about whether the results constitute success, particularly where there has been significant innovation.[11] Resolving such perceptual differences may lead to deeper mutual understanding and collaborative capacity in the partnership.

Benefits Internal to the Partnership

In this section, we consider organizations as well as individuals. As explained in Chapter Two, the value accruing to the partnering organizations can be expressed in terms of four types of value and their corresponding value subsets. All of these have been discussed and illustrated in previous chapters, and they are recapped here:

Associational Value

- Reputational enhancement
- Credibility
- Desirability
- Legitimacy
- Visibility
- Affinity with the organization
- Employee recruitment, retention, motivation, and productivity
- Clients' patronage and loyalty
- Community support
- Government support
- Attractiveness to investors and donors[12]

Transferred-Asset Value

- Depreciable assets
- Durable assets
- Renewable assets[13]

Interaction Value

- Relational capital
- Trust building
- Access to networks
- Diversity management
- Empathy and solidarity
- Joint problem solving
- Conflict resolution
- Communication
- Coordination
- Collaborative leadership
- Risk reduction[14]

Synergistic Value

- Virtuous value circle
- Synergistic resource combinations
- Innovative solutions
- Synergism processes and pathways[15]

Each of these types of value, with their corresponding subcategories, can give rise to economic value in a multitude of forms for the partnering organizations, thereby contributing to "financial sustainability, i.e., an organization's capacity to operate indefinitely," as Márquez, Reficco, and Berger define economic value.[16] In addition to economic value, managers can identify how, in their particular situations, value generation contributes to the attainment of social and environmental missions.

At the micro-level (the level of individuals) there can be two types of value outcomes. One is instrumental in that engagement in the collaboration increases the capabilities and professional development of the involved individuals. For example, individuals may learn new technical or management skills, gain new knowledge, broaden their exposure to other organizational approaches and cultures, increase their interpersonal skills, and strengthen their leadership capacity.[17] A second value outcome at the micro-level is psychological benefits. These can include psychic satisfaction in helping others, new friendships with colleagues in the partnering organization, pride in the organization, and prestige in the community.[18]

Value Generated for Collaborating Businesses and Nonprofits: Case Examples

Georgia Pacific and the Nature Conservancy

When the timber-products company Georgia-Pacific came together with the Nature Conservancy, there was interaction value in the form of joint problem-solving capacity because each side had combined its distinctive and complementary competencies in forest management and environmental sciences. This enabled environmentally superior management of timbering practices for habitat and biodiversity preservation.

La Nación and Red Solidaria

In Argentina, a collaboration was formed between the major newspaper *La Nación* and the NGO Red Solidaria, an organization whose name means "Solidarity Network," and which promoted social solidarity. This collaboration produced an innovative solution to the systemic problem of matching needy people and organizations with those who had the relevant resources.[19] This was a very inefficient "marketplace" fraught with information imperfections. The collaboration resulted in the creation of a free "Solidarity Classifieds" section of the newspaper, where groups on both the supply side and the demand side could place ads and thus create connections, which in turn generated social value. This distinctive feature created competitive advantage as well, and it attracted greater readership, thus generating virtuous social and economic synergism.

Benefits External to the Partnership

Here we consider organizations, individuals, and society outside the partnership. There are many external organizational stakeholders of businesses and nonprofits, including institutional financial supporters interested in knowing the results of their support. Therefore, outcomes that demonstrate the synergistic contribution of the collaboration to the generation of economic, social, and environmental value reveal the enhanced return on the investments of these donors and investors. Other organizations can also benefit by the collaboration. These include governmental entities and community organizations concerned about or involved in the social or environmental problems being addressed by the partners. Similarly, other businesses or nonprofits from the same sector may be assisted indirectly when any of the collaboration's actions improve the situation for everyone engaged in that arena—for example, when new industry standards are created[20]— or when new opportunities for value creation are demonstrated. In effect, these are positive externalities of the collaboration that accrue to those organizations.

The primary external individual beneficiaries will be those receiving the services or goods produced by the collaborating organizations.[21] The nature of the benefit will depend, of course, on the specific problem and client focus of a partnership. Indirect beneficiaries will include individual donors to the nonprofit and individual clients of the business who receive psychological "income" from the enhanced well-being that their patronage has enabled.

At the societal level, collaborations might create economic, social, or environmental value for society in general through systemic changes in societal awareness, values, or priorities, in social or sectoral relationships, in institutional governance arrangements, or in access to new technologies and innovations.[22] Improvements in the environment inherently generate benefits for society at large. Hitt, Ireland, Sirmon, and Trahms refer to such benefits as "meeting social needs in ways that improve the quality of life and increase human development over time," including attempts that "enrich the natural environment and/or are designed to overcome or limit others' negative influences on the physical environment."[23] In the partnership between Alcoa and Greening Australia cited toward the end of Chapter Five,[24] the partners became increasingly rigorous and encompassing in their evaluations. They moved from counting the number of volunteers involved in reforestation (inputs) to trees planted (outputs) to environmental health benefits (outcomes) to impact (ecosystem changes that were due to the collaboration).

In assessing benefits at all levels, partners should also determine the accompanying costs in terms of economic, management, and reputational resources deployed and risks incurred.[25] In so doing, however, partners should operate with the investment and longer-run mindset (see Chapter Three) that recognizes that the gestation period and the process for creating collaborative value are often longer and cumulative.

Outcomes Assessment Mapping for Starbucks and Conservation International: Case Example

Let us return to the partnership between Starbucks and Conservation International,[26] discussed in Chapter Four. Collaborative value was generated in different forms on an ongoing basis as the undertaking evolved. The start-up period required an investment of time and resources, including a three-year $150,000 donation by Starbucks to Conservation International (CI) to institute the production processes for shade-grown organic coffee, to test and ensure that the quality standards were being met, and to organize the export. The output was an initial shipment of 76,000 pounds of coffee.

At the organizational level, the first outcome was that the export attracted unexpectedly high interest from newspapers because of the novelty of a company and a conservation nonprofit working together to produce a new product with benefits for the environment and for small coffee growers. This novel synergistic combination of economic, environmental, and social value resulted in free press coverage, with more than 45 million impressions nationwide. The equivalent commercial value of this coverage probably exceeded the Starbucks donation of $150,000. In effect, both the company and the nonprofit harvested associational value in the form of high visibility contributing to reputational enhancement. Externally, this public dissemination also generated societal value by increasing awareness of an innovative approach to multiple value creation and perhaps planting the seeds for imitation.

Even more important to the partners was the transferred-asset value resulting from the conjoining of their distinctive success-related resources. Their combination of environmental knowledge and marketing systems enabled them to create a new supply system that generated an ongoing stream of synergistic value in which social and environmental benefits produced economic benefits in the form of higher-value coffee for the company and the farmers. Consumers received a new product with the distinctive attributes of social and environmental value. The initial shipment's success led to expansion so that by 2001 Starbucks had established a new product and sold 1.5 million pounds of its shade-grown organic coffee. At a price of $13 per pound, and with the company's average net margin of 6.8 percent, that represented a cumulative profit of $1.3 million.

At the microlevel, the farmers' incomes rose greatly because of the premium price they received—$1.26 per pound, compared to the market price of $0.48. Enhanced income can lead to quality-of-life improvements. Impact studies revealed that 90 percent of the producers who had adopted sustainability standards also improved their homes, and 72 percent of their families consumed meat more than once every ten days, with a rate of only 50 percent for non-participants.[27] Furthermore, more farmers participating in the company's C.A.F.E. Practices sent their children to secondary school. At the meso-level, the farmers' cooperatives were strengthened economically as export sales rose by

(continued)

Outcomes Assessment Mapping for Starbucks and Conservation International: Case Example (*continued*)

100 percent, organizational capacities increased, and social cohesion solidified.

In terms of environmental value, there were benefits at the micro-level, the meso-level, and the macro-level. As farmers adopted organic methods, they ceased to pollute water systems adjacent to their farms, thus improving water quality for all the individual users of those water sources. At the meso-level, CI benefited by achieving its conservation goals, thus increasing its credibility with donors. Mexican authorities in charge of the adjacent El Triunfo biosphere reserve were benefited by a reduction in the encroachment of coffee-producing areas. This preservation meant macro-level value generation in the form of the enhanced environmental services of the reserve as well as expanded habitat for birds and other species because of increased tree coverage with the growth of shade-grown coffee. A 2011 study in Colombia found that farms using the C.A.F.E. Practices had greater diversity in their shade canopies, had more stable natural habitat, and made greater gains in waste and wastewater management.[28]

Of even more strategic value at all levels was the replication and scaling up of the model. The partners intended their formulation of sustainable coffee-production standards to extend across the entire industry, and the geographical extension by Starbucks and CI of the system into Central America and South America magnified the value outcomes already described. In addition, the standards created a more sustainable supply system for the small farmers. This was critical to the aggressive retail-store expansion strategy of Starbucks, given that over half the world's coffee comes from producers who are farming an area of less than twelve acres.

The institutionalization of the system, with its multivalue approach, in the Starbucks operations carried with it another important benefit. The company, by "walking its talk," reinforced its stated values of benefiting producers in their communities of origin and improving the environment. External value generation creates internal value. Starbucks is a values-driven and employee-focused company. Its values and practices, including its community collaborations, contribute to its having a 70 percent turnover rate, by contrast with the industry average of 200 percent. In 2000, it cost the company $500 to recruit and train a new employee (or "partner," as Starbucks refers to an employee). With around 54,000 "partners" in 2000, this meant that annual workforce turnover costs for Starbucks were about $19 million, compared to the industry average of $54 million at that time. This difference of $35 million was equal to about 20 percent of the company's annual profits. Values generate value.

Handling Assessment Perplexities

The Outcomes Assessment Framework, described in the preceding section of this chapter, advances the evaluation task by more systematically and comprehensively identifying who is benefited, and how. But performance measurement is more than just a technical issue, and collaborations, along with all other welfare-enhancing programs, are characterized by a perplexing set of difficulties in measuring outcomes.

Anticipating Challenges

David Hunter, former director of assessment for the Edna McConnell Clark Foundation, observes, "Few people involved in this work have thought deeply about managing toward outcomes. Most put the cart before the horse—focusing on how to measure rather than on why [to] measure and what to measure."[29] Therefore, before plunging into specific measurement difficulties, we should focus on four important precursors: *mindset, clarity of objectives, theory of value creation and change,* and *assessment investment.*

n Chapter Three, partners need to have a robust
ed collaborative value mindset. Central to this
..p and ever-present focus on ensuring that the part-
..ership is generating maximum value, which requires ongoing
assessment. Outcomes measurement is essential. If this mental
framework is not present within each partnering organization, it
is unlikely to emerge in the collaboration. But even if only one
of the partners has a strong value measurement mindset, there
is an opportunity to stimulate and develop that orientation in
the other partner.

Clarity of Objectives

Many companies lack an explicit mission statement or goals for
their social-performance activities (including collaborations),
which is to say that they lack criteria against which they would
have to perform,[30] or they lack consistency in employing outcomes metrics.[31] Previous chapters have stressed the importance of partners' linked interests and alignment. Investing
time in clarifying what the collaboration aspires to achieve is
vital for defining the outcomes objectives. (We referred to this
in Chapter Five as the process of converging value frames.)
These converged objectives, expressed as specifically as possible
in terms of the types of value being sought, then guide the
formulation of what should be measured. The clearer the objectives, the sharper the measurement. Hunter, in a book filled
with detailed examples from his decades of experience in
performance management, prescribes five characteristics for
performance indicators: they must be *clear, relevant, economical,
adequate,* and *monitorable.*[32]

Theory of Value Creation and Change

Hunter observes that the nonprofit sector "suffers generally from
a pervasive case of unjustifiable optimism," that is, a habit of
"over-claiming . . . effectiveness while under-measuring . . . performance," and he contends that this problem can be addressed
if nonprofits formulate "robust theories of change that serve as
blueprints for achieving specific results in well-defined domains"

and "make their strategic visions operational."[33] In collaborations, this means identifying collective sources of value and delineating value-creation pathways (see Chapter Five) so as to project the theoretical value.[34]

Assessment Investment

According to the Center of Effective Philanthropy's 2012 survey, 71 percent of the nonprofits surveyed received no support from their funders for their assessment efforts.[35] Collaborations serious about creating value will ensure that adequate resources are mobilized for carrying out meaningful assessment. Morino stresses the importance of such investment: "Management-oriented data collection and analysis is what managing to outcomes requires. It is a way for leaders and nonprofits to learn and grow. It is essential for achieving lasting impact."[36]

Investing in and Learning from Outcomes Measurement: Case Example

The Strive Initiative

The Strive Initiative, in Cincinnati, was a multiparty, multisector megacollaboration involving over 300 nonprofits, school districts, foundations, and corporations addressing education issues, from birth through college and into a meaningful career. Over two years, with facilitated biweekly meetings, this coalition established common goals, formulated evidence-based strategies, and defined outcome measures and regional impact metrics. The coalition continuously tested and refined performance indicators, eventually reducing a list of 150 indicators down to 10 key ones. As the coalition's executive director, Jeff Edmondson, explained, "People originally just threw out whatever indicators came to mind, but over time we were able to have an honest dialogue about which few would really tell us if we were moving the needle."[37]

Types of Complication

Let us now turn to the complexities of measurement. Austin, Leonard, Reficco, and Wei-Skillern summarize the difficulties concisely: "The challenge of measuring social change is great due to nonquantifiability, multicausality, temporal dimensions, and perspective differences of the social impact created."[38] Others have also cited these and related complexities. Although these measurement problems constitute significant challenges to evaluation, a variety of approaches have emerged to deal with them. For each of the problem areas indicated here, we set forth some of the ways that have been used to deal with them.

Methodological Challenges

Methodological challenges in measurement may be due to the intangible character of many outcomes and to the need for documented, likely, and perceived effects.[39] Quantification is important, but not everything can be quantified. Khandker, Gayatri, Koolwal, and Samad, writing about experience at the World Bank, observe that "a mixture of qualitative and quantitative methods (a mixed-methods approach) might . . . be useful in gaining a comprehensive view of [a] program's effectiveness," as illustrated by the Jamaican Social Investment Fund (JSIF):

> Program evaluators conducted semi-structured, in-depth qualitative interviews with JSIF project coordinators, local government and community leaders, and members of the JSIF committee that helped implement the project in each community. This information revealed important details about social norms, motivated by historical and cultural influences that guided communities' decision making and therefore the way the program ultimately played out in targeted areas. These interviews also helped in matching communities, because focus groups were asked to identify nearby communities that were most similar to them.[40]

Attribution of Results to a Particular Program

The tendency to attribute results to a particular program, especially in companies and nonprofits that have a sophisticated portfolio of social activities or partnerships, may be even more

pronounced with respect to changes in complex systems influenced by a range of factors.[41] Impact evaluation focuses explicitly
on determining causality attribution by using rigorous methodology (for example, randomized-control trial groups). Khandker,
Gayatri, Koolwal, and Samad provide a comprehensive exposi-
tion, with case examples and exercises, of a multitude of quantitative methods for assessing causality.[42] Outcomes assessment, in
contrast to impact evaluation, does not have such randomized
designs or control groups, but Lim suggests that if a collaboration is achieving its intended results, one can reasonably assess
outcomes with the following approach:

1. Existing national and regional datasets can serve as rea-
    sonable comparison benchmarks.
2. Related evaluation studies or social science research offer
    corroborating evidence.
3. There already exists a considerable amount of confidence
    in the quality of the program's theory of change.
4. The measured data align with judgments suggested by
    close knowledge of the grantee and interactions with the
    program's beneficiaries.[43]

Time Required to Effect Social or Environmental Change

It can take a long time to effect social or environmental change.
The long gestation period for creating collaborative value
means that intervening factors can affect outcomes and that
managerial needs for immediate feedback may be frustrated.
One approach to dealing with this situation is to examine the
collaboration's theory of change and, in the words of Lim, to
"apply a model drawn from external evidence and adjusted
to current local conditions pertaining to ultimate effectiveness.
This external evidence includes quantitative data from prior
studies and consultations with sector experts."[44] An example
that comes from a malaria-prevention program is the practice
of multiplying the number of individuals receiving antimalarial
bed nets by a figure (drawn from the results of existing studies)
representing the expected effectiveness of the nets, to yield
a projection of lives saved. That projection then becomes an
intermediate indicator of outcomes.

Subjectivity Associated with Various Stakeholders

Subjectivity on the part of different stakeholders in varying contexts may influence how those stakeholders value outcomes, which is to say that stakeholders may have subjective impressions of what is acceptable, what is appropriate, and what is of value to whom.[45]

There are two dimensions with respect to subjectivity concerns. The first dimension has to do with the fact that different groups will value benefits differently. Rather than being a problem, however, this is a pathway to refined value assessment. Value is and should be in the eyes of the beholders. It is important to identify all the different beneficiaries at the microlevel, the meso-level, and the macro-level, and so the task is not to homogenize value but to recognize its heterogeneity, which provides a more comprehensive view of the value created. The second dimension has to do with the reasonable desire to monetize the different forms of value created so that one can use a common unit of analysis to compare costs/investments with benefits. According to the SROI [Social Return on Investment] Network:

> There will be estimates and assumptions. We prefer to call these professional judgements, which is after all what accountants use to describe their estimates and assumptions . . . There are many outcomes for different stakeholders, some negative and some conflicting. And this means there needs to be a way of deciding which of these are important or, in SROI terms, which are material. Valuation is a way of weighting outcomes in order to help make this decision and cannot be left until the end of the process if used this way. Valuation isn't an end, it's a beginning.[46]

Even if one does not convert the social or environmental value to a financial equivalent, useful cost-effectiveness indicators can be calculated (for example, cost per life saved, or cost per gallon of water saved).

Evaluation Costs

The cost of evaluation may seem too high. Even a staunch supporter of rigorous evaluation like the Roberts Enterprise Development Fund (REDF), a pioneer in developing and applying SROI and blended-value methodologies, confirms that the process of using SROI analysis uses many resources and is not financially feasible for many nonprofits.[47]

But one should consider the cost of not doing evaluation. One researcher cites

> a well-known program, Scared Straight, which arranges for juveniles who are getting in trouble with the law to meet, up close and personal, lifers who let them know that prison is hell. The idea is that this will terrify the kids and propel them back onto the straight and narrow path. But you might want to know that rigorous experimental research shows that Scared Straight is more harmful to teens than doing nothing. What does this mean? It means that Scared Straight has been proven to increase violence among teenagers who participate in its visits to prison. Nevertheless, Scared Straight not only thrives in the U.S. but has spread to at least six other countries.[48]

Similarly, an evaluation by the Latin American Youth Center revealed that its educational program that aimed at decreasing domestic violence actually increased it, which led to a redesign that produced the opposite results.[49] Although rigorous, evidence-based evaluation is desirable, the level of sophistication and the accompanying costs should be adjusted to fit the purpose and the users.

Reviewing the Outcomes Assessment Framework

Clearly, outcomes assessment is filled with challenges, but its importance makes Nike's slogan "Just do it" quite applicable. In fact, that company appears to have applied the slogan to itself:

> A critical task . . . [has been] to focus on impact and develop a systematic approach to measure it. We're still working hard at this. How do we know if a worker's experience on the contract factory floor has improved, or if our community investments helped improve a young person's life? We're not sure anyone has cornered the market in assessing real, qualitative social impact. We are grappling with those challenges now. In FY07–08, we will continue working with key stakeholders to determine the best measures. We aim to have a simple set of agreed-upon indicators that form a baseline and then to measure in sample areas around the world.[50]

In its 2009 CSR report, the company acknowledged that solutions require industry-level and systemic change, which will have to pass through "new approaches to innovation and collaboration"; interestingly, the report states, "Our aim is to measure our performance and report accurate data. At times, that means systems and methodology for gathering information needed to change even as we collect data, as we learn more about whether we are asking the right questions and whether we are getting the information that will help us to answer them rather than just information."[51] The company also reported that it aimed at developing targets and metrics around programs for excluded youth around the world, which demonstrates the policy-type thinking required for the development of impact indicators as well as for the development of processes to monitor, report, and advocate. These are competencies usually associated with nonprofit organizations, but they clearly are needed equally by corporations to assess the creation of multiple types of value.

Nike has embraced an evolutionary and historical approach in understanding the workplace impact on factories.[52] The World Business Council for Sustainable Development has responded to the growing interest in assessment by publishing a guide for measuring socioeconomic impact. As the organization's president, Peter Bakker, has stressed, "Capitalism requires a new operating system, and needs to be re-booted so that we expect and manage the returns on financial, natural, and social capital in a balanced way with a view to future-proofing our economies."[53]

Assessing outcomes is a learning journey. The complications of evaluation can appear overwhelming, but in fact they are manageable. One can begin by using the multilevel outcomes assessment mapping framework to systematically and comprehensively identify who is benefiting, and with what type of value. Approaching the task with the appropriate outcomes-oriented collaborative value mindset, and ensuring that the partners have clarity about their objectives, will provide the necessary focus. Then, delineating a theory of value creation and change, one is able to set forth a guiding logic of transformational pathways toward value creation. Finally, a willingness to invest in assessment efforts enables a meaningful ongoing learning process that is essential to continuous improvement in co-creating value.

This chapter has elaborated the fifth and last component of our Collaborative Value Creation Framework. In the book's final chapter, we extract from the previous chapters a set of smart practices for co-generating collaborative value.

Questions for Reflection

1. Employ the Outcomes Assessment Framework to examine your most important collaboration. What outcomes are internal to the partnership? What outcomes are external to the partnership for individuals, the partnering organizations, and society?

2. Consider one of your collaborations. In terms of outcomes evaluation, how would you characterize its (a) mindset? (b) clarity of objectives? (c) theory of value creation and change? (d) assessment investment?

3. In evaluating the outcomes of your cross-sector collaborations, have you employed (a) a mixed approach (that is, the use of quantitative and qualitative methods)? (b) impact evaluation? (c) a theory of change? (d) third-party assessments?

4. In the analysis of cross-sector collaborations, what are the benefits of using a multilevel approach?

5. Explain the following complexities, which surmount cross-sector social partnerships: (a) nonquantifiability, (b) multicausality, (c) temporality, and (d) difference in perspectives on the social impact that has been created.

Chapter Seven

Twelve Smart Practices for Maximizing Collaborative Value Creation

The purpose of this chapter is to distill from the preceding chapters, and from the underlying literature review, a consolidated set of guidelines for nonprofit and business practitioners involved in designing and managing strategic cross-sector partnerships aimed at generating ever-higher levels of planned and emergent collaborative value.

Twelve Themes

From our analyses, there have emerged twelve interrelated themes of smart collaboration practice:

1. Understanding value creation
2. Achieving a collaborative value mindset
3. Advancing through stages of collaboration
4. Managing value-creation processes
5. Assessing outcomes
6. Seeking partners who fit
7. Bonding
8. Governing and organizing
9. Communicating

10. Building trust
11. Learning
12. Transforming

The first five themes relate directly to the components of the Collaborative Value Creation Framework. The other seven merit spotlighting because they have been repeatedly identified by the practitioners and researchers cited in the previous chapters as especially important to successful collaboration. In this, the final chapter of the book, we will elaborate the salient aspects of each of these twelve smart collaboration practices.

1. Understanding Value Creation

The conceptual cornerstone of constructing a powerful collaboration is to understand where value comes from and what kind of value is created. Therefore, the building blocks in the analytics of collaborative value creation are the four sources and the four types of value.

Identifying Sources of Value

Practitioners can make value analysis more systematic by examining the four core sources of collaborative value. Each source contributes to value creation in distinctive ways. First, *resource directionality* addresses the question of who provides value-generating resources, and how. The value potential of the resources is greater as their mobilization moves from sole creation to dual creation to co-creation. Second, *resource complementarity* addresses the question of how productive the fit is between the collaborators' respective resources. Differences are a source of value, and so the key is to preserve those value-creating differences while avoiding incompatibilities. Third, *resource nature* focuses on the kinds of resources deployed. Practitioners can generate greater value by moving from generic resources to differentiated, organization-specific resources to key success-related resources. Fourth, *linked interests* have to do with the value-creating linkages that tie the partners together. The broader and deeper the partners' shared interests, the greater the value potential.

For each source, practitioners should ask, "Are we tapping to the fullest the value potential embedded in the source in our particular context?" Because value sources are complementary and interrelated, partners should also identify the possibilities of combining the different sources. The question here is "Have we created the optimum value-source mix to move the collaboration toward the highest level on the Collaborative Value Creation Spectrum?" In a high-performance collaboration the resources would flow from both partners, move beyond a bilateral exchange, and achieve a conjoined fusion of resources. The combination of complementary resources would add new capabilities to the integrated effort. Key success-related resources would be deployed, and the distinctive competencies of each partner would thus be leveraged. The collaboration would be propelled and sustained by broad and deep linkages between each partner's self-interest and the creation of value for the other partner and for the larger society.

Assessing Value Types

Ultimately, these sources give rise to economic, social, and environmental value, but the analytics of value creation enable a more refined analysis of the four underlying types of value and their respective constituent value subsets created by the collaboration. *Associational value* emerges from the perceived worthiness of the relationship in the eyes of the partners' stakeholders, both internal and external. Its value subsets include enhanced reputation and credibility of the partnering organizations as well as internal benefits, such as employee recruitment, retention, and motivation, and such external benefits as clients' patronage and loyalty, support from the surrounding community and from governmental sources, and attractiveness to investors and donors. The subsets of *transferred-asset value* are depreciable assets (such as cash, and goods and services that get used up), durable assets (which can be used for a longer time), and renewable assets (which bring new value to the collaboration). *Interaction value* arises from the processes of the partners working together, with resultant value subsets that include relationship capital, trust building, diversity management, joint problem solving, conflict resolution, communication, coordination, empathy, solidarity, and collaborative leadership. All of these are value outputs from the collaboration but also inputs to the collaboration that strengthen its value-generating capacity. *Synergistic value* is the virtuous circle of reciprocal generation of economic, social, and environmental value, whereby complementary resource combinations lead to high-value innovations and ongoing synergism-process pathways.

Practitioners should first reflect on which types of value and value subsets are most important to them. Then they should look at the entire constellation of value as a collaborative value portfolio and assess whether the mix is optimum. The Collaborative Value Creation Spectrum provides a conceptual mapping tool for identifying where a partnership's value creation resides on the spectrum, from a low-performing to a high-performing collaboration, in terms of sources and types of value. The core question is how to produce more collaborative value for individuals, organizations, and society.

2. Achieving a Collaborative Value Mindset

Partners' mental frameworks regarding value and collaboration fundamentally shape collaborative value creation. Partners will have higher potential for the co-generation of value with mindsets that include the following elements:

A *broad view of value.* The starting point is conceiving of value broadly as economic, social, and environmental rather than narrowly focusing on just one category. This broader perspective would also encompass the more refined value types—associational value, transferred-asset value, interaction value, and synergistic value—along with their respective subsets.

A *synergistic and integrative outlook.* Instead of viewing economic, social, and environmental value as trade-offs, one recognizes them as compatible and synergistic. Rather than segregating them, one integrates them.

A *value-adding perspective.* While all partners should expect to harvest benefits, the collaborative mindset is not fixated on extraction but rather on how to add value to the partnership. Generating value for your partner will trigger reciprocity and create a continuous virtuous circle of value creation.

An inclusionary attitude. One needs to move from being exclusionary and internally focused to becoming inclusive and externally oriented in terms of who participates in and benefits from the collaboration. This means moving from a shareholder or a staff mindset to a stakeholder mindset.

A focus on investing. One thinks of outlays not as expenses but as investments aimed at long-term value creation. Interactions are not viewed as transaction costs but rather as activities that generate value.

Interdependence. There is recognition that organizations and individuals are inescapably interdependent rather than isolated and independent.

Multiple motivations. Collaboration motivations are multifaceted and complementary. They are a mix of self-serving and other-serving motivations.

Cooperation. The orientation is toward constructive cooperation rather than antagonistic conflict. Disagreements are dealt with as learning opportunities.

Convergence. Multiple core elements of the organizations, such as mission, strategy, values, and value generation, are perceived as converging rather than diverging.

Innovation. One shifts from a minimal change perspective to a perspective of innovation and system transformation.

3. Advancing through Stages of Collaboration

The dynamics of value creation vary as partner relationships evolve through the philanthropic, transactional, integrative, and transformational collaborative stages. In different ways and to different degrees. each stage taps into the four sources of value (resource direction, complementarity, resource nature, and linked interests) and generates the four types of value (associational value, transferred-asset value, interaction value, and synergistic value), creating economic, social, and environmental value for partners, individuals, and society.

The three interrelated value drivers—alignment, engagement, and leverage—propel the collaboration to increasingly higher value co-creation across the Collaboration Continuum. Each value driver encompasses a constellation of value contributors, which change in their nature and significance from one relationship stage to another and are useful descriptors of the different stages. More important for practitioners, they are variables for analysis and management action, as revealed by the following summarizations of how these drivers and their respective value contributors evolve across the stages, from philanthropic to transformational.

Alignment

The collaboration's relevance to the partners' *missions* moves from being peripheral to central, and its *strategic importance* rises from weak to vital. The connection between the partners' *values* shifts from shallow to profound. The partners' respective *knowledge* of the social or environmental problem, which is often initially unbalanced, becomes synchronous as their joint efforts delve deeper into it. Disparate *value-creation frames* become fused; partners' ways of thinking about co-generation of value become synchronized. The *benefits focus* in the beginning is on the partners but shifts toward the larger betterment of society.

Engagement

An initially modest shared *emotional connection* with the cause and with each other becomes deep. The *focus of the interaction* in the beginning is on procedures but becomes substantive. *Involvement* broadens from a few individuals to encompass personnel throughout the organizations and their external stakeholders. The *interaction frequency* shifts from occasional to intensive. *Trust* deepens as the engagement intensifies and results are produced. The partnership's *scope of activities* broadens as they discover new value-creating opportunities. The dual partnership *structure* may expand to encompass the multiple parties needed to address more complicated and larger undertakings. Correspondingly, *managerial complexity* magnifies.

Leverage

The *magnitude of resources* required by the collaboration increases; larger investments are required to produce greater returns. The *resource nature* is generic at the philanthropic stage, but the more advanced stages mobilize the partners' more powerful specialized organizational resources andkey success-related resources. At each successive stage, the leverage of these assets is magnified as they become more closely *linked*. As the linkages grow, *synergism* multiplies. Mutual *learning* is limited in traditional philanthropic relationships but becomes an increasingly powerful value contributor, especially fueling *innovation*, which becomes predominant and systemic at the transformational stage. Whereas very little *internal organizational change* is required initially, it later becomes critical to the support of high value transformation focused on *external system change*.

4. Managing Value-Creation Processes

Partnering processes are the underlying value-creating mechanisms. Each of the four phases of building and operating a cross-sector partnership—*formation, selection, implementation,* and *institutionalization*—has a distinct value-creation pathway that needs to be carefully managed. The components of each value-creation pathway are managed through vital subprocesses that tap into and convert the sources of value into actual value. Part of this process management is planned, and part is emergent in response to unforeseen events that require adaptive flexibility.

Formation

The process components of the value-creation pathway in this phase aim to assess the potential for collaborative value creation. They consist of articulating the social problem, mapping the potential collaboration in terms of the collaborative value portfolio, determining organizational intentions, charting the value-creation experience, assessing compatibility with respect to visibility, and detecting prepartnership champions.

Selection

This process pathway includes identifying linked interests, determining the value of resources, recognizing organizational capabilities, developing partnership criteria, and assessing risks.

Implementation

The pathway subprocesses focused on design and operation include experimenting, adapting, operationalizing, and evaluating.

Institutionalization

The process elements here include embedding the collaboration, wherein relationships deepen and enable information to become knowledge and then develop into new capabilities. The partners' value frames merge and they govern the partnership in a fully shared manner.

5. Assessing Outcomes

Evaluation is essential to ensuring accountability, measuring progress toward goal attainment, and improving collaborative value generation. Assessing the outcomes of partnering is challenging because of the inherent complexity of measuring the economic, social, and environmental value generated by collaboration. These challenges can be addressed in five ways—through *multilevel mapping,* an *evaluation mindset, clear objectives,* a *theory of value creation and change,* and *investments in assessment.*

Undertaking Multilevel Mapping

To avoid underestimating the true value of collaboration, the partnership should comprehensively identify who is benefiting, and how. This means examining three levels—organizational, individual, and societal—that are internal and external to the partnership. At each level, one can specify which of the four types of value (with their corresponding subsets) are being generated.

Having an Evaluation Mindset

The partners need to be jointly and similarly oriented toward assessing outcomes. It really matters that measurement matters to the collaborators. There needs to be a strong shared commitment to and investment in evaluation.

Clarifying Objectives

The partners need to be very clear on the outcomes they are seeking, what they should be measuring, and the uses to which the evaluation results will be put. Ambiguity and vagueness are to be avoided.

Formulating a Theory of Value Creation and Change

By laying out the value-creation and change processes, the partners will be able to specify the operating mechanisms that will tap into sources of value and convert them to positive change. This activity provides a guiding structure for examining the co-creation process, from inputs to outputs to outcomes to impact.

Investing in Assessment

You get what you pay for. A weak investment will lead to weak returns. One should be pragmatic, of course, about the level of evaluation that is financially feasible, but managerially meaningful results require a meaningful investment of resources. The natural and important inclination is to measure the benefits to the partnering organizations, but the most fundamental and neglected question that partners should attempt to answer is "Are we co-creating meaningful value for society?"

6. Seeking Partners Who Fit

A foundational block for a strong partnership is achieving a solid fit between the partners along multiple dimensions. Four dimensions of fit are particularly critical: (1) between *resource complementarity* and *linked interests*; (2) between *purpose* and *goals*; (3) between *strategy* and *structure*; and (4) between *values* and *culture*.

Fit between Resource Complementarity and Linked interests

An essential starting point for powerful co-creation of value is a solid fit between partners' value sources, particularly the complementarity of the resources that each brings to the alliance and the strength of the linkages between their mutual interests.

Each partner needs to assess what necessary resources the other partner has, and the extent to which its own strengths and weaknesses are complemented by the other. Given these sets of resources, each partner should be asking, "How can I create value for my partner, and vice versa?" A more powerful question for the partners to ask is "How can we combine our core capabilities to co-generate value?" Integral to answering those questions is an understanding of how each organization's interests (and those of its stakeholders) are linked. Structuring the collaboration to optimize mutual benefits will contribute to sustainability and longevity. Partners' resources and interests change over time. Consequently, there is a need for periodic reassessment of the prevailing fit and of the underlying value-creation dynamics. The respective value propositions will need to be adjusted and renewed to ensure productive compatibility. To the extent that these shared interests also encompass producing societal benefits, the external impact of the partnership will be even greater. The challenge is not just how to be better off but also how to make the world a better place.

Fit between Purpose and Goals

There is wide recognition of the importance of having clarity of partnering purpose. Jointly establishing explicit goals for the alliance is essential for clarity, motivation, and evaluation. Ambiguity of purpose fosters confusion and misunderstanding. Having clear and strong shared goals provides resilience to deal with any subsequent and almost inevitable partner friction. These goals will be stronger and more durable to the extent that they emerge from and are compatible with each partner's own mission. Partners must be able to explain readily to any stakeholder how the alliance contributes to the attainment of their respective missions. Without such mission fit, the alliance is unlikely to move beyond being of tactical importance and on to being of strategic importance. This argues for each partner's having explicit objectives that it hopes to achieve through the partnership for its own organization; because these objectives will be different for each partner, they should be communicated to ensure clarity of expectations. To add value to a partner, one should know what the partner values. But there are also shared goals for the collaboration. These should include goals having to do with the hoped-for impact on the social problem being addressed. This requires shared understanding of and agreement on the nature of the problem and how the joint effort can contribute toward its solution. Businesses usually have less understanding of the complexities of social problems, and so a nonprofit partner's experience and knowledge can serve as a compensating strength. But co-creation requires joint understanding. The deeper the mutual comprehension of the problem, the greater the possibility of a clearer vision and more imaginative approaches. The partners should assess the resource-problem fit, that is, the adequacy of their individual and combined resources to achieve a meaningful impact on the problem they wish to address. Being realistic about what is feasible helps avoid the frustration of false expectations.

Fit between Strategy and Structure

Strong alliances achieve strategic fit. Understanding your partner's strategy is important in order to understand how the collaboration fits into it. If you do not take the time to study and comprehend your partner's strategy, you will be unable to shape the strategy for the alliance so that it adds the greatest strategic value to each partner. This requires each partner to learn from the other about its strategy and operations, both at the early stage and continually at later stages. The alliance strategy emerges from this mutual understanding and provides guidance for the most powerful combination of resources so as to attain the shared goals and ensure fit between the partners' respective organizational strategies.

As Chandler's pioneering research reveals, structure follows strategy.[1] Consequently, the collaboration strategy should guide the way the alliance is structured, but underlying this is the issue of the fit between the partners' respective organizational structures. There is, of course, no one correct alliance structure or optimum fit. Rather, each partner's different organizational characteristics, such as those involving hierarchical structures and centralization of decision making, will entail pros and cons for the other partner, depending on the goals of the collaboration and the nature of each partner's organization. Experimentation and adaptation during implementation can achieve organizational fit.

Fit between Values and Culture

A strong partnership is characterized by congruence of values and compatibility of cultures. Such alignment is not readily available. The literature abounds with examples of how the many differences between businesses and nonprofits can constitute barriers to their entering into a partnership. Crossing from one sector into the other is akin to crossing the border of a foreign country and encountering a different language, strange customs, puzzling values, and distinct behavior. But such obstacles are surmountable. One imperative is studying, understanding, respecting, and appreciating the partner's cultural values and comportment. Therefore, fit emerges as this process of comprehension unfolds through collaborative interaction. It is important to remember that differences may seem like impediments but are also a fundamental source of value. Partnering with an identical twin is just more of the same. Complementarity requires diversity. Therefore, we value differences. Screening aims to catch fundamental incompatibilities that are not amenable to adjustment.

7. Bonding

In strong and enduring alliances the partners develop deep bonds. There appear to be four stages in this bonding process: (1) understanding, (2) empathy, (3) emotional connection, and (4) commitment.

Understanding

As mentioned earlier, a prerequisite of achieving fit is understanding your partner. This is seldom instantaneous. Taking the time to get to know your partner well is a good investment. As in most other significant relationships, this entails an ongoing discovery process. The more you interact, the more you discover. It is important to go beyond the narrow boundaries of the specific collaboration activities to understand the partner's other dimensions and practices. Part of this exploration involves understanding differences, why they exist, and how they might serve to build a stronger collaboration.

Empathy

Out of understanding can emerge empathy. You need to break down stereotypes and gain respect for the things your partner does and how your partner does those things. Empathy fosters reciprocity; respect begets respect. In this stage, you begin to identify with your partner and are able to put yourself in your partner's shoes. Being empathetic also sharpens your ability to understand how your partner sees and reacts to you.

Emotional Connection

Two critical forces feed the powerful pool of the partners' emotions. The first is *interpersonal chemistry*. Understanding and empathy foster positive relationships. The quality of the relationships between individuals from the different partner organizations can be a significant determinant of the alliance's effectiveness. If people click, collaboration can flourish. If the chemistry is bad, collaboration can curdle. Consequently, considerable care must be given to choosing the key people who will be managing the interface, and to creating opportunities for them to develop positive relationships. In the course of an ongoing alliance, key individuals inevitably get shifted to other positions or may even leave their organizations. The act of choosing their replacements takes place at a critical juncture, and you would be wise to engage your partner in some prescreening of the candidates to ensure compatibility. Strong relational bonds serve as shock absorbers and risk managers. They enable the partners to work together more effectively in dealing with the unexpected problems and opportunities that will arise. The second force feeding emotional connection grows out of the *social cause* toward which the collaboration is directed. Deep, shared belief in the importance of the cause is a powerful source of energy. This intrinsic motivation transcends the value calculus of the individual partnering organizations and is a primary driver in alliances that have entered the transformational stage.

Commitment

The glue of bonding is commitment. Top leadership must be committed to the collaboration if it is to be strategic. Furthermore, if the collaboration is to be transformative, the leaders must nurture and multiply commitment by motivating, empowering, and enabling individuals throughout the organization. Commitment is institutionalized when appropriate incentive structures are established and when collaborative value-creating behavior continues after the initial champions have moved on. The mindset transformation has evolved from "us and them" to "us." Leadership may change, but organizational integration remains. It is vital for there to be congruence of commitment between the partners. Lopsidedness in the area of commitment leads to an unbalanced, unsustainable alliance. You must start building commitment early in the relationship, since what you are seeking is the long-term commitment essential to transformational change.

8. Governing and Organizing

Collaborative alliances are a form of social enterprise requiring thoughtful governance and careful organization in three areas: (1) *roles and responsibilities,* (2) *planning and decision making,* and (3) *conflict and power management.* According to Bryson, Crosby, and Middleton Stone, "the leadership challenge in cross-sector collaboration may . . . be viewed as the challenge of aligning initial conditions, structures, processes, outcomes and accountabilities such that good things happen in a sustained way over time—indeed, so that public value can be created."[2]

Roles and Responsibilities

Just as it is vital to have clarity of purpose, it is also important to be clear about what roles each partner will play and what each will assume responsibility for. Formulating an explicit agreement together about who will be accountable for what eliminates recriminations due to vagueness. For those roles and responsibilities that are joint, it is important to set ground rules about how the coordinated efforts will be carried out. Reaching such agreements does not mean that roles and responsibilities are static. Processes are both intentional and emergent. They require iterative recalibration as the relationship progresses and as internal and external situations change. These adjustments become more significant contributors to the co-creation of value as they progress from reactive to proactive to adaptive to transformative.

To ensure effective stewardship of the responsibilities and the realization of this maturing process of creative adjustment, it is important to have managers of the collaboration relationship. They need to be highly and broadly respected individuals within their organizations. Furthermore, they need to be endowed with sufficient authority and ability to mobilize and manage the resources, actions, and interactions that are required to perform the designated roles and fulfill the assigned responsibilities.

Planning and Decision Making

As strategic social alliances progress from philanthropic to transactional to integrative to transformational relationships, they become increasingly complex and require ever more careful planning in terms of both design and operation. Nevertheless, the dynamic and organic nature of collaboration means that part of the planning will be emergent as conditions dictate new paths. The decision making involved in planning and operating an alliance needs to be shared and participatory. Clarity about the scope of decision-making authority is important so that the partners will not unknowingly and unduly infringe on each other's separate organizational realms. The degree of collaborative governance is significantly shaped by the amount of decision-making discretion given to each partner. It can be quite beneficial to create multiple mechanisms for engagement and interaction among a broad range of the employees of both partners, as well as for engagement and interaction among a broad range of the partners' external stakeholders. These mechanisms increase the pool of collective knowledge and the opportunities for discovering distinct capabilities and innovative collaborative combinations. Furthermore, fostering that kind of participation promotes the bonding process.

Conflict and Power Management

Conflict is both inevitable and desirable in collaborations. Conflict avoidance can be counterproductive. Disagreements represent potential opportunities for collaborative learning and advancement. The key to a productive outcome lies in how the disagreements are managed. Expecting problems, and being open to jointly finding solutions, will reduce emotional intensity and foster constructive solutions. This requires openness to different points of view and willingness to air conflicts. The supporting mindset aims to build bridges of understanding between the areas of disagreement. A power imbalance between the two partners, either on the side of the business or on the side of the nonprofit, is one source of potential conflict. But conflict may arise for many reasons as well, such as differences in resources, size, and prestige. At the same time, the existence of such differences does not automatically cause conflict. The elephant and the mouse can live happily ever after, but they do need to be careful where they step.[3] The governance of the collaboration should aim to create equal footing and find ways to capture power-based synergies that increase interdependence so as to ensure mutual influence in the decision-making processes.

9. Communicating

Communication lubricates the collaboration machinery. Its quality fundamentally shapes the bonding, governing, and organizing processes, which in turn can also enable or stifle communication. For example, weak bonds or hierarchical relationships can hinder communication, and vice versa. There are three key communication categories: *interorganizational communication, internal communication,* and *external communication.*

Interorganizational Communication

The first and most critical category of communication is communication between the partner organizations. It should be characterized by clarity, honesty, constructiveness, respect, and caring. One of its key functions is to create a distinct and stable identity for the partnership.[4] As for frequency, more is better.

Internal Communication

Each partner needs to communicate to its internal organization about the importance and evolution of the alliance, to ensure comprehension and commitment.

External Communication

The partners need to communicate and engage with their respective external constituencies. For external audiences, the partners need to agree on content and joint communications, to ensure that there is consistency of message. Partners should formulate a communications strategy that deals with content, audiences, form, and timing. To be a good communicator, one should also be a good listener. Empathetic, active listening fosters openness.

10. Building Trust

Trust is earned, not given. It is an output of the actions and interactions of the partners. But once created it in turn becomes an input into the partnership processes. Communication builds trust, as Bruce Burtch has emphasized:

> Effective communication is the platform upon which trust and a strong relationship are built. Your communication should be open, honest, and regular. When challenges arise, you must address them immediately, coming from the position of "What can we do to solve this challenge in such a way that will strengthen the partnership and further our goals?" Your partners, and your own organization, will appreciate your being frank and reacting in a timely way. Indeed, working through such challenges will strengthen the trust among all participants, and prepare you for when future challenges arise.[5]

Trust is one of the most valuable intangible assets of a partnership. You build it continuously by keeping your word by doing what you said you were going to do. Dependability is an early building block. Sharing proprietary information, expertise, knowledge, and relationships adds more blocks. Having confidentiality agreements reduces risk and fosters greater openness. Ensuring that your partner is receiving a fair share of the collaboration's co-created value motivates your partner's greater willingness to increase investments and assume greater risks.

11. Learning

The most vibrant partnerships thrive on continuous collaborative learning. There is an ongoing search, individually and jointly, on two fronts.

Collaborating on Processes

First, the partners must learn how to work and learn together more effectively; that is, they must learn how to push the organizational and operational processes and frontiers outward to create an even more powerful collaboration.

Maximizing Value

Second, the partners must learn how to co-generate even greater value at the individual, organizational, and societal levels. Both partners must be willing to change. As joint solutions to problems are found, the partners must be receptive to expeditiously integrating adaptations into their respective organizations and into their ways of working together. There must be a process of converting new information into knowledge and then creatively generating innovations.

12. Transforming

Collaborations generate multiple types of value at multiple levels, but in their most powerful form they produce transformative effects on societal problems and on partnering organizations. To achieve this aspirational level, one needs to integrate the preceding eleven smart collaborative practices. The scope of collaboration broadens into multiparty, multisector collaborative networks. Priority is placed on system-altering innovation that is life-changing. Resource synergism is leveraged to the maximum. Significant internal organizational changes emerge to enable these transformative processes and outcomes. Value focus is on the societal level; derivative benefits accrue at all other levels. The world is changed for the better.

Toward the Future

This will be the collaboration century. Cross-sector collaboration is experiencing an accelerating upward trajectory. More firms and nonprofits are collaborating, and they are generating more value. Yet the potential exists for even greater collaborative value creation for the partnering organizations and their people, but also for co-creating innovative and transformative solutions to a multitude of major societal problems. It is our hope that this book will contribute to the realization of that critical collective aspiration.

Questions for Reflection

1. Summarize your partnerships by using the twelve smart practices outlined in this chapter to identify the main lessons of your cross-sector collaborations.
2. *A successful partnership needs to make sense at the individual level.* Explain this statement by employing the most relevant elements of the twelve smart practices.
3. In a partnership relationship, what are the roles of the different types of communication (intercommunication, internal communication, and external communication)?
4. What contribution does the Collaborative Value Creation Framework make to facilitating the systematic analysis of value creation?
5. How has the Collaborative Value Creation Framework affected your conceptualization of collaboration and value creation?

Notes

Preface
1. Austin, 2000d.
2. Austin, 2000b.
3. Austin and Seitanidi, 2012a; Austin and Seitanidi, 2012b.
4. Handy, Brudney, and Meijs, 2012, p. 721.

Chapter One
1. Partnerships Resource Centre, 2011, p. 5.
2. Lacy, Cooper, Hayward, and Neuberger, 2010, p. 11.
3. C&E Advisory, 2010.
4. Burtch, 2012.
5. BISC—Benchmarking do Investimento Social Corporativo, 2012, pp. 43–49, 66–67.
6. Austin, Reficco, Berger, Fischer, Gutierrez, Koljatic, Lozano, Ogliastri, and the Social Enterprise Knowledge Network (SEKN) Team, 2004.
7. Den Hond, De Bakker, and Doh, forthcoming.
8. Austin, 2000b; Margolis and Walsh, 2003; Berger, Cunningham, and Drumwright, 2004; Austin, Reficco, Berger, Fischer, Gutierrez, Koljatic, Lozano, Ogliastri, and the Social Enterprise Knowledge Network (SEKN) Team, 2004; Selsky and Parker, 2005; Åhlström and Sjöström, 2005; Galaskiewicz and Sinclair Colman, 2006; Googins, Mirvis, and Rochlin, 2007; Biermann, Chan, Mert, and Pattberg, 2007; Seitanidi, 2010; Kourula and Laasonen, 2010; Kanter, 2011; Porter and Kramer, 2011; London and Hart, 2011.
9. Oppenheim, Bonini, Bielak, Kehm, and Lacy, 2007, p. 6.
10. United Nations General Assembly, 2001.
11. Austin and Seitanidi, 2012a; Austin and Seitanidi, 2012b.
12. Austin and Seitanidi, 2012a.
13. Austin and Seitanidi, 2012a, p. 728.
14. Elkington, 1997.
15. Emerson, 2003.
16. Porter and Kramer, 2011.

17. Rackham, Friedman, and Ruff, 1996.
18. Bryson, Crosby, and Middleton Stone, 2006; Cooper, Bryer, and Meek, 2006; Milne, Iyer, and Gooding-Williams, 1996; Selsky and Parker, 2005; Warner and Sullivan, 2004.

Chapter Two
1. Jamali and Keshishian, 2009.
2. Eweje and Palakshappa, 2009.
3. Austin, 200b.
4. Eweje and Palakshappa, 2009.
5. Austin, 2000b.
6. Pfeiffer and Salancik, 1978; Davis and Cobb, 2010.
7. Cairns and Harris, 2011.
8. De Cooman, De Geiter, Pepermans, and Jegers, 2011; Crane, 2010; Kolk, Van Tulder, and Kostwinder, 2008; Seitanidi and Ryan, 2007; Bryson, Crosby, and Middleton Stone, 2006; Teegen, Doh, and Vachani, 2004; Berger, Cunningham, and Drumwright, 2004; Austin, 2000a; McFarlan, 1999; Di Maggio and Anheier, 1990; Milne, Iyer, and Gooding-Williams, 1996; Crane, 1998; Alsop, 2004; Stafford and Hartman, 2001; Green, Groenewegen, and Hofman, 2001; Shaffer and Hillman, 2000; Westley and Vredenburg, 1997.
9. Le Ber and Branzei, 2010a; Le Ber and Branzei, 2010b.
10. Sagawa and Segal, 2000; Austin and Porraz, 2002.
11. Austin, Reficco, Berger, Fischer, Gutierrez, Koljatic, Lozano, Ogliastri, and the Social Enterprise Knowledge Network (SEKN) Team, 2004.
12. Schiller and Almog-Bar, forthcoming.
13. Holmes and Smart, 2009.
14. Le Ber and Branzei, 2010a.
15. Long and Arnold, 1995.
16. Austin, Reficco, Berger, Fischer, Gutierrez, Koljatic, Lozano, Ogliastri, and the Social Enterprise Knowledge Network (SEKN) Team, 2004.
17. Austin, 2000b.
18. Austin, Reficco, Berger, Fischer, Gutierrez, Koljatic, Lozano, Ogliastri, and the Social Enterprise Knowledge Network (SEKN) Team, 2004.
19. GlobeScan, 2002.
20. Kim, Sung, and Lee, 2011.
21. Kolk, Van Dolen, and Vock, 2010; Bhattacharya, Korschun, and Sen, 2009; Bhattacharya and Sen, 2004; Bhattacharya, Sen, and Korschun, 2008; Bhattacharya, Sen, and Korschun, 2011.

22. Cone Communications, 2002.
23. Cummins, 2004.
24. Conroy, 2007.
25. McDaniel and Malone, 2012.
26. Holmes and Smart, 2009.
27. Bhattacharya, Sen, and Korschun, 2011.
28. Couchman and Fulop, 2009b.
29. Austin, Reficco, Berger, Fischer, Gutierrez, Koljatic, Lozano, Ogliastri, and the Social Enterprise Knowledge Network (SEKN) Team, 2004.
30. Austin, Reficco, Berger, Fischer, Gutierrez, Koljatic, Lozano, Ogliastri, and the Social Enterprise Knowledge Network (SEKN) Team, 2004.
31. Kourula, 2010.
32. Yaziji and Doh, 2009.
33. Jamali, Yianni, and Abdallah, 2011.
34. Holmes and Smart, 2009.
35. Kanter, 1999.
36. Austin and Seitanidi, 2012a.

Chapter Three

1. Bowen, 1953; Carroll, 2006; Rowley and Berman, 2000; Carroll, 1999; Gerde and Wokutch, 1998; Griffin and Mahon, 1997; Aguinis and Glavas, 2012; Matten and Crane, 2005; Elkington, 1999.
2. Elkington, 2004.
3. De Bakker, Groenewegen, and Den Hond, 2005.
4. Garriga and Melé, 2004.
5. Googins, Mirvis, and Rochlin, 2007.
6. Lockett, Moon, and Visser, 2006; Googins, Mirvis, and Rochlin, 2007; Egri and Ralston, 2008.
7. Aguinis and Glavas, 2012, p. 941.
8. Friedman, 1962; Friedman, 1970.
9. Freeman, 1984; Neville and Menguc, 2006; Green and Peloza, 2011.
10. Peter Drucker, quoted in Cohen, 2009, p. 31.
11. Donaldson and Preston, 1995; Jones and Wicks, 1999; Freeman, 1999.
12. Makower, 1994; Burke and Logsdon, 1996; Googins, Mirvis, and Rochlin, 2007.
13. Aguinis and Glavas, 2012.
14. George, 2003.
15. Waddock, 2008.
16. Jensen, 2002.
17. Cotten and Lasprogata, 2012.

18. Barton, 2011, p. 84.
19. Kanter, 2011, p. 71.
20. Jones, 1995; Hill and Jones, 1985.
21. Halal, 2001, p. 28.
22. Margolis and Walsh, 2003, p. 282.
23. Shamir, 2008.
24. Makower, 1994.
25. Wang, Choi, and Li, 2008; Margolis and Walsh, 2003; Emerson, 2003; Walsh, Weber, and Margolis, 2003.
26. Norman and MacDonald, 2004.
27. Orlitzky, Schmidt, and Rynes, 2003.
28. Eccles, Ioannou, and Serafeim, 2012a; Eccles, Ioannou, and Serafeim, 2012b.
29. SAM and PricewaterhouseCoopers, 2010, p. 12.
30. Barnett, 2007, p. 803.
31. Peloza and Papania, 2008.
32. Schuler and Cording, 2006.
33. Ling, Forrest, Fox, and Feilhauer, 2007, p. 7.
34. Barnett, 2007, p. 805.
35. Margolis and Walsh, 2003, pp. 278, 289.
36. Googins, Mirvis, and Rochlin, 2007, p. 22.
37. McKinsey & Company, 2006.
38. Galaskiewicz, 1997; Austin, Reficco, Berger, Fischer, Gutierrez, Koljatic, Lozano, Ogliastri, and the Social Enterprise Knowledge Network (SEKN) Team, 2004; Bansal and Roth, 2000; Goodpaster and Matthews, 1982.
39. Aguilera, Rupp, Williams, and Ganapathi, 2007.
40. Marquis, Glynn, and Davis, 2007.
41. Campbell, 2007.
42. GlobeScan, 2002.
43. Paine, 2003.
44. Peloza, 2009; Peloza and Shang, 2010.
45. Martin, 2002.
46. Porter and Kramer, 2011.
47. Aakhus and Bzdak, 2012.
48. Kanter, 2011, p. 73.
49. Leo Scott, quoted in Schell, 2011, p. 86.
50. Walsh, Weber, and Margolis, 2003.
51. Zadek, 2004.
52. Quelch and Jocz, 2009.
53. Cone Communications, 2010.
54. Fleishman-Hillard/National Consumers League, 2007, p. 7.
55. Oppenheim, Bonini, Bielak, Kehm, and Lacy, 2007.
56. Ling, Forrest, Fox, and Feilhauer, 2007, p. 26.

57. Investor Network on Climate Risk, 2013.
58. http://www.femsa.com/es/social
59. De Beers Family of Companies, 2009, p. 2.
60. Oppenheim, Bonini, Bielak, Kehm, and Lacy, 2007, pp. 17, 21.
61. Kanter, 2009, p. 2.
62. Porter and Kramer, 2011, p. 15.
63. Prahalad, 2005; Prahalad and Hamel, 1990; Prahalad and Hart, 2002; Rangan, Quelch, Herrero, and Barton, 2007; Hammond, Kramer, Katz, Tran, and Walker, 2007.
64. London and Hart, 2011.
65. London and Anupindi, 2012.
66. Ryan, Richardson, and Voutier, 2012.
67. Salamon, 2010, p. 58.
68. World Economic Forum Global Corporate Citizenship Initiative, 2005, p. 4.
69. Slawinski and Bansal, 2012.
70. World Economic Forum Global Corporate Citizenship Initiative, 2005, p. 4.
71. Andrioff and Waddock, 2002, p. 42.
72. Porter and Kramer, 2002.
73. Gosling and Mintzberg, 2003.
74. Den Hond, De Bakker, and Doh, forthcoming.
75. Goldsmith, 2011.
76. Seelos and Mair, 2007.
77. Tormod Hermansen, quoted in Seelos and Mair, 2007, p. 56.
78. Selsky and Parker, 2010.
79. Porter and Kramer, 2011; Austin, 2000a.
80. Kolk, Van Tulder, and Westdijk, 2006.
81. Crane and Matten, 2007; Pearce and Doh, 2005; Heath, 1997; Salamon and Anheier, 1997.
82. Van Tulder and Kolk, 2007.
83. Austin and Reavis, 2002.
84. Le Ber and Branzei, 2010a, p. 163.
85. "Corporate Philanthropy More Strategic, Deloitte Report Reveals," 2011.
86. Porter and Kramer, 2011, p. 4.
87. Polman, 2011.
88. Halal, 2001.
89. Zadek, 2001.
90. Kaku, 1997, p. 55.
91. Márquez, Reficco, and Berger, 2010.
92. Rivera-Santos, Rufin, and Kolk, 2012.
93. Googins, Mirvis, and Rochlin, 2007, p. 8.
94. Business in the Community, 2012.

95. Seitanidi and Crane, 2009.
96. Grant and Crutchfield, 2007, p. 34.
97. Marsden, 2000, p. 9.
98. Kotler and Zaltman, 1971.
99. Kotler and Lee, 2009.
100. Reis, 1999; Thompson, 2008; Boschee and McClurg, 2003.
101. Dees, 1998; Austin, Stevenson, and Wei-Skillern, 2006; Billis, 2010; Bromberger, 2011; Fruchterman, 2011.
102. Austin, Leonard, Reficco, and Wei-Skillern, 2006.
103. Emerson, 2003.
104. Levenson Keohane, 2013.
105. Dees and Anderson, 2003; Glasbergen, Biermann, and Mol, 2007; Crane, 2010; Seitanidi, 2010.
106. Social Enterprise Knowledge Network (SEKN), 2006; Austin, Gutiérrez, Ogliastri, and Reficco, 2007; Seitanidi, 2010; Bulloch, Lacy, and Jurgens, 2011.
107. Grolin, 1998; Waygood and Wehrmeyer, 2003; Rehbein, Waddock, and Graves, 2004; Hendry, 2006; Baur and Schmitz, 2012; Laasonen, Fougere, and Kourula, 2012.
108. MacKay and Munro, 2012.
109. Yaziji, 2004; Yaziji and Doh, 2009; Den Hond, 2010; Ählström and Sjöström, 2005; Stafford, Polonsky, and Hartman, 2000.
110. Taylor and Scharlin, 2004.
111. Oppenheim, Bonini, Bielak, Kehm, and Lacy, 2007, p. 24.
112. Argenti, 2004.
113. John Mackey, quoted in Koehn and Miller, 2007.
114. Mackey and Sisodia, 2013, p. 26.
115. Porter and Kramer, 2006, p. 7.
116. Seelos and Mair, 2007, p. 61.
117. Swartz, 2010, p. 43.
118. Eccles, Newquist, and Schatz, 2007, p. 113.
119. Covey and Brown, 2001.
120. Seitanidi, 2010.
121. Koschmann, Kuhn, and Pfarrer, 2012, p. 340.
122. Yaziji, 2004.
123. Hyatt and Berente, 2011.
124. Arya and Salk, 2006.
125. Conroy, 2007.
126. Hustvedt and Bernard, 2010.
127. Levy, Brown, and de Jong, 2010.
128. Crilly, Zollo, and Hansen, 2012.
129. Haack, Schoeneborn, and Wickert, 2012, p. 837.
130. Heugens, 2003.

131. Joutsenverta, 2011.
132. Visser, 2011, p. 5.
133. Seitanidi, 2010.

Chapter Four

1. Austin, 2000b; Austin, 2000d.
2. Schiller and Almog-Bar, forthcoming; Ross, 2012; Vaschon, 2012; Edmond, Raghavan, and Smith, 2011; Jiang and Cai, 2011; Selsky and Parker, 2010; Le Ber and Branzei, 2010a; Le Ber and Branzei, 2010b; Seitanidi and Lindgreen, 2010; Bowen, Newenham-Kahindi, and Herremans, 2010; Seitanidi, 2010; Kourula and Laasonen, 2010; Jamali and Keshishian, 2009; Peloza and Falkenberg, 2009; Seitanidi and Crane, 2009; Glasbergen, Biermann, and Mol, 2007; Brickson, 2007; Googins, Mirvis, and Rochlin, 2007; Seitanidi and Ryan, 2007; Galaskiewicz and Sinclair Colman, 2006; Selsky and Parker, 2005; Berger, Cunningham, and Drumwright, 2004; Rondinelli and London, 2003; Wymer and Samu, 2003; Margolis and Walsh, 2003.
3. Austin and Seitanidi, 2012a; Bryson, Crosby, and Middleton Stone, 2006; Rondinelli and London, 2003; Bowen, Newenham-Kahindi, and Herremans, 2010; Googins, Mirvis, and Rochlin, 2007; Galaskiewicz and Sinclair Colman, 2006.
4. Perrini, 2006.
5. Lakotos and Candea, 2012.
6. Fuller and Tian, 2006.
7. Giving USA Foundation, 2012.
8. Sonia de Avelar, 2002, quoted in Sanborn and Portocarrero, 2005, p. 3.
9. *2004 Deloitte Volunteer IMPACT Survey*, 2004.
10. Godfrey, Merrill, and Hansen, 2009.
11. Galaskiewicz and Wasserman, 1989.
12. Oppenheim, Bonini, Bielak, Kehm, and Lacy, 2007, p. 8.
13. Opinion Leader Research, 2005, p. 3.
14. Nelson and Prescott, 2005, p. 26.
15. "Global RepTrak® Pulse Complimentary Reports—2011," 2011.
16. Ross, 2012, p. 84.
17. Austin, 1998c, p. 42.
18. Porter and Kramer, 2002; Sagawa and Segal, 2000.
19. Nelson and Prescott, 2005, p. 26.
20. "Coca-Cola Aids in Mexico's Reforestation," 2009.
21. Porter and Kramer, 2002.
22. Chênevert and Bonini, 2008, p. 9.
23. Nelson and Prescott, 2005, p. 14.
24. Galaskiewicz and Sinclair Colman, 2006.
25. Austin, 2006.

26. "Health Authorities Plan and Pledge to Overcome River Blindness," 1997.
27. George W. Merck Jr., quoted in Weber, Austin, and Barrett, 2001a, p. 1.
28. Austin, 2000b, pp. 173–175.
29. Committee Encouraging Corporate Philanthropy, 2012, p. 4.
30. Seitanidi, 2009.
31. Lim, 2010.
32. Points of Light Foundation, 2007.
33. Preston, 2011.
34. Sagawa and Segal, 2000, p. 58.
35. Goodwill NCW, 2005.
36. "Corporate Philanthropy More Strategic, Deloitte Report Reveals," 2011.
37. Fleishman-Hillard/National Consumers League, 2007, p. 4.
38. "Avon Foundation for Women Announces Avon Walk for Breast Cancer's 10th Birthday Season," 2011.
39. Sagawa and Segal, 2000, pp. 48–56.
40. Porter and Kramer, 2002, p. 6.
41. Beta San Miguel and Colegio San Ignacio de Loyola Vizcaínas, 2008.
42. Liu and Ko, 2011.
43. Alex Gourlay, quoted in Business in the Community, 2012.
44. Lim, 2010.
45. Cone Communications, 2010.
46. Parceiros Voluntários, 2011, p. 17.
47. Allen, Galiano, and Hayes, 2011, p. 7.
48. Kramer, 2009.
49. Conference Board, 1993.
50. Cone Communications, 2010.
51. Steckel and Simons, 1992, p. 25.
52. Bartel, 2001; Jones, 2006; Sagawa and Segal, 2000; Aguinis and Glavas, 2012.
53. Points of Light Foundation, 2007.
54. CDC Development Solutions, 2011.
55. Austin, 1998c, p. 39.
56. Bonini, Koller, and Mirvis, 2009.
57. Kanter, 1999; Vian, Feeley, MacLeod, Richards, and McCoy, 2007.
58. Grant, 2012.
59. Austin, 1998c.
60. Epstein and McFarlan, 2011; McFarlan, 1999; Korngold, 2005.
61. Austin, 1998a, p. 47.
62. Austin, Leonard, and Quinn, 2004, p. 4.
63. Cone Communications, 2010, p. 20.
64. Frisk, 2012.

65. Tariq and Tenneyson, 2009.
66. Austin, 1998c, p. 41.
67. Austin, 1998c, p. 39.
68. Cone Communications, 2010, p. 4.
69. Cone Communications, 2010, p. 5.
70. *Edelman goodpurpose® Study*, 2012.
71. Gourville and Rangan, 2004, p. 56.
72. Andreasen, 1996.
73. Gray and Hall, 1998; "Proving That Cause Marketing Is a Win-Win," 2010.
74. Hiscox and Smyth, 2008.
75. Austin, 2000d.
76. "Race for the Cure National Sponsors," 2013.
77. Seitanidi and Ryan, 2007; Galaskiewicz and Sinclair Colman, 2006, pp. 191–193.
78. Ukman, 2012.
79. Chansky, 2010.
80. Ukman, 2012.
81. Conroy, 2007.
82. Yaziji, 2004.
83. Arya and Salk, 2006.
84. Watanatada and Mak, 2011.
85. Nelson and Prescott, 2005, p. 27.
86. Maon, Lindgreen, and Vanhamme, 2009.
87. Peter F. Drucker Foundation for Nonprofit Management, 2002, p. 61.
88. "McDonald's and Environmental Defense Fund Celebrate 20 Years of Partnerships for Sustainability," 2010.
89. "McDonald's and Environmental Defense Fund Mark 20 Years of Partnerships for Sustainability," 2010.
90. Couchman and Fulop, 2009a.
91. "McDonald's and Environmental Defense Fund Mark 20 Years of Partnerships for Sustainability," 2010.
92. "Proving That Cause Marketing Is a Win-Win," 2010.
93. Sagawa and Segal, 2000, pp. 117–120.
94. "Kraft American Cheese Teams Up," 2012.
95. Cone Communications, 2010.
96. "Walmart Giving in Last Fiscal Year Exceeds $1 Billion for the First Time," 2013.
97. Gourville and Rangan, 2004, p. 49.
98. Haddad and Nanda, 2001; Bartling, 1998, p. 12; "Broken Deal Costs AMA $9.9 Million," 1998.
99. "KFC Presents," 2010.
100. Schwartz, 2010.

101. "Save Lids to Save Lives," 2012.
102. Cone Communications, 2010.
103. Grau and Folse, 2007.
104. Austin, Reficco, Berger, Fischer, Gutierrez, Koljatic, Lozano, Ogliastri, and the Social Enterprise Knowledge Network (SEKN) Team, 2004, p. 38.
105. Austin, Reficco, Berger, Fischer, Gutierrez, Koljatic, Lozano, Ogliastri, and the Social Enterprise Knowledge Network (SEKN) Team, 2004, p. 134.
106. Austin, Reficco, Berger, Fischer, Gutierrez, Koljatic, Lozano, Ogliastri, and the Social Enterprise Knowledge Network (SEKN) Team, 2004, p. 138.
107. Austin, Reficco, Berger, Fischer, Gutierrez, Koljatic, Lozano, Ogliastri, and the Social Enterprise Knowledge Network (SEKN) Team, 2004, p. 167.
108. Cone Communications, 2010.
109. Neff, 2011.
110. Zwick, Bonsu, and Darmody, 2008; Prahalad and Ramaswamy, 2004.
111. Keller, 1993.
112. Doyle, 2000.
113. Quelch, Austin, and Laidler-Kylander, 2004; Quelch and Laidler-Kylander, 2005.
114. Laidler-Kylander, Quelch, and Simonin, 2007.
115. *Edelman goodpurpose® Study*, 2012.
116. Austin, 2000d, p. 97.
117. "Our Story," n.d.
118. Dybul, 2013.
119. Rosenman, 2007.
120. Knoepke, 2011.
121. Austin, 2000d, p. 26.
122. Le Ber and Branzei, 2010b.
123. Austin, 2000d, pp. 26–27.
124. Kanter, 1999, p. 129.
125. Bowen, Newenham-Kahindi, and Herremans, 2010, p. 311.
126. Austin, 2003a.
127. Le Ber and Branzei, 2010a, p. 161.
128. Austin, 2000b, p. 80.
129. Kanter, 1999, p. 130.
130. Rondinelli and London, 2003, p. 72.
131. Brugmann and Prahalad, 2007, p. 83.
132. Drayton and Budinich, 2010.
133. Drayton, 2011.
134. Drayton and Budinich, 2010, p. 58.

135. Googins, Mirvis, and Rochelin, 2007, p. 122.
136. Conservation International and Starbucks, 2011.
137. Conservation International and Starbucks, 2011.
138. Orin Smith, personal interview conducted by James E. Austin, June 10, 2002.
139. Austin and Reavis, 2002, p. 1.
140. Austin and Reavis, 2002, p. 3.
141. Howard Schultz, personal interview conducted by James E. Austin, February 7, 2007.
142. Christopher, 2012.
143. Howard Schultz, personal interview conducted by James E. Austin, February 7, 2007.
144. Austin and Reavis, 2002, p. 9.
145. Austin and Reavis, 2002, p. 9.
146. Howard Schultz, personal interview conducted by James E. Austin, February 7, 2007.
147. Perez-Aleman and Sandilands, 2008.
148. Austin and Reavis, 2002, p. 13.
149. Perez-Aleman and Sandilands, 2008.
150. Prahalad and Hammond, 2002; Prahalad and Hart, 2002.
151. Peter Seligmann, quoted in Austin and Reavis, 2002, p. 12.
152. "Coffee," 2013.
153. Martin and Osberg, 2007.
154. Nelson and Jenkins, 2006.
155. Oppenheim, Bonini, Bielak, Kehm, and Lacy, 2007, p. 6.
156. Selsky and Parker, 2010.
157. Waddock, 1989.
158. Kanter, 2011, pp. 74, 67.
159. Vurro, Dacin, and Perrini, 2010.
160. Mahoney, McGahan, and Pitelis, 2009.
161. Guilherme Peirão Leal, quoted in Salamon, 2010, p. 103.
162. Business in the Community, 2012.
163. Howard Schultz, personal interview conducted by James E. Austin, February 7, 2007.
164. Austin and Reavis, 2002, p. 13.
165. Austin and Reavis, 2002.
166. "Starbucks Coffee Company," 2013.
167. Howard Schultz, personal interview conducted by James E. Austin, February 7, 2007.
168. Howard Schultz, personal interview conducted by James E. Austin, February 7, 2007.
169. Austin, 2000b; Austin and Elias, 2001; Austin, Leonard, and Quinn, 2004.
170. Austin, Leonard, and Quinn, 2004, p. 10.

171. Cikaliuk, 2011, p. 292.
172. Peloza and Falkenberg, 2009, p. 107.
173. Wittneben, Okereke, Banerjee, and Levy, 2012.
174. Kania and Kramer, 2011.
175. Eggers and Macmillan, 2013.
176. Austin, 2000d.
177. General Electric, 2012.
178. Starbucks, 2012.
179. Orin Smith, personal interview conducted by James E. Austin, June 10, 2002.
180. Conroy, 2007.
181. Conroy, 2007.
182. Peloza and Falkenberg, 2009.
183. Kohl Kaufman, 2005.
184. ISEAL Alliance, 2009.
185. Potter, 2006.
186. Austin, 2000d.
187. Austin, 1998b.
188. Nambisan, 2009.
189. Crosby and Bryson, 2010.
190. Weber, Austin, and Barrett, 2001a, p. 1.
191. Balderston, 2012.
192. Yeatman, 2012.
193. Zedlmayer, 2012.
194. Christensen, Baumann, Ruggles, and Sadtler, 2006.
195. Phills, Deiglmeier, and Miller, 2008, p. 38.
196. Pol and Ville, 2009, p. 880.
197. General Electric, 2012.
198. Zadek, 2004.
199. Deiglmeier, 2012.
200. Holmes and Moir, 2007.
201. Bojer, 2008, p. 3.
202. Samuel J. Palmisano, quoted in Corporate Citizenship and Corporate Affairs, IBM Corporation, 2012.
203. Corporate Citizenship and Corporate Affairs, IBM Corporation, 2012.
204. Corporate Citizenship and Corporate Affairs, IBM Corporation, 2012.
205. William Foege, quoted in Weber, Austin, and Barrett, 2001b, p. 2.
206. Ramiah and Reich, 2006.
207. Barrett, Austin, and McCarthy, 2000.
208. Waddell, 2011.
209. Nambisan, 2009.
210. Nambisan, 2009.

211. Patricia Hoven, quoted in Austin, 2000c, p. 49.
212. Brainerd, Campbell, and Davis, 2013.
213. Cozzolino, 2012.

Chapter Five

1. C&E Advisory, 2010.
2. Austin and Seitanidi, 2012a; Austin and Seitanidi, 2012b.
3. McCann, 1983; Gray, 1989; Bryson, Crosby, and Middleton Stone, 2006.
4. Mintzberg, 1978.
5. Brest, 2012; Seitanidi, 2010.
6. Mintzberg, 1978.
7. Vurro, Dacin, and Perrini, 2010; McCann, 1983; Gray, 1989; Seitanidi and Ryan, 2007.
8. Selsky and Parker, 2005.
9. Bryson, Crosby, and Middleton Stone, 2006.
10. McCann, 1983; Gray, 1989.
11. Waddock, 1989.
12. Waddell and Brown, 1997.
13. McCann, 1983; Gray, 1989; Waddock, 1989.
14. McCann, 1983.
15. Clarke and Fuller, 2010; Waddell and Brown, 1997; Seitanidi, Koufopoulos, and Palmer, 2010; Seitanidi and Crane, 2009; Seitanidi, 2010.
16. Vurro, Dacin, and Perrini, 2010.
17. Bryson, Crosby, and Middleton Stone, 2006.
18. Bryson, Crosby, and Middleton Stone, 2006, p. 51.
19. Berger, Cunningham, and Drumwright, 2004; Jamali and Keshishian, 2009.
20. C&E Advisory, 2010.
21. Austin, 2000b; Jamali and Keshishian, 2009.
22. Seitanidi, 2010.
23. Seitanidi, Koufopoulos, and Palmer, 2010.
24. Berger, Cunningham, and Drumwright, 2004; Gourville and Rangan, 2004; Austin and Seitanidi, 2012b.
25. Seitanidi, Koufopoulos, and Palmer, 2010.
26. Seitanidi, Koufopoulos, and Palmer, 2010.
27. Austin, 2000b; Austin and Seitanidi, 2012a; Austin and Seitanidi, 2012b.
28. Austin and Seitanidi, 2012a.
29. McCann, 1983.
30. Gray, 1989.
31. McCann, 1983; Gray, 1989.
32. Austin and Seitanidi, 2012b.
33. Lubbers, 2002, p. 38.

34. Lubbers, 2002.
35. Seitanidi, 2010.
36. Lubbers, 2002, p. 27.
37. Browne, 1997.
38. Seitanidi, 2010.
39. Austin, 2000b.
40. Gourville and Rangan, 2004.
41. Baur and Palazzo, 2011.
42. Berger, Cunningham, and Drumwright, 2004; Gourville and Rangan, 2004.
43. Berger, Cunningham, and Drumwright, 2004.
44. http://www.earthwatch.org/europe/aboutus/our_mission
45. Seitanidi, 2010.
46. Hardy, Phillips, and Lawrence, 2003.
47. Barnett, 2007.
48. Seitanidi, Koufopoulos, and Palmer, 2010.
49. Brickson, 2007; Plowman, Baker, Kulkarni, Solansky, and Travis, 2007.
50. Bryson, Crosby, and Middleton Stone, 2006.
51. Jones, Hesterly, and Borgatti, 1997; Ring and Van de Ven, 1994.
52. Seitanidi, Koufopoulos, and Palmer, 2010.
53. Goffman, 1983; Seitanidi, Koufopoulos, and Palmer, 2010.
54. Seitanidi, 2010.
55. Seitanidi, 2010.
56. Austin, 2000b.
57. Nestlé, 2011.
58. Hewlett-Packard Company, 2011, p. 157.
59. Sakarya, Bodur, Yildirim-Öktem, and Selekler-Göksen, 2012.
60. Tully, 2004.
61. Heap, 1998; Alsop, 2004.
62. Milne, Iyer, and Gooding-Williams, 1996.
63. Greenall and Rovere, 1999; Heap, 1998.
64. Gourville and Rangan, 2004.
65. Heap, 1998; Seitanidi, 2010.
66. Andrioff, 2000; Andrioff and Waddock, 2002; Heap, 1998.
67. Tran, 2005.
68. Austin, 2000b; Austin, 2000d; Austin, 2003b; Austin and Seitanidi, 2012a.
69. Austin and Seitanidi, 2012a; Austin and Seitanidi, 2012b.
70. Austin and Seitanidi, 2012a; Austin and Seitanidi, 2012b.
71. Austin, 2003b.
72. Austin, 2003b.
73. Ryan, Richardson, and Voutier, 2012.

74. Muthuri, 2007.
75. Austin, 2003b.
76. Bockstette and Stamp, 2011.
77. Nestlé, 2011.
78. Muthuri, 2007.
79. Rondinelli and London, 2003; Alsop, 2004.
80. Weiser, Kahane, Rochlin, and Landis, 2006, p. 6.
81. Weiss, Anderson, and Lasker, 2002.
82. Winchester, 2014.
83. Seitanidi and Crane, 2009.
84. Seitanidi, 2010; Gray, 1989.
85. Holmberg and Cummings, 2009.
86. Huxham, 1996.
87. Simonin, 1997; Austin, 2000b; Gray, 1989; Rondinelli and London, 2003.
88. Draulans, deMan, and Volberda, 2003.
89. Kumar and Nti, 1998.
90. Rondinelli and London, 2003; Seitanidi, 2010.
91. Harbison and Pekar, 1998.
92. Pangarkar, 2003.
93. Austin and Seitanidi, 2012a; Austin and Seitanidi, 2012b.
94. Clarke and Fuller, 2010.
95. Le Ber and Branzei, 2010b.
96. Austin, 2010.
97. Crane, 2010.
98. Seitanidi and Crane, forthcoming.
99. Austin and Reavis, 2002.
100. Seitanidi, Koufopoulos, and Palmer, 2010; Berger, Cunningham, and Drumwright, 2004.
101. Berger, Cunningham, and Drumwright, 2004.
102. Seitanidi, Koufopoulos, and Palmer, 2010.
103. Austin and Reavis, 2002.
104. Seitanidi, 2010.
105. Holmberg and Cummings, 2009; Seitanidi and Crane, 2009; Seitanidi, 2010.
106. Crane, 2010; Kolk, Van Tulder, and Kostwinder, 2008; Seitanidi and Ryan, 2007; Teegen, Doh, and Vachani, 2004; Berger, Cunningham, and Drumwright, 2004; Austin, 2000b; Austin, 2000d.
107. McFarlan, 1999.
108. Di Maggio and Anheier, 1990; Milne, Iyer, and Gooding-Williams, 1996; Crane, 1998; Alsop, 2004.
109. Heap, 1998; Stafford and Hartman, 2001; Green, Groenewegen, and Hofman, 2001.

110. Shaffer and Hillman, 2000; Westley and Vredenburg, 1997.

111. Berger, Cunningham, and Drumwright, 2004.

112. Berger, Cunningham, and Drumwright, 2004.

113. Berger, Cunningham, and Drumwright, 2004.

114. Berger, Cunningham, and Drumwright, 2004.

115. http://www.legislation.gov.uk/ukpga/2012/3/enacted

116. Seitanidi, 2010; Seitanidi and Crane, 2009.

117. Seitanidi, 2010; Seitanidi and Crane, 2009.

118. Selsky and Parker, 2005; Tully, 2004; Warner and Sullivan, 2004; Wymer and Samu, 2003; Bendell, 2000; Heap, 2000; Andrioff and Waddock, 2002; Heap, 1998; Le Ber and Branzei, 2010a.

119. Seitanidi, 2010; Le Ber and Branzei, 2010a; Andrioff and Waddock, 2002.

120. Le Ber and Branzei, 2010c.

121. Seitanidi and Crane, 2009.

122. Hamann and Acutt, 2003.

123. Austin and Reavis, 2002.

124. Austin and Reavis, 2002.

125. C&E Advisory, 2010.

126. Clarke and Fuller, 2010.

127. World Economic Forum Global Corporate Citizenship Initiative, 2005, p. 5.

128. World Economic Forum Global Corporate Citizenship Initiative, 2005, p. 17.

129. Godfrey and Hatch, 2007; Clarke, 2007a; Clarke, 2007b; Waddock, 1989.

130. Selsky and Parker, 2005.

131. Seitanidi and Crane, 2009.

132. Seitanidi, 2010; Seitanidi and Crane, 2009.

133. Clarke and Fuller, 2010; Hood, Logsdon, and Thompson, 1993; Dalal-Clayton and Bass, 2002.

134. Bryson, Crosby, and Middleton Stone, 2006; Berger, Cunningham, and Drumwright, 2004; Googins and Rochlin, 2000; Wilson and Charlton, 1993; Westley and Vredenburg, 1997; McCann, 1983.

135. Vurro, Dacin, and Perrini, 2010.

136. Pressman and Wildavsky, 1973.

137. Seitanidi and Crane, 2009.

138. Clarke and Fuller, 2010.

139. Gray, 1989; Barr and Huxham, 1996.

140. Gray, 1989; Barr and Huxham, 1996.

141. Gray, 1989.

142. Glasbergen, 2007; Arya and Salk, 2006; Bryson, Crosby, and Middleton Stone, 2006; Andreasen, 1996; Halal, 2001; Austin, 2000d; Googins and Rochlin, 2000.
143. Das and Teng, 1998; Gray, 1989.
144. Seitanidi and Crane, 2009.
145. Austin, 2000b; Waddock, 1986.
146. Berger, Cunningham, and Drumwright, 2004; McCann, 1983.
147. Seitanidi and Crane, 2009; Austin and Reavis, 2002.
148. Clarke and Fuller, 2010; Bowen, Newenham-Kahindi, and Herremans, 2010; Bryson, Crosby, and Middleton Stone, 2006.
149. Andreasen, 1996, pp. 47–50, 55–59.
150. Seitanidi, 2008; Bryson, Crosby, and Middleton Stone, 2006; Selsky and Parker, 2005; Brinkerhoff, 2002; Milne, Iyer, and Gooding-Williams, 1996.
151. Kroeger, 2012.
152. McCarter, Mahoney, and Northcraft, 2011.
153. Business in the Community, 2012.
154. Austin and Reavis, 2002, p. 10.
155. Seitanidi, 2010; Seitanidi and Crane, 2009.
156. Seitanidi, 2008.
157. Murphy, Perrot, and Rivera-Santos, 2012.
158. Le Ber and Branzei, 2010a.
159. Le Ber and Branzei, 2010a.
160. Stadtler, 2011, p. 99.
161. Business in the Community, 2012.
162. Austin, 2000b.
163. Seitanidi and Crane, 2009.
164. Das and Teng, 1998.
165. Orlitzky, Schmidt, and Rynes, 2003.
166. Waddock, 1991.
167. Harris and Crane, 2002.
168. Harris and Crane, 2002.
169. Arya and Salk, 2006.
170. Wilkof, Brown, and Selsky, 1995.
171. Bhattacharya, Sen, and Korschun, 2008; Berger, Cunningham, and Drumwright, 2004; Andreasen, 1996.
172. Austin, 2000b; Googins and Rochlin, 2000.
173. Austin, 2000b; Googins and Rochlin, 2000.
174. Bowen, Newenham-Kahindi, and Herremans, 2010; Senge, Dow, and Neath, 2006; Austin, 2000b; Rondinelli and London, 2003.
175. Seitanidi, 2010; Gray, 1989.
176. Elkington and Fennell, 2000.

177. Hunter, 2013.
178. Seitanidi and Crane, 2009.
179. Seitanidi, 2010; Seitanidi and Crane, 2009.
180. Kroeger, 2012.
181. Eng, Liu, and Sekhorn, 2012.
182. Le Ber and Branzei, 2010c; Kaplan, 2008.
183. Noy, 2009.
184. Le Ber and Branzei, 2010a.
185. Le Ber and Branzei, 2010a.
186. Wiltbank, Dew, Read, and Sarasvathy, 2006, p. 983.
187. Kaplan, 2008.
188. Balogun and Johnson, 2004.
189. Croteau and Hicks, 2003; Kaplan and Murray, 2010.
190. Le Ber and Branzei, 2010c.
191. Crane, 1998; Dalal-Clayton and Bass, 2002.
192. Stafford, Polonsky, and Hartman, 2000.
193. Stafford and Hartman, 2001.
194. Rondinelli and London, 2003; Austin, 2000b.
195. Gray, 1989.
196. Kaplan 2008, p. 744.
197. Hamann, Pienaar, Boulogne, and Kranz, 2011.
198. Seitanidi, 2010; Le Ber and Branzei, 2010c; Heap, 2000.
199. Utting, 2005; Tully, 2004; Millar, Choi, and Chen, 2004; Hamann and Acutt, 2003.
200. Kaplan, 2008.
201. Seitanidi and Lindgreen, 2010.
202. Le Ber and Branzei, 2010c.
203. Seitanidi and Crane, 2009.
204. Reed and Reed, 2009.
205. Brown, 1991.
206. Austin, 2000b; Ashman, 2000.
207. Elbers, 2004.
208. Utting, 2005.
209. Seitanidi and Ryan, 2007.
210. Schiller and Almog-Bar, forthcoming.
211. Clarke and Fuller, 2010.
212. Newell, 2002.
213. Collier and Esteban, 1999; Heuer, 2011.
214. Gray, 1989; Murphy and Arenas, 2010.
215. Cornelious and Wallace, 2010; Fiol, Pratt, and O'Connor, 2009; Barrett, Austin, and McCarthy, 2000; Israel, Schulz, Parker, and Becker, 1998.
216. Wei-Skillern, Silver, and Heitz, 2013, p. 2.

217. McDonald and Young, 2012.
218. Sharfman, Gray, and Yan, 1991.

Chapter Six
1. Maas and Liket, 2011.
2. Porter and Kramer, 2006, p. 3.
3. Peloza, 2009.
4. Morariu, Athanasiades, and Emery, 2012, pp. 2, 6.
5. Morino, 2011, p. 4.
6. Campos, Andion, Serva, Rossetto, and Assumpção, 2010, p. 238.
7. Mulgan, 2010, p. 42.
8. Austin and Seitanidi, 2012a.
9. Porter and Kramer, 2011.
10. Porter, Hills, Pfitzer, Patscheke, and Hawkins, 2012, p. 1.
11. Jay, 2013.
12. Austin, 2000b; Elkington and Fennell, 2000; Gourville and Rangan, 2004; Seitanidi, 2010; Austin, 2000d; Googins and Rochlin, 2000; Heap, 1998; Huxham, 1996; Yaziji and Doh, 2009; Waddock and Post, 1995; Warner and Sullivan, 2004; Pearce and Doh, 2005; Alsop, 2004; Greenall and Rovere, 1999; Heugens, 2003; Andreasen, 1996; Bowen, Newenham-Kahindi, and Herremans, 2010.
13. Brown and Kalegaonkar, 2002; Galaskiewicz, 1985; Googins and Rochlin, 2000; Yaziji and Doh, 2009; Vock, Van Dolen, and Kolk, forthcoming; Austin and Seitanidi, 2012a; Austin and Seitanidi, 2012b; Milne, Iyer, and Gooding-Williams, 1996; Porter and Kramer, 2002; Seitanidi, 2010.
14. Austin, 2000d; Googins and Rochlin, 2000; Huxham, 1996; Yaziji and Doh, 2009; Gray, 1989; Hardy, Phillips, and Lawrence, 2003; Porter and Kramer, 2011; Heap, 1998; Millar, Choi, and Chen, 2004; Austin 2000b; Seitanidi, 2010; Vock, Van Dolen, and Kolk, forthcoming; Polonsky and Ryan, 1996; Seitanidi and Lindgreen, 2010; Pearce and Doh, 2005; Crane, 1998; Newell, 2002; Bishop and Green, 2008; Googins and Rochlin, 2000; Porter and Kramer, 2002; Gourville and Rangan, 2004; Kanter, 1999; Bendell, 2000; Das and Teng, 1998; Selsky and Parker, 2005; Tully, 2004; Wymer and Samu, 2003; Le Ber and Branzei, 2010a; Le Ber and Branzei, 2010b; Stafford, Polonsky, and Hartman, 2000.
15. Austin, 2000b; Kanter, 1999; Seitanidi, 2010; Stafford, Polonsky, and Hartman, 2000; Yaziji and Doh, 2009; Tully, 2004; Drucker, 1989; Austin, 2000d; Holmes and Moir, 2007; Glasbergen, 2007; Murphy and Bendell, 1999; Waddock and Post, 1995; Bryson, Crosby, and Middleton Stone, 2006; Le Ber and Branzei, 2010a; Le Ber and Branzei, 2010b; Gourville and Rangan, 2004.

16. Márquez, Reficco, and Berger, 2010, p. 6.
17. Burchell and Cook, 2011; Austin, 2000b; Austin and Seitanidi, 2012a; Bartel, 2001; Jones, 2006; Vock, Van Dolen, and Kolk, forthcoming.
18. Bhattacharya and Sen, 2004; Green and Peloza, 2011; Vock, Van Dolen, and Kolk, forthcoming; Bhattacharya, Sen, and Korschun, 2008; Kolk, Van Dolen, and Vock, 2010; Bhattacharya, Korschun, and Sen, 2009.
19. Austin, Reficco, Berger, Fischer, Gutierrez, Koljatic, Lozano, Ogliastri, and the Social Enterprise Knowledge Network (SEKN) Team, 2004.
20. Stafford, Polonsky, and Hartman, 2000.
21. Bockstette and Stamp, 2011.
22. Waddock and Post, 1995; Crane, 2010.
23. Hitt, Ireland, Sirmon, and Trahms, 2011, p. 68.
24. McDonald and Young, 2012.
25. Austin and Seitanidi, 2012b.
26. Austin and Reavis, 2002.
27. Millard, 2005; Zettelmeyer and Maddison, 2004.
28. Conservation International and Starbucks, 2011.
29. Hunter, 2011, p. 6.
30. Austin, Gutiérrez, Ogliastri, and Reficco, 2007.
31. Peloza and Shang, 2010; Peloza, 2009.
32. Hunter, 2013.
33. Hunter, 2011, p. 99.
34. White, 2009.
35. Brock, Buteau, and Herring, 2012, p. 6.
36. Morino, 2011, p. 4.
37. Jeff Edmondson, quoted in Eckhart-Queenan and Forti, 2011.
38. Austin, Leonard, Reficco, and Wei-Skillern, 2006.
39. Jorgensen, 2006; Sullivan and Skelcher, 2002.
40. Khandker, Gayatri, Koolwal, and Samad, 2010, p. 19.
41. Peloza and Shang, 2010; Peloza, 2009; Brinkerhoff, 2002; Austin, 2003b; Hoffman, 2005; O'Flynn, 2010.
42. Khandker, Gayatri, Koolwal, and Samad, 2010.
43. Lim, 2010, p. 15.
44. Lim, 2010, p. 15.
45. Mulgan, 2010; Lepak, Smith, and Taylor, 2007; Austin, 2003b; Endacott, 2003; Amabile, 1996.
46. SROI Network, 2012, pp. 2–3.
47. Javits, 2008.
48. Morino, 2011, p. 43.
49. Morino, 2011, p. 96.

50. Nike, 2005, p. 11.
51. Nike, 2009, p. 18.
52. Nike, 2005, p. 37.
53. World Business Council for Sustainable Development, 2013.

Chapter Seven
1. Chandler, 2003.
2. Bryson, Crosby, and Middleton Stone, 2006, p. 52.
3. Austin and Leonard, 2008.
4. Koschmann, Kuhn, and Pfarrer, 2012.
5. Burtch, 2013, p. 136.

References

Aakhus, M., and Bzdak, M. (2012). "Revisiting the Role of 'Shared Value' in the Business-Society Relationship." *Business & Professional Ethics Journal*, 31(2), 231–246.

Aguilera, R. V., Rupp, D. E., Williams, C. A., and Ganapathi, J. (2007). "Putting the S Back in Corporate Social Responsibility: A Multilevel Theory of Social Change in Organizations." *Academy of Management Review*, 32(3), 836–863.

Aguinis, H., and Glavas, A. (2012). "What We Know and Don't Know about Corporate Social Responsibility: A Review and Research Agenda." *Journal of Management*, 38(4), 932–968.

Ählström, J., and Sjöström, E. (2005). "CSOs and Business Partnerships: Strategies for Interaction." *Business Strategy and the Environment*, 14(4), 230–240.

Allen, K., Galiano, M., and Hayes, S. (2011). *Global Companies Volunteering Globally: The Final Report of the Global Corporate Volunteering Research Project.* Dulles, VA: International Association for Volunteer Effort.

Alsop, R. J. (2004). *The 18 Immutable Laws of Corporate Reputation: Creating, Protecting, and Repairing Your Most Valuable Asset.* New York: Free Press.

Amabile, T. M. (1996). *Creativity in Context: Update to the Social Psychology of Creativity.* Boulder, CO: Westview Press.

Andreasen, A. R. (1996). "Profits for Nonprofits: Find a Corporate Partner." *Harvard Business Review*, 74(6), 47–59.

Andreasen, A. R. (2009). "Cross-Sector Marketing Alliances." In J. J. Cordes and C. E. Steuerle, eds., *Nonprofits and Business*, pp. 155–192. Washington, DC: Urban Institute Press.

Andrioff, J. (2000). "Managing Social Risk through Stakeholder Partnership Building: Empirical Descriptive Process Analysis of Stakeholder Partnerships from British Petroleum in Colombia and Hoechst in Germany for the Management of Social Risk." Doctoral dissertation, Warwick University.

Andrioff, J., and Waddock, S. (2002). "Unfolding Stakeholder Management." In J. Andrioff and S. Waddock, eds., *Unfolding Stakeholder Thinking*, pp. 19–42. Sheffield, England: Greenleaf.

Argenti, P. A. (2004). "Collaborating with Activists: How Starbucks Works with NGOs." *California Management Review*, 47(1), 91–116.

Arya, B., and Salk, J. E. (2006). "Cross-Sector Alliance Learning and Effectiveness of Voluntary Codes of Corporate Social Responsibility." *Business Ethics Quarterly*, 16(2), 211–234.

Ashman, D. (2000). *Promoting Corporate Citizenship in the Global South: Towards a Model of Empowered Civil Society Collaboration with Business.* IDR [Institute for Developmental Research] Reports, 16(3). Boston: IDR Publications.

Austin, J. E. (1998a). "Business Leaders and Nonprofits." *Nonprofit Management & Leadership*, 9(1), 39–51.

Austin, J. E. (1998b). "Business Leadership Lessons from the Cleveland Turnaround." *California Management Review*, 41(1), 86–106.

Austin, J. E. (1998c). "The Invisible Side of Leadership." *Leader to Leader*, 8, 38–46.

Austin, J. E. (2000a). "Business Leadership Coalitions." *Business and Society Review*, 105(3), 305–322.

Austin, J. E. (2000b). *The Collaboration Challenge: How Nonprofits and Businesses Succeed through Strategic Alliances.* San Francisco: Jossey-Bass.

Austin, J. E. (2000c). "Principles for Partnership." *Leader to Leader*, 22, 44–50.

Austin, J. E. (2000d). "Strategic Collaboration between Nonprofits and Businesses." *Nonprofit and Voluntary Sector Quarterly*, 29(suppl. 1), 69–97.

Austin, J. E. (2003a). "Institutional Collaboration." In D. R. Young, ed., *Effective Economic Decision-Making by Nonprofit Organizations*, pp. 149–166. New York: Foundation Center.

Austin, J. E. (2003b). "Strategic Alliances: Managing the Collaboration Portfolio." *Stanford Social Innovation Review*, 1(2), 49–55.

Austin, J. E. (2010). "From Organization to Organization: On Creating Value." *Journal of Business Ethics*, 94(suppl. 1), 13–15.

Austin, J. E., and Elias, J. (2001). *Timberland and Community Involvement.* HBS case no. 796156. Boston: Harvard Business School.

Austin, J. E., Gutiérrez, R., Ogliastri, E., and Reficco, E. (2007). "Capitalizing on Convergence." *Stanford Social Innovation Review*, 5(1), 24–31.

Austin, J. E., and Leonard, H. B. (2008). "Can the Virtuous Mouse and the Rich Elephant Live Happily Ever After?" *California Management Review*, 41(1), 77–102.

Austin, J. E., Leonard, H. B., and Quinn, J. W. (2004). *Timberland: Commerce and Justice.* HBS case no. 305002. Boston: Harvard Business School.

Austin, J. E., Leonard, H. B., Reficco, E., and Wei-Skillern, J. (2006). "Social Entrepreneurship: It's for Corporations, Too." In A. Nicholls, ed., *Social Entrepreneurship: New Models of Sustainable Social Change*, pp. 169–180. Oxford, England: Oxford University Press.

Austin, J. E., and Porraz, J. M. (2002). *KaBOOM!* HBS case no. 303025. Boston: Harvard Business School.

Austin, J. E., and Reavis C. (2002). *Starbucks and Conservation International.* HBS case no. 9303055. Boston: Harvard Business School.

Austin, J. E., Reficco, E., Berger, G., Fischer, R. M., Gutierrez, R., Koljatic, M., Lozano, G., Ogliastri, E., and the Social Enterprise Knowledge Network (SEKN) Team (2004). *Social Partnering in Latin America: Lessons Drawn from Collaborations of Business and Civil Society Organizations.* Cambridge, MA: Harvard University Press.

Austin, J. E., and Seitanidi, M. M. (2012a). "Collaborative Value Creation: A Review of Partnering Between Nonprofits and Businesses," part 1: "Value Creation Spectrum and Collaboration Stages. *Nonprofit and Voluntary Sector Quarterly*, 41(5), 723–755.

Austin, J. E., and Seitanidi, M. M. (2012b). "Collaborative Value Creation: A Review of Partnering between Nonprofits and Businesses," part 2: "Partnering Processes and Outcomes." *Nonprofit and Voluntary Sector Quarterly*, 41(6), 929–968.

Austin, J. E., Stevenson, H., and Wei-Skillern, J. (2006). "Social Entrepreneurship and Commercial Entrepreneurship: The Same, Different, or Both?" *Entrepreneurship Theory and Practice*, 30(1), 1–22.

Avelar, S. de (2002). "On Corporate Giving and Philanthropy in Brazil: An Overview." *ReVista: Harvard Review of Latin America*, Spring, 66–69.

"Avon Foundation for Women Announces Avon Walk for Breast Cancer's 10th Birthday Season" (2011, Dec. 28). Available at http://www .avonwalk.org/press/avon-foundation-for-women-announces-avon-walk-for-breast-cancer-s-10th-birthday-season.html (retrieved Oct. 14, 2013).

Balderston, K. (2012). "Creating Value through Uncommon Alliances." *Stanford Review of Social Innovation*, 10(4), 23–24.

Balogun, J., and Johnson, G. (2004). "Organizational Restructuring and Middle Manager Sensemaking." *Academy of Management Journal*, 47(4), 523–549.

Bansal, P., and Roth, K. (2000). "Why Companies Go Green: A Model of Ecological Responsiveness." *Academy of Management Journal*, 43(4), 717–736.

Barnett, M. L. (2007). "Stakeholder Influence Capacity and the Variability of Financial Returns to Corporate Social Responsibility." *Academy of Management Review*, 32(3), 794–816.

Barr, C., and Huxham, C. (1996). "Involving the Community: Collaboration for Community Development." In C. Huxham, ed., *Creating Collaborative Advantage*, pp. 110–125. London: Sage.

Barrett, D., Austin, J. E., and McCarthy, S. (2000). "Cross-Sector Collaboration: Lessons from the International Trachoma Initiative." In M. R. Reich, ed., *Public-Private Partnerships for Public Health.* Cambridge, MA: Harvard University Press.

Bartel, C. A. (2001). "Social Comparisons in Boundary-Spanning Work: Effects of Community Outreach on Members' Organizational Identity and Identification." *Administrative Science Quarterly,* 46(3), 379–413.

Bartling, C.E. (1998). *Strategic Alliances for Nonprofit Organizations.* Washington, DC: American Society of Association Executives.

Barton, D. (2011). "Capitalism for the Long Term." *Harvard Business Review,* 89(3), 84–91.

Baur, D., and Palazzo, G. (2011). "The Moral Legitimacy of NGOs as Partners of Corporations." *Business Ethics Quarterly,* 21(4), 579–604.

Baur, D., and Schmitz, H. P. (2012). "Corporations and NGOs: When Cooperation Leads to Co-optation." *Journal of Business Ethics,* 106(1), 9–21.

Bendell, J. (2000). "Civil Regulation: A New Form of Democratic Governance for the Global Economy?" In J. Bendell, ed., *Terms of Endearment: Business, NGOs and Sustainable Development,* pp. 239–254. Sheffield, England: Greenleaf.

Berger, I. E., Cunningham, P. H., and Drumwright, M. E. (2004). "Social Alliances: Company/Nonprofit Collaboration." *California Management Review,* 47(1), 58–90.

Beta San Miguel and Colegio San Ignacio de Loyola Vizcaínas (2008). *Programa Emalur Informe Anual 2008* [2008 annual report, Emalur Program]. Mexico City, Mexico: Beta San Miguel.

Bhattacharya, C. B., Korschun, D., and Sen, S. (2009). "Strengthening Stakeholder–Company Relationships through Mutually Beneficial Corporate Social Responsibility Initiatives." *Journal of Business Ethics,* 85(suppl. 2), 257–272.

Bhattacharya, C. B., and Sen, S. (2004). "Doing Better at Doing Good: When, Why and How Consumers Respond to Social Initiatives." *California Management Review,* 47(1), 9–24.

Bhattacharya, C. B., Sen, S., and Korschun, D. (2008). "Using Corporate Social Responsibility to Win the War for Talent." *MIT Sloan Management Review,* 49(2), 37–44.

Bhattacharya, C. B., Sen, S., and Korschun, D. (2011). *Leveraging Corporate Responsibility: The Stakeholder Route to Maximizing Business and Social Value.* Cambridge, England: Cambridge University Press.

Biermann, F., Chan, M., Mert, A., and Pattberg, P. (2007). "Multi-Stakeholder Partnerships for Sustainable Development: Does the

Promise Hold?" In P. Glasbergen, F. Biermann, and A.P.J. Mol, eds., *Partnerships, Governance and Sustainable Development: Reflections on Theory and Practice*, pp. 239–260. Cheltenham, England: Edward Elgar.

Billis, D., ed. (2010). *Hybrid Organizations and the Third Sector: Challenges for Practice, Theory and Policy*. London: Palgrave Macmillan.

BISC—Benchmarking do Investimento Social Corporativo (2012). *Relatório 2001*. São Paulo, Brazil: COMUNITAS.

Bishop, M., and Green, M. (2008). *Philanthrocapitalism: How the Rich Can Save the World*. New York: Bloomsbury Press.

Bockstette, V., and Stamp, M. (2011). *Creating Shared Value: A How-to Guide for the New Corporate (R)evolution*. Boston: FSG. Available at http://www.fsg.org/Portals/0/Uploads/Documents/PDF/Shared_Value_Guide.pdf (retrieved Aug. 11, 2013).

Bojer, M. (2008). "We Can't Keep Meeting Like This: Developing the Capacity for Cross-Sector Collaboration." *The Systems Thinker*, 19(9), 2–6.

Bonini, S., Koller, T. M., and Mirvis, P. H. (2009). "Valuing Social Responsibility Programs." *McKinsey Quarterly*, 4, 65–73.

Boschee, J. and McClurg, J. (2003). "Toward a Better Understanding of Social Entrepreneurship: Some Important Distinctions." Unpublished paper. Available at http://www.caledonia.org.uk/papers/Social-Entrepreneurship.pdf (retrieved Oct. 9, 2013).

Bowen, F., Newenham-Kahindi, A., and Herremans, I. (2010). "When Suits Meet Roots: The Antecedents and Consequences of Community Engagement Strategy." *Journal of Business Ethics*, 95(2), 297–318.

Bowen, H. R. (1953). *Social Responsibilities of the Businessman*. New York: Harper & Row.

Brainerd, M., Campbell, J., and Davis, R. (2013, Sept.). "Doing Well by Doing Good: A Leader's Guide." *McKinsey Quarterly*. Available at http://www.mckinsey.com/insights/social_sector/doing_well_by_doing_good_a_leaders_guide (retrieved Oct. 14, 2013).

Brest, P. (2012). "A Decade of Outcome-Oriented Philanthropy." *Stanford Social Innovation Review*, 10(2), 42–47. Available at http://www.ssireview.org/articles/entry/a_decade_of_outcome_oriented_philanthropy (retrieved Oct. 14, 2013).

Brickson, S. L. (2007). "Organizational Identity Orientation: The Genesis of the Role of the Firm and Distinct Forms of Social Value." *Academy of Management Review*, 32(3), 864–888.

Brinkerhoff, J. M. (2002). "Assessing and Improving Partnership Relationships and Outcomes: A Proposed Framework." *Evaluation and Program Planning*, 25(3), 215–231.

Brock, A., Buteau, E., and Herring, A. (2012). *Room for Improvement: Foundations' Support of Nonprofit Performance Assessment*. Cambridge, MA: Center for Effective Philanthropy.

"Broken Deal Costs AMA $9.9 Million" (1998, Aug. 2). *New York Times.* Available at http://www.nytimes.com/1998/08/03/us/broken-deal-costs-ama-9.9-million.html (retrieved October 15, 2013).

Bromberger, A. R. (2011). "A New Type of Hybrid." *Stanford Social Innovation Review,* 9(2), 48–53.

Brown, L. D. (1991). "Bridging Organizations and Sustainable Development." *Human Relations,* 44(8), 807–831.

Brown, L. D., and Kalegaonkar, A. (2002). "Support Organizations and the Evolution of the NGO Sector." *Nonprofit and Voluntary Sector Quarterly,* 31(2), 231–258.

Browne, J. (1997, May 19). "Addressing Global Climate Change." Transcript of speech delivered at Stanford University. Available at http://www.aral.de/assets/bp_internet/globalbp/STAGING/global_assets/complex_flash/bp_complex/GlobalClimate_full.pdf (retrieved Aug. 13, 2013).

Brugmann, J., and Prahalad, C. K. (2007). "Cocreating Businesses' New Social Compact." *Harvard Business Review,* 85(2), 80–90.

Bryson, J. M., Crosby, B. C., and Middleton Stone, M. (2006). "The Design and Implementation of Cross-Sector Collaborations: Propositions from the Literature." *Public Administration Review,* 66, 44–55.

Bulloch, G., Lacy, P., and Jurgens, C. (2011). *Convergent Economy: Rethinking International Development in a Converging World.* Accenture paper no. 10–2270/11–2682. Available at http://www.accenture.com/SiteCollectionDocuments/PDF/Accenture_Development_Partnerships_Rethinking_International_Development_in_a_Converging%20World.pdf (retrieved Aug. 8, 2013).

Burchell, J., and Cook, J. (2011). "Deconstructing the Myths of Employer-Sponsored Volunteering Schemes." Paper presented at 27th European Group for Organizational Studies (EGOS) colloquium, Gothenburg, Sweden.

Burke, L., and Logsdon, J. M. (1996). "How Corporate Social Responsibility Pays Off." *Long Range Planning,* 29(4), 495–502.

Burtch, B. W. (2012). *The 2012 Burtch Report.* San Francisco: Bruce W. Burtch, Inc.

Burtch, B. W. (2013). *Win-Win for the Greater Good.* San Francisco: Bruce W. Burtch, Inc.

Business in the Community (BITC) (2012). *Shared Goals, Shared Solutions: Research on Collaboration for a Sustainable Future.* London: Business in the Community. Available at http://www.csreurope.org/sites/default/files/Wellbeing%20for%20Older%20Employees%20-%20Corporate%20Practices%202010.pdf (retrieved Aug. 6, 2013).

C&E Advisory (2010). *C&E Corporate-NGO Partnership Barometer, Summary Report 2010.* Available at http://www.candeadvisory.com/sites/default/files/report_abridged.pdf (retrieved Aug. 2, 2013).

Cairns, B., and Harris, M. (2011). "Local Cross-Sector Partnerships. Tackling the Challenges Collaboratively." *Nonprofit Management & Leadership*, 21(3), 311–324.

Campbell, J. L. (2007). "Why Would Corporations Behave in Socially Responsible Ways? An Institutional Theory of Corporate Social Responsibility." *Academy of Management Review*, 32(3), 946–967.

Campos, L., Andion, C., Serva, M., Rossetto, A., and Assumpção, J. (2011). "Performance Evaluation in Non-Governmental Organizations (NGOs): An Analysis of Evaluation Models and Their Applications in Brazil." *Voluntas*, 22, 238–258.

Carroll, A. B. (1999). "Corporate Social Responsibility: Evolution of a Definitional Construct." *Business & Society*, 38(3), 268–295.

Carroll, A. B. (2006). "Corporate Social Responsibility: A Historical Perspective." In M. J. Epstein and K. O. Hanson, eds., *The Accountable Corporation: Corporate Social Responsibility*, pp. 3–30. Westport, CT: Praeger.

CDC Development Solutions (2011, Apr. 14). "Global Citizenship and Volunteerism: CDS Second Annual ICV Workshop a Hit." Available at http://www.cdcdevelopmentsolutions.org/newsletter/april2011-icv-workshop (retrieved Aug. 10, 2013).

Chandler, A. D. Jr. (2003). *Strategy and Structure: Chapters in the History of the American Industrial Enterprise*. Washington, DC: Beard Books.

Chansky, E. (2010). "For Goodness' Sake: Legal Regulation and Best Practices in the Field of Cause-Related Marketing." *NYBSA Inside*, 28, 1.

Chênevert, S., and Bonini, S. (2008). *The State of Corporate Philanthropy*. Report based on results of a survey conducted by McKinsey and Company. Available at http://www.disabilityfunders.org/webfm_send/13 (retrieved Aug. 9, 2013).

Christensen, C. M., Baumann, H., Ruggles, R., and Sadtler, T. M. (2006). "Disruptive Innovation for Social Change." *Harvard Business Review*, 84(12), 96–101.

Christopher, T. (2012, Oct. 9). "CI at 25: Making Business a Positive Force for Conservation." *HumaNature* (blog). Available at http://blog.conservation.org/2012/10/ci-at-25-making-business-a-positive-force-for-conservation (retrieved Aug. 10, 2013).

Cikaliuk, M. (2011). "Cross-Sector Alliances for Large-Scale Health Leadership Development in Canada: Lessons for Leaders." *Leadership in Health Services*, 24(4), 281–294.

Clarke, A. (2007a, May). "Cross-Sector Collaborative Strategic Management: Regional Sustainable Development Strategies." Paper presented at scoping symposium on future challenges of cross-sector interactions, Brunel Business School, Brunel University, London.

Clarke, A. (2007b, Apr.). "Furthering Collaborative Strategic Management Theory: Process Model and Factors per Phase." Paper presented at

Sprott Doctoral Symposium, Sprott School of Business, Carleton University, Ottawa.

Clarke, A., and Fuller, M. (2010). "Collaborative Strategic Management: Strategy Formulation and Implementation by Multi-organizational Cross-Sector Social Partnerships." *Journal of Business Ethics*, 94 (supp. 1), 85–101.

"Coca-Cola Aids in Mexico's Reforestation" (2009). Available at http://infosurhoy.com/en_GB/articles/saii/features/2009/11/12/feature-01 (retrieved Oct. 13, 2013).

"Coffee" (2013). Available at http://www.starbucks.com/responsibility/sourcing/coffee (retrieved Oct. 6, 2013).

Cohen, W. A. (2009). "What Drucker Taught Us about Social Responsibility." *Leader to Leader*, 51, 29–34.

Collier, J., and Esteban, R. (1999). "Governance in the Participative Organization: Freedom, Creativity and Ethics." *Journal of Business Ethics*, 21, 173–188.

Committee Encouraging Corporate Philanthropy (2012). *Giving in Numbers: 2012 Edition*. New York: Committee Encouraging Corporate Philanthropy.

Cone Communications (2002). *Cone Corporate Citizenship Study: The Role of Cause Branding*. Boston: Cone Communications. Available at http://www.conecomm.com/stuff/contentmgr/files/0/7c6165bb378273babd958415d58ec980/files/2002_cone_corporate_citizenship_study.pdf (retrieved Aug. 6, 2013).

Cone Communicattions (2010). *2010 Cone Cause Evolution Study*. Boston: Cone Communications. Available at http://www.ppqty.com/2010_Cone_Study.pdf (retrieved Oct. 13, 2013).

Conference Board (1993). *Corporate Volunteer Programs: Benefits to Business*. Report no. 1029. New York: Conference Board.

Conroy, M. E. (2007). *Branded! How the "Certification Revolution" is Transforming Global Corporations*. Gabriola Island, British Columbia, Canada: New Society Publishers.

Conservation International and Starbucks (2011, Nov.). *Measuring the Impact of C.A.F.E. Practices: Colombia Field Survey*. Overview and key findings. Available at http://www.conservation.org/global/celb/Documents/2011.09_Starbucks_Colombia_Overview_HR.PDF (retrieved Aug. 10, 2013).

Cooper, T. L., Bryer, T. A., and Meek, J. W. (2006). "Citizen-Centered Collaborative Public Management." *Public Administration Review*, 66, 76–88.

Cornelious, N., and Wallace, J. (2010). "Cross-Sector Partnerships: City Regeneration and Social Justice." *Journal of Business Ethics*, 94 (suppl. 1), 71–84.

Corporate Citizenship and Corporate Affairs, IBM Corporation (2012). *World Community Grid: Innovation That Matters for the World.* Available at http://www.worldcommunitygrid.org/bg/partner.pdf (retrieved Aug. 9, 2013).

"Corporate Philanthropy More Strategic, Deloitte Report Reveals" (2011, July 15). Philanthropy Impact. Available at http://www.philanthropy-impact.org/news/corporate-philanthropy-more-strategic-deloitte-report-reveals (retrieved Aug. 8, 2013).

Cotten, M. N., and Lasprogata, G. A. (2012). "Corporate Citizenship and Creative Collaboration: Best Practice for Cross-Sector Partnerships." *Journal of Law, Business and Ethics,* 18, 9–39.

Couchman, P. K., and Fulop, L. (2009a). "Examining Partner Experience in Cross-Sector Collaborative Projects Focused on the Commercialization of R&D." *Innovation: Management, Policy and Practice,* 11, 85–103.

Couchman, P. K., and Fulop, L. (2009b). "Risk and Trust in Cross-Sector R&D Projects." Paper presented at the 23rd conference of the Australian and New Zealand Academy of Management (ANZAM), Melbourne, Australia.

Covey, J., and Brown, L. D. (2001). *Critical Cooperation: An Alternative Form of Civil Society–Business Engagement.* IDR [Institute for Developmental Research] Reports, 17(1). Boston: IDR Publications.

Cozzolino, A. (2012). *Cross-Sector Cooperation in Disaster Relief Management.* London: Springer.

Crane, A. (1998). "Exploring Green Alliances." *Journal of Marketing Management,* 14(6), 559–579.

Crane, A. (2010). "From Governance to Governance: On Blurring Boundaries." *Journal of Business Ethics,* 94(suppl. 1), 17–19.

Crane, A., and Matten, D. (2007). *Business Ethics: Managing Corporate Citizenship and Sustainability in the Age of Globalization.* Oxford, England: Oxford University Press.

Crilly, D., Zollo, M., and Hansen, M. T. (2012). "Faking It or Muddling Through? Understanding Decoupling in Response to Stakeholder Pressures." *Academy of Management Journal,* 55(6), 1429–1448.

Crosby, B. C., and Bryson, J. M. (2010). "Integrative Leadership and the Creation and Maintenance of Cross-Sector Collaborations." *Leadership Quarterly,* 21, 211–30.

Croteau, D., and Hicks, L. (2003). "Coalition Framing and the Challenge of a Consonant Frame Pyramid: The Case of Collaborative Response to Homelessness." *Social Problems,* 50(2), 251–272.

Cummins, A. (2004). "The Marine Stewardship Council: A Multi-Stakeholder Approach to Sustainable Fishing." *Corporate Social Responsibility and Environmental Management,* 11, 85–94.

Dalal-Clayton, B., and Bass, S. (2002). *Sustainable Development Strategies: A Resource Handbook.* London: Earthscan.

Das, T. K., and Teng, B. (1998). "Between Trust and Control: Developing Confidence in Alliances." *Academy of Management Review,* 23(3), 491–512.

Davis, G. F., and Cobb, J. A. (2010). "Resource Dependence Theory: Past and Future." *Research in the Sociology of Organizations,* 28, 21–42.

De Bakker, F.G.A., Groenewegen, P., and Den Hond, F. (2005). "A Bibliometric Analysis of 30 Years of Research and Theory on Corporate Social Responsibility and Corporate Social Performance." *Business & Society,* 44(3), 283–317.

De Beers Family of Companies (2009). *Living Up to Diamonds: Report to Society 2009.* Luxembourg: De Beers. Available at http://www.angloamerican.com/~/media/Files/A/Anglo-American-Plc/docs/ImageVaultHandler.pdf (retrieved Aug. 7, 2013).

De Cooman, R., De Geiter, S., Pepermans, R., and Jegers, M. (2011). "A Cross-Sector Comparison of Motivation-Related Concepts in For-Profit and Not-for-Profit Service Organizations." *Nonprofit and Voluntary Sector Quarterly,* 40(2), 296–317.

Dees, J. G. (1998). "Enterprising Nonprofits." *Harvard Business Review,* 76(1), 54–67.

Dees, J. G., and Anderson, B. B. (2003). "Sector-Bending: Blurring Lines between Nonprofit and For-Profit." *Society,* 40(4), 16–27.

Deiglmeier, K., (2012). "'Sustainable Conversation' and the Long View of Cross-Sector Partnerships." Interview with Ashley Boren. Available at http://csi.gsb.stanford.edu/sustainable-conservation-and-long-view-cross-sector-partnerships (retrieved Aug. 9, 2013).

Den Hond, F. (2010). "Review Essay: Reflections on Relationships Between NGOs and Corporations." *Business & Society,* 49(1), 173–178.

Den Hond, F., De Bakker, F.G.A., and Doh, J. (forthcoming). "What Prompts Companies to Collaboration with NGOs? Recent Evidence from The Netherlands." *Business & Society.* Abstract available at http://bas.sagepub.com/content/early/2012/06/06/0007650312 439549 (retrieved Oct. 9, 2013).

Devinney, T. M., Auger, P., Eckhardt, G., and Birtchnell, T. (2006). "The Other CSR." *Stanford Social Innovation Review,* 4(3), 30–37.

Dew, N., Read, S., Sarasvathy, S. D., and Wiltbank, R (2008). "Outlines of a Behavioral Theory of the Entrepreneurial Firm." *Journal of Economic Behavior & Organization,* 66(1), 37–59.

Di Maggio, P., and Anheier, H. (1990). "The Sociology of the Non-Profit Sector." *Annual Review of Sociology,* 16, 137–159.

Donaldson, T., and Preston, L. E. (1995). "The Stakeholder Theory of the Corporation: Concepts, Evidence, and Implications." *Academy of Management Review,* 20(1), 65–69.

Doyle, P. (2000). *Value-Based Marketing.* Hoboken, NJ: Wiley.

Draulans, J., deMan, A.-P., and Volberda, H. W. (2003). "Building Alliance Capability: Management Techniques for Superior Alliance Performance." *Long Range Planning*, 36, 151–166.

Drayton, B. (2011). "Collaborative Entrepreneurship: How Social Entrepreneurs Have Learned to Tip the World by Working in Global Teams." *Innovations*, spring, 1–5.

Drayton, B, and Budinich, V. (2010). "A New Alliance for Global Change." *Harvard Business Review*, 88(9), 56–64.

Drucker, P. E. (1989). "What Business Can Learn from Nonprofits." *Harvard Business Review*, 67(4), 88.

Dybul, M. (2013). "The Role of (RED) in Defeating AIDS." *The Global Fund* (blog). Available at http://www.theglobalfund.org/en/blog/32404 (retrieved Oct. 6, 2013).

Eccles, R. G., Ioannou, I., and Serafeim, G. (2012a). "Essay: Is There an Optimal Degree of Sustainability?" Available at http://www.ethicalcorp.com/governance-regulation/essay-there-optimal-degree-sustainability (retrieved Aug. 7, 2013).

Eccles, R. G., Ioannou, I., and Serafeim, G. (2012b). *The Impact of a Corporate Culture of Sustainability on Corporate Behavior and Performance*, rev. ed. HBS working paper no. 12-035. Boston: Department of Accounting and Management, Harvard Business School.

Eccles, R. G., Newquist, S. C., and Schatz, R. (2007). "Reputation and Its Risks." *Harvard Business Review*, 85(2), 104–114.

Eckhart-Queenan, J., and Forti, M. (2011, Apr. 25). *Measurement as Learning: What Nonprofit CEOs, Board Members, and Philanthropists Need to Know to Keep Improving.* Boston: The Bridgespan Group. Available at http://www.bridgespan.org/Publications-and-Tools/Performance-Measurement/Section1/Measurement-as-Learning-What-Nonprofit-CEOs,-B.aspx#.Ugh0mW2DzIU (retrieved Aug. 11, 2013).

Edelman good purpose® Study (2012). Executive summary. Available at http://www.scribd.com/doc/90411623/Executive-Summary-2012-Edelman-goodpurpose%C2%AE-Study (retrieved Aug. 10, 2013).

Edmond, T, Raghavan, K., and Smith, P. C. (2011). "Cross-Sector Collaborations and Enterprise Risk-Management: Strategies for Nonprofit Organizations to Effectively Partner with For-Profit Organizations." *Journal of Business and Accounting*, 4(1), 24–36.

Eggers, W. D., and Macmillan, P. (2013). *The Solution Revolution: How Business, Government, and Social Enterprises Are Teaming Up to Solve Society's Toughest Problems.* Boston: Harvard Business Review Press.

Egri, C. P., and Ralston, D. A. (2008). "Corporate Responsibility: A Review of International Management Research from 1998 to 2007." *Journal of International Management*, 14(4), 319–339.

Elbers, W. (2004). *Doing Business with Business: Development NGOs Interacting with the Corporate Sector.* Nijmegen, The Netherlands: Centre for International Development Issues, Radboud University.

Elkington, J. (1997). *Cannibals with Forks: The Triple Bottom Line of 21st-Century Business.* Oxford, England: Capstone.

Elkington, J. (1999). *Cannibals with Forks: The Triple Bottom Line of 21st Century Business.* Oxford, England: Capstone.

Elkington, J. (2004). "The Triple Bottom Line: Sustainability's Accountants." In M. J. Epstein and K. O. Hanson, eds., *The Accountable Corporation: Corporate Social Responsibility*, pp. 97–109. Westport, CT: Praeger.

Elkington, J., and Fennell, S. (2000). "Partners for Sustainability." In J. Bendell, ed., *Terms of Endearment: Business, NGOs and Sustainable Development*, pp. 150–162. Sheffield, England: Greenleaf.

Emerson, J. (2003). "The Blended-Value Proposition: Integrating Social and Financial Returns." *California Management Review*, 45(4), 35–51.

Endacott, R.W.J. (2003). "Consumers and CSRM: A National and Global Perspective." *Journal of Consumer Marketing*, 21(3), 183–189.

Eng, T., Liu, C. G., and Sekhorn, Y. K. (2012). "The Role of Relationally Embedded Network Ties in Resource Acquisition of British Nonprofit Organizations." *Nonprofit and Voluntary Sector Quarterly* 41(6), 1092–1115.

Epstein, M. J., and McFarlan, F. W. (2011). *Joining a Nonprofit Board: What You Need to Know.* San Francisco: Jossey-Bass.

Eweje, G., and Palakshappa, N. (2009). "Business Partnerships with Nonprofits: Working to Solve Mutual Problems in New Zealand." *Corporate Social Responsibility and Environmental Management*, 16, 337–351.

Fiol, C. M., Pratt, M. G., and O'Connor, E. J. (2009). "Managing Intractable Identity Conflicts." *Academy of Management Review*, 34(1), 32–55.

Fleishman-Hillard/National Consumers League (2007, May). *Rethinking Corporate Social Responsibility.* St. Louis/Washington, DC: Fleishman-Hillard/National Consumers League. Available at http://www.franchise-kwt.com/mazeedi/mazeedi/media/pdf/mosoh5.pdf (retrieved Aug. 7, 2013).

Freeman, R. E. (1984). *Strategic Management: A Stakeholder Approach.* Boston: Pitman Publishing.

Freeman, R. E. (1999). "Divergent Stakeholder Theory." *Academy of Management Review*, 24(2), 233–236.

Friedman, M. (1962). *Capitalism and Freedom.* Chicago: University of Chicago Press.

Friedman, M. (1970, Sept. 13). "The Social Responsibility of Business Is to Increase Its Profits." *New York Times Magazine*, pp. 122–126.

Frisk, P. (2012). "Our Journey & Commitment." Available at http://responsibility.timberland.com/executive-commitment (retrieved Oct. 13, 2013).

Fruchterman, J. (2011). "For Love or Lucre." *Stanford Social Innovation Review*, 9(2), 42–47.

FTSE Group (n.d.). *FTSE4Good Index Series Inclusion Criteria*. London: FTSE Group. Available at http://www.ftse.com/Indices/FTSE4Good_Index_Series/Downloads/FTSE4Good_Inclusion_Criteria.pdf (retrieved Aug. 13, 2013).

Fuller, T., and Tian, Y. (2006). "Social and Symbolic Capital and Responsible Entrepreneurship: An Empirical Investigation of SME Narratives." *Journal of Business Ethics*, 67, 287–304.

Galaskiewicz, J. (1985). "Interorganizational Relations." *Annual Review of Sociology*, 11, 281–304.

Galaskiewicz, J. (1997). "An Urban Grants Economy Revisited: Corporate Charitable Contributions in the Twin Cities, 1979–81, 1987–89." *Administrative Science Quarterly*, 42, 445–471.

Galaskiewicz, J., and Sinclair Colman, M. (2006). "Collaboration between Corporations and Nonprofit Organizations." In W. W. Powell and R. Steinberg, eds., *The Nonprofit Sector: A Research Handbook*, 2nd ed., pp. 180–206. New Haven: Yale University Press.

Galaskiewicz, J., and Wasserman, S. (1989). "Mimetic Processes within an Interorganizational Field: An Empirical Test." *Administrative Science Quarterly*, 34, 454–479.

Garriga, E., and Melé, D. (2004). "Corporate Social Responsibility Theories: Mapping the Territory." *Journal of Business Ethics*, 53, 51–71.

General Electric (2012). *GE Global Innovation Barometer 2011: An Overview on Messaging, Data and Amplification*. Available at http://files.gereports.com/wp-content/uploads/2011/01/GIB-results.pdf (retrieved Aug. 10, 2013).

George, B. (2003). *Authentic Leadership: Rediscovering the Secrets to Creating Lasting Value*. San Francisco: Jossey-Bass.

Gerde, V. W., and Wokutch, R. E. (1998). "Twenty-Five Years and Going Strong: A Content Analysis of the First Twenty-Five Years of the Social Issues in Management Division Proceedings." *Business & Society*, 37(4), 414–446.

Giving USA Foundation (2012). *Giving USA 2012: The Annual Report of Philanthropy for the Year 2011*. Indianapolis: Center on Philanthropy, Indiana University.

Glasbergen, P. (2007). "Setting the Scene: The Partnership Paradigm in the Making." In P. Glasbergen, F. Biermann, and A.P.J. Mol, eds., *Partnerships, Governance, and Sustainable Development: Reflections on Theory and Practice*, pp. 1–28. Cheltenham, England: Edward Elgar.

Glasbergen, P., Biermann, F., and Mol, A.P.J., eds. (2007). *Partnerships, Governance and Sustainable Development: Reflections on Theory and Practice*. Cheltenham, England: Edward Elgar.

"Global RepTrak® Pulse Complimentary Reports—2011" (2011). Details available at http://www.reputationinstitute.com/thought-leadership/complimentary-reports-2011 (retrieved Oct. 13, 2013).

GlobeScan (2002). "What Do 25,000 People Say about CSR?" Press release. Available at http://www.globescan.com/news_archives/csr02_press_release.html (retrieved Oct. 9, 2013).

Godfrey, P. C., and Hatch, N. W. (2007). "Researching Corporate Social Responsibility: An Agenda for the 21st Century." *Journal of Business Ethics*, 70, 87–98.

Godfrey, P. C., Merrill, C. B., and Hansen, J. M. (2009). "The Relationship between Corporate Social Responsibility and Shareholder Value: An Empirical Test of the Risk-Management Hypothesis." *Strategic Management Journal*, 30(4), 425–445.

Goffman, E. (1983). "The Interaction Order." *American Sociological Review*, 48(1), 1–17.

Goldsmith, A. A. (2011). "Profits and Alms: Cross-Sector Partnerships for Global Poverty Reduction." *Public Administration and Development*, 31, 15–24.

Goodpaster, K. E., and Matthews, J. B. Jr. (1982). "Can a Corporation Have a Conscience?" *Harvard Business Review*, 60(1), 132–141.

Goodwill NCW (2005). *Ten Collaborations That Have Changed Our Corner of the World*. Menasha, WI: Goodwill Industries of North Central Wisconsin.

Googins, B. K., Mirvis, P. H., and Rochlin, S. A. (2007). *Beyond Good Company: Next-Generation Corporate Citizenship*. New York: Palgrave MacMillan.

Googins, B. K., and Rochlin, S. A. (2000). "Creating the Partnership Society: Understanding the Rhetoric and Reality of Cross-Sectoral Partnerships." *Business and Society Review*, 105(1), 127–144.

Gosling, J., and Mintzberg, H. (2003). "The Five Minds of a Manager." *Harvard Business Review*, 81(11), 54–63.

Gourville, J. T., and Rangan, V. K. (2004). "Valuing the Cause Marketing Relationship." *California Management Review*, 47(1), 38–57.

Grant, A. M. (2012). "Giving Time, Time after Time: Work Design and Sustained Employee Participation in Corporate Volunteering." *Academy of Management Review*, 37(4), 589–615.

Grant, H. M., and Crutchfield, L. R. (2007). "Creating High-Impact Nonprofits." *Stanford Social Innovation Review*, 5(3), 32–41.

Grau, S. L., and Folse, J.A.G. (2007). "Cause-Related Marketing (CRM): The Influence of Donation Proximity and Message-Framing Cues on the Less-Involved Consumer." *Journal of Advertising*, 36(4), 19–33.

Gray, B. (1989). *Collaborating*. San Francisco: Jossey-Bass.

Gray, S., and Hall, H. (1998). "Cashing In on Charity's Good Name." *Chronicle of Philanthropy*, 25, 27–29.

Green, K., Groenewegen, P., and Hofman, P. S. (Eds.) (2001). *Ahead of the Curve: Cases of Innovation in Environmental Management*. Dordrecht, The Netherlands: Kluwer Academic Publishers.

Green, T., and Peloza, J. (2011). "How Does Corporate Social Responsibility Create Value for Consumers?" *Journal of Consumer Marketing*, 28(1), 48–56.

Greenall, D., and Rovere, D. (1999). *Engaging Stakeholders and Business–NGO Partnerships in Developing Countries*. Toronto: Centre for innovation in Corporate Social Responsibility.

Griffin, J. J., and Mahon, J. F. (1997). "The Corporate Social Performance and Corporate Financial Performance Debate: Twenty-Five Years of Incomparable Research." *Business & Society*, 36(1), 5–31.

Grolin, J. (1998). "Corporate Legitimacy in Risk Society: The Case of Brent Spar." *Business Strategy and the Environment*, 7(4), 213–222.

Haack, P., Schoeneborn, D., and Wickert, C. (2012). "Talking the Talk, Moral Entrapment, Creeping Commitment? Exploring Narrative Dynamics in Corporate Responsibility Standardization." *Organization Studies*, 83(5–6), 815–845.

Haddad, K. A., and Nanda, A. (2001). *The American Medical Association–Sunbeam Deal (A–D)*. HBS case no. 9801326. Boston: Harvard Business School.

Halal, W. E. (2001). "The Collaborative Enterprise: A Stakeholder Model Uniting Probability and Responsibility." *Journal of Corporate Citizenship*, 1(2), 27–42.

Hamann, R., and Acutt, N. (2003). "How Should Civil Society (and the Government) Respond to 'Corporate Social Responsibility'? A Critique of Business Motivations and the Potential for Partnerships." *Development Southern Africa*, 20(2), 255–270.

Hamann, R., Pienaar, S., Boulogne, P., and Kranz, N. (2011). *What Makes Cross-Sector Partnerships Successful? A Comparative Case Study Analysis of Diverse Partnership Types in an Emerging Economy Context*. Research report no. 03/11. Dakar, Senegal: Investment Climate and Business Environment Research Fund.

Hammond, A. L., Kramer, W. J., Katz, R. S., Tran, J. T., and Walker, C. (2007). *The Next Four Billion: Market Size and Business Strategy at the Base of the Pyramid*. Washington, DC: International Finance Corporation/World Resources Institute.

Handy, F., Brudney, J. L., and Meijs, L.C.P.M. (2012). "From the Editors' Desk." *Nonprofit and Voluntary Sector Quarterly*, 41(5), 721.

Harbison, J. R., and Pekar, P. (1998). *Smart Alliances: A Practical Guide to Repeatable Success*. San Francisco: Jossey-Bass.

Hardy, C., Phillips, N., and Lawrence, T. B. (2003). "Resources, Knowledge and Influence: The Organizational Effects of Interorganizational Collaboration." *Journal of Management Studies*, 40, 321–47.

Harris, L. C., and Crane, A. (2002). "The Greening of Organizational Culture: Managers' Views on the Depth, Degree and Diffusion of Change." *Journal of Organizational Change Management*, 15(3), 214–234.

Heal, G. (2008). *When Principles Pay: Corporate Social Responsibility and the Bottom Line*. New York: Columbia University Press.

"Health Authorities Plan and Pledge to Overcome River Blindness" (1997, Nov. 5). Press release. Available at http://www.prnewswire.co.uk/news-releases/health-authorities-plan-and-pledge-to-overcome-river-blindness-156832265.html (retrieved Aug. 9, 2013).

Heap, S. (1998). *NGOs and the Private Sector: Potential for Partnerships?* Oxford, England: INTRAC Publications.

Heap, S. (2000). *NGOs Engaging with Business: A World of Difference and a Difference to the World*. Oxford, England: INTRAC Publications.

Heath, R. L. (1997). *Strategic Issues Management: Organizations and Public Policy Challenge*. Thousand Oaks, CA: Sage.

Hendry, J. R. (2006). "Taking Aim at Business: What Factors Lead Environmental Non-Governmental Organizations to Target Particular Firms?" *Business & Society*, 45(1), 47–86.

Heuer, M. (2011). "Ecosystem Cross-Sector Collaboration: Conceptualizing an Adaptive Approach to Sustainable Governance." *Business Strategy and the Environment*, 20, 211–221.

Heugens, P.P.M.A.R. (2003). "Capability Building through Adversarial Relationships: A Replication and Extension of Clarke and Roome (1999)." *Business Strategy and the Environment*, 12, 300–312.

Hewlett-Packard Company (2011). *HP 2011 Global Citizenship Report*. Palo Alto, CA: Hewlett-Packard Company. Available at http://www8.hp.com/us/en/pdf/hp_fy11_gcr_tcm_245_1357670.pdf (retrieved Aug. 13, 2013).

Hill, C.W.L., and Jones, T. M. (1985). "Stakeholder Agency Theory." *Journal of Management Studies*, 29(2), 131–154.

Hiscox, M., and Smyth, N. (2008). "Is There Consumer Demand for Improved Labor Standards? Evidence from Field Experiments in Social Product Labeling." Unpublished paper, Department of Government, Harvard University. Available at http://www.people.fas.harvard.edu/~hiscox/SocialLabeling.pdf (retrieved October 15, 2013).

Hitt, M. A., Ireland, R. D., Sirmon, D. G., and Trahms, C. (2011). "Strategic Entrepreneurship: Creating Value for Individuals, Organizations, and Society." *Academy of Management Perspectives*, 25(2), 57–75.

Hoeffler, S., and Keller, K. L. (2002). "Building Brand Equity through Corporate Societal Marketing." *Journal of Public Policy & Marketing,* 21(1), 78–89.

Hoffman, W. H. (2005). "How to Manage a Portfolio of Alliances." *Long Range Planning,* 38(2), 121–143.

Holmberg, S. R., and Cummings, J. L. (2009). "Building Successful Strategic Alliances: Strategic Process and Analytical Tool for Selecting Partner Industries and Firms." *Long Range Planning,* 42(2), 164–193.

Holmes, S., and Moir, L. (2007). "Developing a Conceptual Framework to Identify Corporate Innovations through Engagement with Non-Profit Stakeholders." *Corporate Governance,* 7(4), 414–422.

Holmes, S., and Smart, P. (2009). "Exploring Open Innovation Practice in Firm–Nonprofit Engagements: A Corporate Social Responsibility Perspective." *R&D Management,* 39(4), 394–409.

Hood, J. N., Logsdon, J. M., and Thompson, J. K. (1993). "Collaboration for Social Problem-Solving: A Process Model." *Business and Society,* 32(1), 1–17.

Hunter, D.E.K. (2011). "Using a Theory-of-Change Approach to Helping Nonprofits Manage to Outcomes." In M. Morino, ed., *Leap of Reason: Managing to Outcomes in an Era of Scarcity.* Washington, DC: Venture Philanthropy Partners.

Hunter, D.E.K. (2013). *Working Hard and Working Well: A Practical Guide to Performance Management.* Hamden, CT: Hunter Consulting. Available at http://www.vppartners.org/sites/default/files/documents/WorkingWellBook_Full_Version_SinglePage.pdf (retrieved Aug. 11, 2013).

Hustvedt, G., and Bernard, J. C. (2010). "Effects of Social Responsibility Labelling and Brand on Willingness to Pay for Apparel." *International Journal of Consumer Studies,* 34(6), 619–626.

Huxham, C. (1996). "Collaboration and Collaborative Advantage." In C. Huxham, ed., *Creating Collaborative Advantage,* pp. 1–18. London: Sage.

Hyatt, D. G., and Berente, N. (2011, June). "Proactive Environmental Strategies: An Exploration of the Effects of Cross-Sector Partnerships." Paper presented at the First International Conference on Engaged Management Scholarship, Weatherhead School of Management, Case Western Reserve University.

Investor Network on Climate Risk (INCR) (2013, Apr.). *INCR Listing Standards Drafting Committee Consultation Paper: Proposed Sustainability Disclosure Listing Standards for Global Stock Exchanges.* Boston: Investor Network on Climate Risk.

ISEAL Alliance (2009). *ISEAL Alliance Strategic Plan 2009–2013.* London: ISEAL Alliance.

Israel, B., Schulz, A. J., Parker, E. A., and Becker, A. B. (1998). "Review of Community-Based Research: Assessing Partnership Approaches to Improve Public Health." *Annual Review of Public Health*, 19, 173–202.

Jamali, D., and Keshishian, T. (2009). "Uneasy Alliances: Lessons Learned from Partnerships between Businesses and NGOs in the Context of CSR." *Journal of Business Ethics*, 84(2), 277–295.

Jamali, D., Yianni, M., and Abdallah, H. (2011). "Strategic Partnerships, Social Capital and Innovation: Accounting for Social Alliance Innovation." *Business Ethics: A European Review*, 20(4), 375–391.

Javits, C. I. (2008). *REDF's Current Approach to SROI*. San Francisco: Roberts Enterprise Development Fund [REDF].

Jay, J. (2013). "Navigating Paradox as a Mechanism of Change and Innovation in Hybrid Organizations." *Academy of Management Journal*, 56, 137–159.

Jensen, M. C. (2002). "Value Maximization, Stakeholder Theory, and the Corporate Objective Function." *Business Ethics Quarterly*, 12(2), 235–256.

Jiang, L., and Cai, N. (2011). "Cross-Sector Cooperation and Its Risk Management: Review." In *Proceedings of the 2011 International Conference on Business Computing and Global Informatization*, pp. 138–141. Washington, DC: IEEE Computer Society.

Jones, C., Hesterly, W., and Borgatti, S. (1997). "A General Theory of Network Governance: Exchange Conditions and Social Mechanisms." *Academy of Management Review*, 22(4), 911–945.

Jones, D. A. (2006). "Corporate Volunteer Programs and Employee Responses: How Serving the Community Also Serves the Company." Paper presented at the 67th annual meeting of the Academy of Management, Philadelphia.

Jones, T. M. (1995). "Instrumental Stakeholder Theory: A Synthesis of Ethics and Economics." *Academy of Management Review*, 20(2), 404–437.

Jones, T. M., and Wicks, A. C. (1999). "Convergent Stakeholder Theory." *Academy of Management Review*, 24(2), 206–221.

Jorgensen, M. (2006, Aug. 14). "Evaluating Cross-Sector Partnerships." Paper presented at conference on public-private partnerships in the post-WWSD context, Copenhagen Business School.

Joutsenverta, M. (2011). "Setting Boundaries for Corporate Social Responsibility: Firm–NGO Relationship as Discursive Legitimation Struggle." *Journal of Business Ethics*, 102(1), 57–75.

Kaku, R. (1997). "The Path of Kyosei." *Harvard Business Review*, 75(4), 55–63.

Kania, J., and Kramer, M. (2011). "Collective Impact." *Stanford Social Innovation Review*, 9(1), 36–41.

Kanter, R. M. (1999). "From Spare Change to Real Change: The Social Sector as Beta Site for Business Innovation." *Harvard Business Review*, 77(3), 122–132.

Kanter, R. M. (2009). *Supercorp: How Vanguard Companies Create Innovation, Profits, Growth, and Social Good*. New York: Random House.

Kanter, R. M. (2011). "How Great Companies Think Differently." *Harvard Business Review*, 89(11), 64–80.

Kaplan, S. (2008). "Framing Contests: Strategy Making under Uncertainty." *Organization Science*, 19, 729–752.

Kaplan, S., and Murray, F. (2010). "Entrepreneurship and the Construction of Value in Biotechnology." In N. Phillips, G. Sewell, and D. Griffiths, eds., *Technology and Organization: Essays in Honor of Joan Woodward*. Research in the Sociology of Organizations, vol. 29. Bingley, England: Emerald.

Keller, K. (1993). "Conceptualizing, Measuring, and Managing Customer-Based Brand Equity." *Journal of Marketing*, 57(1), 1–22.

"KFC Presents to Susan G. Komen for the Cure® a Check for More Than $4.2 Million" (2010, Aug. 24). Available at http://ww5.komen.org/KomenNewsArticle.aspx?id=6442452377&terms=Buckets (retrieved Aug. 10, 2013).

Khandker, S. R., Gayatri B., Koolwal, G. B., and Samad, H. A. (2010). *Handbook on Impact Evaluation: Quantitative Methods and Practices*. Washington, DC: World Bank.

Kim, N., Sung, Y., and Lee, M. (2011). "Consumer Evaluations of Social Alliances: The Effects of Perceived Fit between Companies and Non-Profit Organizations." *Journal of Business Ethics*, 78(4), 611–622.

Knoepke, D. (2011, Apr.). *(im)Proving Cause*. Arlington, VA: Association of Fundraising Professionals. Available at http://www.afpnet.org/files/ContentDocuments/AFPInfoExchange_imProvingCause_IEG.pdf (retrieved Aug. 10, 2013).

Koehn, N. F., and Miller, K. (2007). *John Mackey and Whole Foods Market*. HBS case no. 807111. Boston: Harvard Business School.

Kohl Kaufman, E. (2005). "Common Ground: The Collaborative Approach to Ethical Working Standards." *Corporate Responsibility Management*, 2(2), 20–23.

Kolk, A., Van Dolen, W., and Vock, M. (2010). "Trickle Effects of Cross-Sector Social Partnerships." *Journal of Business Ethics*, 94(suppl. 1), 123–137.

Kolk, A., Van Tulder, R., and Kostwinder, E. (2008). "Business and Partnerships for Development." *European Management Journal*, 26(4), 262–274.

Kolk, A., Van Tulder, R. and Westdijk, B. (2006). "Poverty Alleviation as Business Strategy? Evaluating Commitments of Frontrunner Multinational Enterprises." *World Development*, 34(5), 789–801.

Korngold, A. (2005). *Leveraging Goodwill: Strengthening Nonprofits by Engaging Businesses*. San Francisco: Jossey-Bass.

Koschmann, M. A., Kuhn, T. R., and Pfarrer, M. D. (2012). "A Communicative Framework of Value in Cross-Sector Partnerships." *Academy of Management Review*, 37(3), 332–354.

Kotler, P., and Lee, N. R. (2009). *Up and Out of Poverty: The Social Marketing Solution*. Upper Saddle River, NJ: Pearson Education Publishing.

Kotler, P., and Zaltman, G. (1971). "Social Marketing: An Approach to Planned Social Change." *Journal of Marketing*, 35(3), 3–12.

Kourula, A. (2010). "Corporate Engagement With Non-Governmental Organizations in Different Institutional Contexts: A Case Study of a Forest Products Company." *Journal of World Business*, 45, 395–404.

Kourula, A., and Laasonen, S. (2010). "Nongovernmental Organizations in Business and Society, Management, and International Business: Review and Implications, 1998–2007." *Business & Society*, 49(1), 3–5.

"Kraft American Cheese Teams Up with Five Guys and Feeding America for National Cheeseburger Day" (2012, Sept. 17). Press release. Available at http://www.prnewswire.com/news-releases/kraft-american-cheese-teams-up-with-five-guys-and-feeding-america-for-national-cheeseburger-day-170011366.html (retrieved Aug. 10, 2013).

Kramer, M. (2009). "Catalytic Philanthropy." *Stanford Social Innovation Review*, 7(4), 30–35.

Kroeger, F. (2012). "Trusting Organizations: The Institutionalization of Trust in Interorganizational Relationships." *Organization*, 19(6) 743–763.

Kumar, R., and Nti, K. O. (1998). "Differential Learning and Interaction in Alliance Dynamics: A Process and Outcome Discrepancy Model." *Organization Science*, 9, 356–367.

Laasonen, S., Fougere, M., and Kourula, A. (2012). "Dominant Articulations in Academic Business and Society Discourse On NGO–Business Relations: A Critical Assessment." *Journal of Business Ethics*, 109(4), 521–545.

Lacy, P., Cooper, T., Hayward, R., and Neuberger, L. (2010). *A New Era of Sustainability*. United Nations Global Compact–Accenture CEO Study 2010. Available at http://www.unglobalcompact.org/docs/news_events/8.1/UNGC_Accenture_CEO_Study_2010.pdf (retrieved Aug. 2, 2013).

Laidler-Kylander, N., Quelch, J. A. and Simonin, B. L. (2007). "Building and Valuing Global Brands in the Nonprofit Sector." *Nonprofit Management & Leadership*, 17(3), 253–277.

Lakotos, E., and Candea, D. (2012). "A Study of Partnering between SMEs and NGOs in Support of Business Sustainability." *Revista de Management si Inginerie Económica*, 11(4), 57–72.

Le Ber, M. J., and Branzei, O. (2010a). "(Re)forming Strategic Cross-Sector Partnerships: Relational Processes of Social Innovation." *Business & Society*, 49(1), 140–172.

Le Ber, M. J., and Branzei, O. (2010b). "Towards a Critical Theory of Value Creation in Cross-Sector Partnerships." *Organization*, 17(5), 599–629.

Le Ber, M. J., and Branzei, O. (2010c). "Value Frame Fusion in Cross-Sector Interactions." *Journal of Business Ethics*, 94(suppl. 1), 163–195.

Lepak, D. P., Smith, K. G., and Taylor, M. S. (2007). "Value Creation and Value Capture: A Multilevel Perspective." *Academy of Management Review*, 32(1), 180–194.

Levenson Keohane, G. (2013). *Social Entrepreneurship for the 21st Century: Innovation across the Nonprofit, Private, and Public Sectors.* New York: McGraw-Hill.

Levy, D. L., Brown, S. H., and de Jong, M. (2010). "The Contested Politics of Corporate Governance: The Case of the Global Reporting Initiative." *Business & Society*, 49(1), 88–115.

Lim, T. (2010). *Measuring the Value of Corporate Philanthropy: Social Impact, Business Benefits, and Investor Returns.* New York: Committee Encouraging Corporate Philanthropy.

Ling, A., Forrest, S., Fox, M., and Feilhauer, S. (2007). *The GS SUSTAIN Focus List.* Goldman Sachs global investment research. Available at http://www.unglobalcompact.org/docs/summit2007/gs_esg_embargoed_until030707pdf.pdf (retrieved Aug. 7, 2013).

Liu, G., and Ko, W. W. (2011). Social Alliance and Employee Voluntary Activities: A Resource-Based Perspective. *Journal of Business Ethics*, 104, 251–268.

Lockett, A., Moon, J., and Visser, W. (2006). "Corporate Social Responsibility in Management Research: Focus, Nature, Salience, and Sources of Influence." *Journal of Management Studies*, 43(1), 115–136.

London, T., and Anupindi, R. (2012). "Using the Base-of-the-Pyramid Perspective to Catalyze Interdependence-Based Collaborations." *Proceedings of the National Academy of Sciences*, 109(31), 12338–12343. Abstract available at http://www.pnas.org/content/109/31/12338 (retrieved Oct. 9, 2013).

London, T., and Hart, S. L. (2011). *Next-Generation Business Strategies for the Base of the Pyramid: New Approaches for Building Mutual Value.* Upper Saddle River, NJ: Pearson Education.

Long, F. J., and Arnold, M. B. (1995). *The Power of Environmental Partnerships.* Orlando, FL: Harcourt, Brace & Company.

Lubbers, E., ed. (2002). *Battling Big Business: Countering Greenwash, Infiltration, and Other Forms of Corporate Bullying.* Monroe, ME: Common Courage Press.

Maas, K.E.H., and Liket, K. C. (2011). "Talk the Walk: Impact Measurement of Corporate Philanthropy." *Journal of Business Ethics,* 100(3), 445–464.

MacKay, B., and Munro, I. (2012). "Information Warfare and New Organizational Landscapes: An Inquiry into the ExxonMobil–Greenpeace Dispute over Climate Change." *Organization Studies,* 33(11), 1507–1536.

Mackey, J., and Sisodia, R. (2013). *Conscious Capitalism: Liberating the Heroic Spirit of Business.* Boston: Harvard Business Review Press.

Mahoney, J. T., McGahan, A. N., and Pitelis, C. N. (2009). "The Interdependence of Public and Private Interests." *Organizational Science,* 20(6), 1034–1052.

Makower, J. (1994). *Beyond the Bottom Line: Putting Social Responsibility to Work for Your Business and the World.* New York: Simon & Schuster.

Maon, F., Lindgreen, A., and Vanhamme, N. (2009). "Developing Supply Chains in Disaster-Relief Operations through Cross-Sector Socially Oriented Collaborations: A Theoretical Model." *Supply Chain Management: An International Journal,* 14(2),149–64.

Margolis, J. D., and Walsh, J. P. (2003). "Misery Loves Companies: Rethinking Social Initiatives by Business." *Administrative Science Quarterly,* 48(2), 268–305.

Marin, L., Ruiz, S., and Rubio, A. (2009). "The Role of Identity Salience in the Effects of Corporate Social Responsibility on Consumer Behavior." *Journal of Business Ethics,* 84, 65–78.

Márquez, P., Reficco, E., and Berger, G. (2010). *Socially Inclusive Business: Engaging the Poor Through Market Initiatives In Iberoamerica.* Cambridge, MA: Harvard University Press.

Marquis, C., Glynn, M. A., and Davis, G. F. (2007). "Community Isomorphism and Corporate Social Action." *Academy of Management Review,* 32(3), 925–945.

Marsden, C. (2000). "The New Corporate Citizenship of Big Business: Part of the Solution to Sustainability?" *Business and Society Review,* 105(1), 9–25.

Martin, R. L. (2002). "The Virtue Matrix: Calculating the Return on Corporate Social Responsibility." *Harvard Business Review,* 80(3), 68–75.

Martin, R. L., and Osberg, S. (2007). "Social Entrepreneurship: The Case for Definition." *Stanford Social Innovation Review,* 5(2), 29–39.

Matten, D., and Crane, A. (2005). "Corporate Citizenship: Towards an Extended Theoretical Conception." *Academy of Management Review,* 30(1): 166–79.

McCann, J. E. (1983). "Design Guidelines for Social Problem–Solving Interventions." *Journal of Applied Behavioural Science*, 19(2), 177–189.

McCarter, M. W., Mahoney, J. T., and Northcraft, S. B. (2011). "Testing the Waters: Using Collective Real Options to Manage the Social Dilemma of Strategic Alliances." *Academy of Management Review*, 36,(4), 621–640.

McDaniel, P. A., and Malone, R. E. (2012). "British American Tobacco's Partnership with Earthwatch Europe and Its Implications for Public Health." *Global Public Health: An International Journal for Research, Policy and Practice*, 7(1), 14–28.

McDonald, S., Young, S. (2012). "Cross-Sector Collaboration Shaping Corporate Social Responsibility Best Practice within the Mining Industry." *Journal of Cleaner Production*, 37, 54–67.

"McDonald's and Environmental Defense Fund Mark 20 Years of Partnerships for Sustainability" (2010, Nov. 15). Available at http://www.edf.org/news/mcdonald%E2%80%99s-and-environmental-defense-fund-mark-20-years-partnerships-sustainability (retrieved Oct. 14, 2013).

McFarlan, F. W. (1999). "Working on Nonprofit Boards: Don't Assume the Shoe Fits." *Harvard Business Review*, 77(6), 65–80.

McKinsey & Company (2006). "The McKinsey Global Survey of Business Executives: Business and Society." *McKinsey Quarterly*, 2, 33–39.

Millar, C., Choi, J. C., and Chen, S. (2004). "Global Strategic Partnerships between MNEs and NGOs: Drivers of Change and Ethical Issues." *Business and Society Review*, 109(4), 395–414.

Millard, E. (2005). *Sustainable Coffee: Increasing Income of Small-Scale Coffee Farmers in Mexico through Upgrading and Improved Transparency in the Value Chain.* Washington, DC: United States Agency for International Development [USAID].

Milne, G. R., Iyer, E., and Gooding-Williams, S. (1996). "Environmental Organization Alliance Relationships within and across Nonprofit, Business, and Government Sectors." *Journal of Public Policy & Marketing*, 15(2), 203–215.

Mintzberg, H. (1978). "Patterns in Strategy Formation." *Management Science*, 24(9), 934–948.

Morariu, J., Athanasiades, K., and Emery, A. (2012). *State of Evaluation 2012: Evaluation Capacity and Practice in the Nonprofit Sector.* Washington, DC: Innovation Network.

Morino, M., ed. (2011). *Leap of Reason: Managing to Outcomes in an Era of Scarcity.* Washington, DC: Venture Philanthropy Partners.

Mulgan, G. (2010). "Measuring Social Value." *Stanford Social Innovation Review*, 8(3), 38–43.

Murphy, D. F., and Bendell, J. (1999). *Partners in Time? Business, NGOs, and Sustainable Development.* Discussion paper no. 109. Washington, DC: United Nations Research Institute for Social Development.

Murphy, M., and Arenas, D. (2010). "Through Indigenous Lenses: Cross-Sector Collaborations with Fringe Stakeholders." *Journal of Business Ethics*, 94(suppl. 1), 103–121.

Murphy, M., Perrot, F., and Rivera-Santos, M. (2012). "New Perspectives on Learning and Innovation in Cross-Sector Collaborations." *Journal of Business Research*, 65(12), 1700–1709.

Muthuri, J. N. (2007). "Corporate Citizenship and Sustainable Community Development: Fostering Multi-Sector Collaboration in Magadi Division in Kenya." *Journal of Corporate Citizenship*, 28, 73–84.

Nambisan, S. (2009). "Platforms for Collaboration." *Stanford Social Innovation Review*, 7(3), 44–49.

Neff, J. (2011, Aug. 15). "Secret's Anti-Bullying Campaign Appears to Get Facebook Fans Engaged." Available at http://adage.com/article/news/secret-s-anti-bullying-push-engage-facebook-fans/229195 (retrieved Aug. 10, 2013).

Nelson, J., and Jenkins, B. (2006). "Investing in Social Innovation: Harnessing the Potential for Partnership between Corporations and Social Entrepreneurs." In F. Perrini, ed., *The New Social Entrepreneurship: What Awaits Social Entrepreneurial Ventures?*, pp. 272–280. Cheltenham, England: Edgar Elgar.

Nelson, J., and Prescott, D. (2005). *Partnering for Success: Business Perspectives on Multistakeholder Partnerships*. Cambridge, MA: World Economic Forum/John F. Kennedy School of Government, Harvard University.

Nestlé (2011). *Nestlé Creating Shared Value Summary Report: Meeting the Global Water Challenge*. Vevey, Switzerland: Nestlé. Available at http://www.nestle.com/info/contactus/contact-us-landing (retrieved Aug. 13, 2013).

Neville, B. A., and Menguc, B. (2006). "Stakeholder Multiplicity: Toward and Understanding of the Interactions between Stakeholders." *Journal of Business Ethics*, 66, 377–391.

Newell, P. (2002). "From Responsibility to Citizenship: Corporate Accountability for Development." *IDS Bulletin*, 33(2), 91–100.

Nike, Inc. (2005). *Corporate Social Responsibility Report 2005*. Beaverton, OR: Nike, Inc.

Nike, Inc. (2009). *Corporate Social Responsibility Report 2009*. Beaverton, OR: Nike, Inc.

Norman, W., and MacDonald, C. (2004). "Getting to the Bottom of 'Triple Bottom Line.'" *Business Ethics Quarterly*, 14(2), 243–262.

Noy, E. (2009). "Corporate Long-Range Quantitative Goals: Profit or Growth?" *Journal of Wealth Management* 12(1), 75–89.

O'Flynn, M. (2010). "Impact Assessment: Understanding and Assessing Our Contributions to Change." M&E paper no. 7. Oxford, England: INTRAC–International NGO Training and Research Centre.

Opinion Leader Research (2005). *Report of Findings of a Survey of Public Trust and Confidence in Charities.* London: The Charities Commission.

Oppenheim, J., Bonini, S., Bielak, D., Kehm, T., and Lacy, P. (2007). *Shaping the New Rules of Competition: UN Global Compact Participant Mirror.* Report based on results of a survey conducted by McKinsey & Company. Available at http://www.unglobalcompact.org/docs/summit2007/mckinsey_embargoed_until020707.pdf (retrieved Aug. 2, 2013).

Orlitzky, M., Schmidt, F. L., and Rynes, S. L. (2003). "Corporate Social and Financial Performance: A Meta-analysis." *Organization Studies,* 24(3), 403–441.

"Our Story" (n.d.). Available at http://www.red.org/en/about (retrieved Oct. 13, 2013).

Paine, L. S. (2003). *Value Shift: Why Companies Must Merge Social and Financial Imperatives to Achieve Superior Performance.* New York: McGraw-Hill.

Pangarkar, N. (2003). "Determinants of Alliance Duration in Uncertain Environments: The Case of the Biotechnology Sector." *Long Range Planning,* 36(3), 269–284.

Parceiros Voluntários (2011). *2011 Annual Report* [English translation of *Relatório Anual 2011*]. Porto Alegre, Brazil: Parceiros Voluntários.

Partnerships Resource Centre (2011). *The State of the Partnerships Report, 2010.* Rotterdam, The Netherlands: Erasmus University.

Pearce, J. A., and Doh, J. P. (2005). "The High Impact of Collaborative Social Initiatives." *Sloan Management Review,* 46(3), 30–38.

Peloza, J. (2009). "The Challenge of Measuring Financial Impacts from Investments in Corporate Social Performance." *Journal of Management,* 25(6), 1518–1541.

Peloza, J., and Falkenberg, L. (2009). "The Role of Collaboration in Achieving Corporate Social Responsibility Objectives." *California Management Review,* 51(3), 95–113.

Peloza, J., and Papania, L. (2008). "The Missing Link between Corporate Social Responsibility and Financial Performance: Stakeholder Salience and Identification." *Corporate Reputation Review,* 11(2), 169–181.

Peloza, J., and Shang, J. (2010). "How Can Corporate Social Responsibility Activities Create Value for Stakeholders? A Systematic Review." *Journal of the Academy of Marketing Science,* 39, 117–135.

Perez-Aleman, P., and Sandilands, M. (2008). "Building Value at the Top and the Bottom of the Global Supply Chain: MNC–NGO Partnerships." *California Management Review,* 51(1), 24–49.

Perrini, F. (2006). "SMEs and CSR Theory: Evidence and Implications from an Italian Perspective." *Journal of Business Ethics,* 67, 305–316.

Peter F. Drucker Foundation for Nonprofit Management (2002). *Meeting the Collaboration Challenge Workbook: Developing Strategic Alliances between Nonprofit Organizations and Businesses.* San Francisco: Jossey-Bass.

Pfeiffer, J., and Salancik, G. R. (1978). *The External Control of Organizations: A Resource-Dependence Perspective.* New York: Harper & Row.

Phills, J. A. Jr., Deiglmeier, K., and Miller, D. T. (2008). "Rediscovering Social Innovation." *Stanford Social Innovation Review,* 6(4), 34–43.

Plowman, D. A., Baker, L. T., Kulkarni, M., Solansky, S. T., and Travis, D. V. (2007). "Radical Change Accidentally: The Emergence and Amplification of Small Change." *Academy of Management Journal,* 50, 512–543.

Points of Light Foundation (2007, March 28). "National Council on Workplace Volunteerism Achieves Important Milestone." Press release. Available at http://www.csrwire.com/press_releases/16770-National-Council-on-Workplace-Volunteerism-Achieves-Important-Milestone (retrieved Aug. 9, 2013).

Pol, E., and Ville, S. (2009). "Social Innovation: Buzz Word or Enduring Term?" *Journal of Socio-Economics,* 38, 878–885.

Polman, R. (2011). "The Remedies for Capitalism." Available at http://www.mckinsey.com/features/capitalism/paul_polman (retrieved Aug. 7, 2013).

Polonsky, M. J., and Ryan, P. J. (1996). "The Implications of Stakeholder Statutes for Socially Responsible Managers." *Business & Professional Ethics Journal,* 15(3), 3–36.

Porter, M. E., and Kramer, M. R. (2002). "The Competitive Advantage of Corporate Philanthropy." *Harvard Business Review,* 80(12), 56–69.

Porter, M. E., and Kramer, M. R. (2006). "Strategy and Society: The Link between Competitive Advantage and Corporate Social Responsibility." *Harvard Business Review,* 84(12), 78–92.

Porter, M. E., and Kramer, M. R. (2011). "Creating Shared Value: How to Reinvent Capitalism—and Unleash a Wave of Innovation and Growth." *Harvard Business Review,* 89(1/2), 62–77.

Porter, M. E., Hills, G., Pfitzer, M., Patscheke, S., and Hawkins, E. (2012). *Measuring Shared Value: How to Unlock Value by Linking Social and Business Results.* Boston: FSG.

Potter, C. (2006). "Weaving Businesses Together." *Stanford Social Innovation Review,* 4(3), 66–67.

Prahalad, C. K. (2005). *The Fortune at the Bottom of the Pyramid: Eradicating Poverty through Profits.* Upper Saddle River, NJ: Wharton School Publishing.

Prahalad, C. K., and Hamel, G. (1990). "The Core Competence of the Corporation." *Harvard Business Review,* 89(1/2), 71–91.

Prahalad, C. K., and Hammond, A. (2002) "Serving the World's Poor, Profitably." *Harvard Business Review*, 80(9), 4–11.

Prahalad, C. K., and Hart, S. (2002). "The Fortune at the Bottom of the Pyramid." *Strategy + Management*, 26, 54–67.

Prahalad, C. K., and Ramaswamy, V. (2004). "Co-Creation Experiences: The Next Practice in Value Creation." *Journal of Interactive Marketing*, 18(3), 5–14.

Pressman, J. L., and Wildavsky, A. B. (1973). *Implementation*. Berkeley: University of California Press.

Preston, J. (2011, Jan. 30). "Pepsi Bets on Local Grants, Not the Super Bowl." *New York Times*. Available at http://www.nytimes.com/2011/01/31/business/media/31pepsi.html?_r=0 (retrieved Aug. 9, 2013).

"Proving That Cause Marketing Is a Win-Win" (2010). Available at http://ww2.causemarketingforum.com/page.asp?ID=345 (retrieved Aug. 10, 2013).

Quelch, J., Austin, J., and Laidler-Kylander, N. (2004). "Mining for Gold in Nonprofits." *Harvard Business Review*, 82(4), 24.

Quelch, J. A., and Jocz, K. E. (2009). "Can Corporate Social Responsibility Survive Recession?" *Leader to Leader*, 53, 37–43.

Quelch, J. A., and Laidler-Kylander, N. (2005). *The New Global Brands: Managing Non-Governmental Organizations in the 21st Century*. Belmont, CA.: Thomson/South-Western.

"Race for the Cure National Sponsors" (2013). Available at http://ww5.komen.org/nationalRacefortheCureSponsors.aspx (retrieved Oct. 13, 2013).

Rackham, N., Friedman, L., and Ruff, R. (1996). *Getting Partnering Right: How Market Leaders Are Creating Long-Term Competitive Advantage*. New York: McGraw-Hill.

Ramiah, I., and Reich, M. R. (2006). "Building Effective Public–Private Partnerships: Experiences and Lessons from the African Comprehensive HIV/AIDS Partnerships (ACHAP)." *Social Science & Medicine*, 63, 397–408.

Rangan, V. K., Quelch, J. A., Herrero, G., and Barton, B. (2007). *Business Solutions for the Global Poor: Creating Social and Economic Value*. San Francisco: Jossey-Bass.

Reed, A. M., and Reed, D. (2009). "Partnerships for Development: Four Models of Business Involvement." *Journal of Business Ethics*, 90, 3–37.

Rehbein, K., Waddock, S., and Graves, S. B. (2004). "Understanding Shareholder Activism: Which Corporations Are Targeted?" *Business & Society*, 43(3), 239–267.

Reis, T. (1999). *Unleashing the New Resources and Entrepreneurship for the Common Good: A Scan, Synthesis and Scenario for Action.* Battle Creek, MI: W. K. Kellogg Foundation.

Ring, P. S., and Van de Ven, A. H. (1994). "Developmental Processes of Cooperative Interorganizational Relationships." *Academy of Management Review,* 19(1), 90–118.

Rivera-Santos, M., and Rufin, C. (2010). "Odd Couples: Understanding the Governance of Firm–NGO Alliances." *Journal of Business Ethics,* 94(suppl. 1), 55–70.

Rivera-Santos, M., Rufin, C., and Kolk, A. (2012). "Bridging the Institutional Divide: Partnerships in Subsistence Markets." *Journal of Business Research,* 65(12), 1721–1727.

Rondinelli, D. A., and London, T. (2003). "How Corporations and Environmental Groups Cooperate: Assessing Cross-Sector Alliances and Collaborations." *Academy of Management Executive,* 17(1), 61–76.

Rosenman, M. (2007, Apr. 11). "The Patina of Philanthropy." *Stanford Social Innovation Review* (blog). Available at http://www.ssireview.org/blog/entry/the_patina_of_philanthropy (retrieved Aug. 10, 2013).

Ross, S. R. (2012). *Expanding the Pie: Fostering Effective Non-Profit and Corporate Partnerships.* Sterling, VA: Kumarian Press.

Rowley, T. J., and Berman, S. (2000). "A Brand-New Brand of Corporate Social Performance." *Business & Society,* 39(4), 397–418.

Ryan, M., Richardson, S., and Voutier, P. (2012). *Business in Development Study 2012: Australian Business Leaders Provide Insight into Delivering Business Outcomes with Social Benefit in Developing Countries.* Melbourne: Accenture/Business for Millennium Development. Available at http://www.accenture.com/SiteCollectionDocuments/PDF/Accenture-Business-Development-Study-2012.pdf#zoom=50 (retrieved Aug. 7, 2013).

Sagawa, S., and Segal, E. (2000). *Common Interest, Common Good: Creating Value through Business and Social Sector Partnerships.* Boston: Harvard Business School Press.

Sakarya, S., Bodur, M., Yildirim-Öktem, Ö., and Selekler-Göksen, N. (2012). "Social Alliances: Business and Social Enterprise Collaboration for Social Transformation." *Journal of Business Research,* 65, 1710–1720.

Salamon, L. M. (2010). *Rethinking Corporate Social Engagement: Lessons from Latin America.* Sterling, VA: Kumarian Press.

Salamon, L. M., and Anheier, H. K. (1997). *Defining the Non-Profit Sector: A Cross-National Analysis.* Manchester, England: Manchester University Press.

SAM (Sustainable Asset Management) and PricewaterhouseCoopers (2010). *The Sustainability Yearbook 2009.* Available at http://petrofed

.winwinhosting.net/upload/Sustainability%20Yearbook_2009.pdf (retrieved Aug. 7, 2013).

Sanborn, C., and Portocarrero, F., eds. (2005). *Philanthropy and Social Change in Latin America.* Cambridge, MA: Harvard University Press.

"Save Lids to Save Lives" (2012). Available at http://yoplait.com/yoplait-in-action/save-lids-to-save-lives (retrieved Oct. 6, 2013).

Schell, O. (2011, Dec.). "How Walmart Is Changing China." *The Atlantic,* pp. 81–98. Available at http://www.theatlantic.com/magazine/archive/2011/12/how-walmart-is-changing-china/308709 (retrieved Aug. 7, 2013).

Schiller, R. S., and Almog-Bar, M. (forthcoming). "Revisiting Collaborations between Nonprofits and Businesses: An NPO-Centric View and Typology." *Nonprofit and Voluntary Sector Quarterly.* Abstract available at http://nvs.sagepub.com/content/early/2013/01/17/0899764012471753.abstract (retrieved Oct. 13, 2013).

Schuler, D. A., and Cording, M. (2006). "A Corporate Social Performance–Corporate Financial Performance Behavioral Model for Consumers." *Academy of Management Review,* 31(3), 540–558.

Schwartz, N. (2010). "Busted Nonprofit Brand: Anatomy of a Corporate Sponsorship Meltdown." Available at http://www.causemarketingforum.com/site/c.bkLUKcOTLkK4E/b.6452355/apps/s/content.asp?ct=8971353 (retrieved Aug. 10, 2013).

Seelos, C., and Mair, J. (2007). "Profitable Business Models and Market Creation in the Context of Deep Poverty: A Strategic View." *Academy of Management Perspectives,* 21(4), 49–63.

Seitanidi, M. M. (2008). "Adaptive Responsibilities: Non-Linear Interactions across Social Sectors: Cases from Cross-Sector Social Partnerships." *Emergence: Complexity & Organization (E:CO) Journal,* 10(3), 51–64.

Seitanidi, M. M. (2009). "Missed Opportunities of Employee Involvement in CSR Partnerships." *Corporate Reputation Review,* 12(2), 90–105.

Seitanidi, M. M. (2010). *The Politics of Partnerships: A Critical Examination of Nonprofit–Business Partnerships.* London: Springer.

Seitanidi, M. M., and Crane, A. (2009). "Implementing CSR through Partnerships: Understanding the Selection, Design, and Institutionalisation of Nonprofit–Business Partnerships." *Journal of Business Ethics,* 85, 413–429.

Seitanidi, M. M., and Crane, A., eds. (forthcoming). *Social Partnerships and Responsible Business: A Research Handbook.* London: Routledge.

Seitanidi, M. M., Koufopoulos, D., and Palmer, P. (2010.) "Partnership Formation for Change: Indicators for Transformative Potential in Cross-Sector Social Partnerships." *Journal of Business Ethics,* 94(suppl. 1), 139–161.

Seitanidi, M. M., and Lindgreen, A. (2010). "Cross-Sector Social Interactions." *Journal of Business Ethics*, 94(suppl. 1), 1–7.

Seitanidi, M. M., and Ryan, A. M. (2007). "A Critical Review of Forms of Corporate Community Involvement: From Philanthropy to Partnerships." *International Journal of Nonprofit and Voluntary Sector Marketing*, 12(3), 247–266.

Selsky, J. W., and Parker, B. (2005). "Cross-Sector Partnerships to Address Social Issues: Challenges to Theory and Practice." *Journal of Management*, 31(6), 849–873.

Selsky, J. W., and Parker, B. (2010). "Platforms for Cross-Sector Social Partnerships: Prospective Sensemaking Devices for Social Benefit." *Journal of Business Ethics*, 94(suppl. 1), 21–37.

Senge, P. M., Dow, M., and Neath, G. (2006). "Learning Together: New Partnerships for New Times." *Corporate Governance*, 6(4), 420–430.

Shaffer, B., and Hillman, A. (2000). "The Development of Business–Government Strategies by Diversified Firms." *Strategic Management Journal.* 21(2), 175–190.

Shamir, R. (2008). "The Age of Responsibilization: On Market Embedded Morality." *Economy and Society*, 37(1), 1–19.

Sharfman, M. P., Gray, B., and Yan, A. (1991). "The Context of Interorganizational Collaboration in the Garment Industry: An Institutional Perspective." *Journal of Applied Behavioral Science*, 27(2), 181–208.

Simonin, B. L. (1997). "The Importance of Collaborative Know-How: An Empirical Test of the Learning Organization." *Academy of Management Journal*, 40(5), 1150–1174.

Singh, S., Kristensen, L., and Villseñor, E. (2009). "Overcoming Skepticism toward Cause-Related Claims: The Case of Norway." *International Marketing Review*, 26(3), 312–326.

Slawinski, N., & Bansal, P. (2012). "A Matter of Time: The Temporal Perspectives of Organizational Responses to Climate Change." *Organization Studies*, 33(11), 1537–1563.

Smith, V., and Langford, P. (2009). "Evaluating the Impact of Corporate Social Responsibility Programs on Consumers." *Journal of Management and Organization*, 15(1), 97–109.

Social Enterprise Knowledge Network (SEKN) (2006). *Effective Management of Social Enterprise: Lessons from Business and Civil Society Organizations in Iberoamerica.* Cambridge, MA: Harvard University Press.

SROI Network (2012). *SROI: Myths and Challenges.* Available at http://www.thesroinetwork.org/images/SROI_Myths_and_Challenges.pdf (retrieved Aug. 11, 2013).

Stadtler, L. (2011). "Aligning a Company's Economic and Social Interests in Cross-Sector Partnerships." *Journal of Corporate Citizenship*, 44, 85–106.

Stafford, E. R., and Hartman, C. L. (2001). "Greenpeace's 'Greenfreeze Campaign': Hurdling Competitive Forces in the Diffusion of Environmental Technology Innovation." In K. Green, P. Groenewegen, and P. S. Hofman, eds., *Ahead of the Curve: Cases of Innovation in Environmental Management.* Dordrecht, The Netherlands: Kluwer Academic Publishers.

Stafford, E. R., Polonsky, M. J., and Hartman, C. L. (2000). "Environmental NGO–Business Collaboration and Strategic Bridging: A Case Analysis of the Greenpeace–Foron Alliance." *Business Strategy and the Environment,* 9(2), 122–135.

Starbucks (2012). *Starbucks Global Responsibility Report: Goals and Progress, 2011.* Seattle: Starbucks, 2012. Available at http://www.starbucks.com/assets/19c68ea6c48a473d865c7327c08d817f.pdf (retrieved Oct. 6, 2013).

"Starbucks Coffee Company" (2013). Available at http://www.conservation.org/how/partnership/corporate/Pages/starbucks.aspx (retrieved Oct. 6, 2013).

Steckel, R., and Simons, R. (1992). *Doing Best by Doing Good: How to Use Public Purpose Partnerships to Boost Profits and Benefit Your Community.* New York: Dutton.

Strahilevitz, M. (1999). "The Effects of Product Type and Donation Magnitude on Willingness to Pay More for a Charity-Linked Brand." *Journal of Consumer Psychology,* 8(3), 215–241.

Strahilevitz, M. (2003). "The Effects of Prior Impressions of a Firm's Ethics on the Success of a Cause-Related Marketing Campaign: Do the Good Look Better While the Bad Look Worse?" *Journal of Nonprofit & Public Sector Marketing,* 11(1), 77–92.

Strahilevitz, M., and Myers, J. G. (1998). "Donations to Charity as Purchase Incentives: How Well They Work May Depend on What You Are Trying to Sell." *Journal of Consumer Research,* 24(4), 434–446.

Sullivan, H., and Skelcher, C. (2002). *Working across Boundaries: Collaboration in Public Services.* New York: Palgrave Macmillan.

Swartz, J. (2010). "Timberland's CEO on Standing Up to 65,000 Angry Activists." *Harvard Business Review,* 88(9), 39–127.

Tariq, H., and Tenneyson, R. (2009). *In the Bank's Best Interests: A Case Study of an Ambitious Partnership.* London: The Partnering Initiative, International Business Leaders Forum.

Taylor, J. G., and Scharlin, P. J. (2004). *Smart Alliance: How a Global Corporation and Environmental Activists Transformed a Tarnished Brand.* New Haven: Yale University Press.

Teegen, H., Doh, J. P., and Vachani, S. (2004). "The Importance of Nongovernmental Organizations (NGOs) in Global Governance and Value Creation: An International Business Research Agenda." *Journal of International Business Studies,* 35, 463–483.

Thompson, J. L. (2008). "Social Enterprise and Social Entrepreneurship: Where Have We Reached? A Summary of Issues and Discussion Points." *Social Enterprise Journal*, 4(2), 149–161.

Tran, M. (2005, Sept. 1). "Branded." *Business Insight* (blog sponsored by *The Guardian*). Available at http://blogs.guardian.co.uk/businessinsight/archives/2005/09/01/branded.html (retrieved Aug. 13, 2013).

Tully, S. (2004). *Corporate-NGO Partnerships as a Form of Civil Regulation: Lessons from the Energy and Biodiversity Initiative*. Economic and Social Research Council (ESRC) Centre for Analysis of Risk and Regulation (CARR) discussion paper no. 22, London School of Economics and Political Science.

2004 Deloitte Volunteer IMPACT Survey: Complete Survey Results (2004). Available at http://www.deloitte.com/view/en_us/us/039d899a961fb110VgnVCM100000ba42f00aRCRD.htm (retrieved Aug. 10, 2013).

Ukman, L. (2012). *A Sponsorship Measurement Solution: Applying Marketing Science to Evaluating Performance*. Chicago: IEG.

United Nations General Assembly (2001). *Cooperation between the United Nations and All Relevant Partners, in Particular the Private Sector: Report of the Secetary-General*. 56th session, agenda item 39: Towards Global Partnerships. New York: United Nations General Assembly. Available at http://www.un.org/partnerships/Docs/partnershipreport_a-56–323.pdf (retrieved Aug. 2, 2013).

Utting, P. (2005). *Rethinking Business Regulation: From Self-Regulation to Social Control*. Geneva: United Nations Research Institute for Social Development.

Van Tulder, R., and Kolk, A. (2007). *Poverty Alleviation as a Business Issue*. In C. Wankel, ed., *21st-Century Management: A Reference Handbook*, pp. 95–105. London: Sage.

Varadarajan, P. R., and Menon, A. (1988). "Cause-Related Marketing: A Coalignment of Marketing Strategy and Corporate Philanthropy." *Journal of Marketing*, 52(3), 58–74.

Vaschon, C. J. (2012). "Scratch My Back, and I'll Scratch Yours: Scratching the Surface of the Duty of Care in Cross-Sector Collaborations—Are For-Profits Obligated to Ensure the Sustainability of their Partner Nonprofits?" *Hastings Business Law Journal*, 8, 1.

Vian, T., Feeley, F., MacLeod, W., Richards, S. C., and McCoy, K. (2007). *Measuring the Impact of International Corporate Volunteering: Lessons Learned from the Global Health Fellows Program of Pfizer Corporation*. Boston: Center for International Health, School of Public Health, Boston University.

Visser, W. (2011). *The Age of Responsibility: CSR 2.0 and the New DNA of Business*. New York: Wiley.

Vock, M., Van Dolen, W., and Kolk, A. (forthcoming). "Micro-Level Interactions in Business Nonprofit Partnerships." *Business & Society*. Abstract available at http://papers.ssrn.com/sol3/papers .cfm?abstract_id=1873503 (retrieved Oct. 13, 2013).

Vurro, C., Dacin, M. T., and Perrini, F. (2010). "Institutional Antecedents of Partnering for Social Change: How Institutional Logics Shape Cross-Sector Social Partnerships." *Journal of Business Ethics*, 94, 39–53.

Waddell, S. (2011). *Global Action Networks: Creating Our Future Together*. New York: Palgrave Macmillan.

Waddell, S., and Brown, L. D. (1997). "Fostering Intersectoral Partnering: A Guide to Promoting Cooperation among Governments, Business, and Civil Society Actors." *IDRC Reports*, 13(3), entire issue. Available at http://commdev.org/files/1305_file_fostering_intersectoral_ partnering.pdf (retrieved Oct. 13, 2013).

Waddock, S. A. (1986). "Public–Private Partnerships as Social Product and Process." *Research in Corporate Social Performance and Policy*, 8, 273–300.

Waddock, S. A. (1989). "Understanding Social Partnerships: An Evolutionary Model of Partnership Organizations." *Administration & Society*, 21(1), 78–100.

Waddock, S. A. (1991). "A Typology of Social Partnership Organizations." *Administration & Society*, 22(4), 480–516.

Waddock, S. (2008). *The Difference Makers: How Social and Institutional Entrepreneurs Built the Corporate Responsibility Movement*. Sheffield, England: Greenleaf.

Waddock, S. A., and Post, J. (1995). "Catalytic Alliances for Social Problem Solving." *Human Relations*, 48(8), 951–973.

"Walmart Giving in Last Fiscal Year Exceeds $1 Billion for the First Time" (2013, Apr. 22). Available at http://news.walmart.com/news-archive/2013/04/22/walmart-giving-in-last-fiscal-year-exceeds-1-billion-for-the-first-time (retrieved Oct. 6, 2013).

Walsh, J. P., Weber, K., and Margolis, J. D. (2003). "Social Issues and Management: Our Lost Cause Found." *Journal of Management*, 29(6), 859–881.

Wang, H., Choi, J., and Li, J. (2008). "Too Little or Too Much? Untangling the Relationship between Corporate Philanthropy and Firm Financial Performance." *Organization Science*, 19(1), 143–159.

Warner, M., and Sullivan, R. (2004). *Putting Partnerships to Work: Strategic Alliances for Development between Government and Private Sector and Civil Society*. Sheffield, England: Greenleaf Publishing.

Watanatada, P., and Mak, H. (2011). *Signed, Sealed . . . Delivered? Behind Certifications and beyond Labels*. London: SustainAbility Ltd.

Waygood, S., and Wehrmeyer, W. (2003). "A Critical Assessment of How Non-Governmental Organizations Use the Capital Markets to Achieve Their Aims: A UK study." *Business Strategy and the Environment*, 12(6), 372–385.

Weber, J., Austin, J. E., and Barrett, D. (2001a). *Merck Global Health Initiatives (A)*. HBS case no. 9301088. Boston: Harvard Business School.

Weber, J., Austin, J. E., and Barrett, D. (2001b). *Merck Global Health Initiatives (B): Botswana*. HBS case no. 9301089. Boston: Harvard Business School.

Wei-Skillern, J., Silver, N., and Heitz, E. (2013). *Cracking the Network Code: Four Principles for Grantmakers*. Washington, DC: Grantmakers for Effective Organizations.

Weiser, J., Kahane, M., Rochlin, S., and Landis, J. (2006). *Untapped: Creating Value in Underserved Markets*. San Francisco: Berrett-Koehler.

Weiss, E. S., Anderson, R. M., and Lasker, R. D. (2002). "Making the Most of Collaboration: Exploring the Relationship between Partnership Synergy and Partnership Functioning." *Health Education & Behavior*, 29(6), 683–698.

Westley, F., and Vredenburg, H. (1997). "Interorganizational Collaboration and the Preservation of Global Biodiversity." *Organization Science*, 8(4), 381–403.

White, H. (2009). "Theory-Based Impact Evaluation: Principles and Practice." *Journal of Development Effectiveness*, 1(3), 271–284.

Wilkof, M., Brown, D., and Selsky, J. (1995). "When the Stories Are Different: The Influence of Corporate Culture Mismatches on Interorganizational Relations." *Journal of Applied Behavioral Science*, 31(3), 373–388.

Wiltbank, R, Dew, N., Read, S., and Sarasvathy, S. D. (2006) "What to Do Next? The Case of Non-predictive Strategy." *Strategic Management Journal*, 27(10), 981–988.

Wilson A., and Charlton, K. (1993). *Making Partnerships Work*. London: J. Roundtree Foundation.

Winchester, S. (2014). "Cross-Sector Collaborations: Challenges in Aligning Perspectives in Partnership Committees and Co-Developing Funding Proposals." In M. M. Seitanidi and A. Crane, eds., *Social Partnerships and Responsible Business: A Research Handbook*. London: Routledge.

Wittneben, B.B.F., Okereke, C., Banerjee, S. B., and Levy, D. L. (2012). "Climate Change and the Emergence of New Organizational Landscapes." *Organization Studies*, 33(11) 1431–1450.

World Business Council for Sustainable Development (2013). *Measuring Socio-Economic Impact: A Guide for Business.* Washington, DC: World Business Council for Sustainable Development.

World Economic Forum Global Corporate Citizenship Initiative (2005). *Partnering for Success: Business Perspectives on Multistakeholder Partnerships.* Geneva: World Economic Forum.

Wymer, W. W. Jr., and Samu, S. (2003). "Dimensions of Business and Nonprofit Collaborative Relationships." *Journal of Nonprofit & Public Sector Marketing,* 11(1), 3–22.

Yaziji, M. (2004). "Turning Gadflies into Allies." *Harvard Business Review,* 82(2), 110–115.

Yaziji, M., and Doh, J. (2009). *NGOs and Corporations: Conflict and Collaboration.* New York: Cambridge University Press.

Yeatman, P. (2012, Apr. 25). "Kraft Foods' Cocoa Partnership in Ghana." *Stanford Social Innovation Review* (blog). Available at http://www.ssireview.org/blog/entry/kraft_foods_cocoa_partnership_in_ghana (retrieved Aug. 10, 2013).

Zadek, S. (2001). *The Civil Corporation: The New Economy of Corporate Citizenship.* London: Earthscan Publications.

Zadek, S. (2004). "The Path to Corporate Responsibility." *Harvard Business Review,* 82(12), 125–132.

Zedlmayer, S. (2012, Apr. 25). "H-P's Cross-Sector Health Partnership In Kenya." *Stanford Social Innovation Review* (blog). Available at http://www.ssireview.org/blog/entry/hps_cross_sector_health_partnership_in_kenya (retrieved Aug. 10, 2013).

Zettelmeyer, W., and Maddison, A. (2004). *Agroforestry-Based Enterprise Development as a Biodiversity Conservation Intervention in Mexico and Ghana.* Final evaluation report for USAID/PVC matching grant no. FAO-A-00-00-00012-00. Washington, DC: United States Agency for International Development (USAID).

Zwick, D., Bonsu, S. K., and Darmody, A. (2008). "Putting Consumers to Work." *Journal of Consumer Culture,* 8(2), 163–196.

About the Authors

Professor **James E. Austin** is the Eliot I. Snider and Family Professor of Business Administration, Emeritus, at the Harvard Business School, having joined the faculty in 1972. He was the Co-Founder and Chairman of the HBS Social Enterprise Initiative. Having authored and edited two dozen books, dozens of articles, and hundreds of case studies, Dr. Austin is recognized internationally as an expert on cross-sector collaboration and social enterprise. Among various awards, Professor Austin received the 2012 Lifetime Achievement Award in Collaboration Research by the International Symposium in Cross Sector Social Interactions, the 2008 Faculty Pioneer Award in Social Entrepreneurship Education by the Aspen Institute and Ashoka, and The Virginia A. Hodgkinson Research Prize-2001, by The Independent Sector for his *The Collaboration Challenge* book. He has been an advisor to corporations, nonprofit organizations, and governments throughout the world, including serving as a Special Advisor to the White House. He is also one of the founding leaders of the Social Enterprise Knowledge Network (SEKN).

Dr. **M. May Seitanidi** (FRSA) is Associate Professor of Strategy at Kent Business School, University of Kent, and Visiting Fellow at the International Centre for Corporate Social Responsibility (ICCSR) at Nottingham University Business School, University of Nottingham, UK. She has published extensively on cross-sector social partnerships in academic journals as well as popular press. Her work for over 20 years, as a practitioner and academic, focused on all types of cross-sector social interactions, previously on philanthropy and socio-sponsorship and currently on social partnerships. She was the founder of the Hellenic Sponsorship Centre (1994), of the magazine *Sponsors and Sponsorships* (1995), and more recently (2005) of a group focused on nonprofit-business partnerships with 400 academic and practitioner members interested in partnerships: http://tech.groups.yahoo.com/group/NPO-BUSPartnerships/. In 2007 she founded the International Symposia Series on "Cross Sector Social Interactions," organized by academics at leading universities around the world. Since 2006 she edits the "Annual Review of Social Partnerships" (ARSP), promoting cross-sector collaboration for the social good. She has served as a consultant and trainer for many private, public, and non-governmental organizations. Books include *The Politics of Partnerships* (2010, short-listed for the SIM 2013 Best Book Award) and *Social Partnerships and Responsible Business: A Research Handbook* (2013, coedited with Andrew Crane).

Index

collaborations with nonprofits, 1–2; influence of NGOs on, 59–60; linking interests with nonprofits, 20–22; mastering relationships with partners, 166–167; mindsets of, 42–43; multiple motivations in mindsets of, 43, 47–48; nature of resources used by, 17–20; problem-focused projects by, 86–88; promoting employee volunteer programs, 76–78; question of partnering visibility, 140–141; recognizing organizational capabilities of, 149–151; sponsorships and licensing by, 83–84; synergistic values with health-related nonprofits, 34; taking operational measures with partners, 163–164; using empiricism in evaluating performance, 42, 46–47; value generated for collaboration by, 184. *See also* CEOs

C

C.A.F.E. (Coffee and Farmer Equity) Practices, 106, 108, 109, 187, 188

Calvert Social Index, 50

Cancer Society of New Zealand, 13, 14, 27

Canon, 83

Canon USA, 96

Cape Town partnership example, 169

Carter Center, 121

Carter, Jimmy, 71

Case examples: alignment within partnerships, 88–93; articulating social problems, 134–136; assessing risks of partnering, 155; associational values, 27–28; Cape Town multisector partnership, 169; creating value with process pathways, 172–174; detecting prepartnership champions, 133, 144–145; developing insights into partner organization, 138–140; developing partnership-specific criteria, 153–154; directional flows, 13–14; drafting memorandum of understanding, 160–161; employee volunteer programs, 79–81; engagement as value driver, 114–116; evaluating partnership's performance, 165; finding complementarity, 151; interaction value, 31–32; linked interests, 22; mapping outcomes assessment, 186–189; nature of resources for collaborative use, 19–20; personal familiarization, 169–170; reflecting resource complementarity, 16–17; synergistic values, 33–34; transferred-asset value, 29–30; using outcomes measurement, 191

Casey, Carolyn, 113

Cause-related marketing (CRM): AMA and Sunbeam's, 91–92; antihunger, 89–91; bonding